Marie NDiaye
Inhospitable Fictions

LEGENDA

LEGENDA is the Modern Humanities Research Association's book imprint for new research in the Humanities. Founded in 1995 by Malcolm Bowie and others within the University of Oxford, Legenda has always been a collaborative publishing enterprise, directly governed by scholars. The Modern Humanities Research Association (MHRA) joined this collaboration in 1998, became half-owner in 2004, in partnership with Maney Publishing and then Routledge, and has since 2016 been sole owner. Titles range from medieval texts to contemporary cinema and form a widely comparative view of the modern humanities, including works on Arabic, Catalan, English, French, German, Greek, Italian, Portuguese, Russian, Spanish, and Yiddish literature. Editorial boards and committees of more than 60 leading academic specialists work in collaboration with bodies such as the Society for French Studies, the British Comparative Literature Association and the Association of Hispanists of Great Britain & Ireland.

The MHRA encourages and promotes advanced study and research in the field of the modern humanities, especially modern European languages and literature, including English, and also cinema. It aims to break down the barriers between scholars working in different disciplines and to maintain the unity of humanistic scholarship. The Association fulfils this purpose through the publication of journals, bibliographies, monographs, critical editions, and the MHRA Style Guide, and by making grants in support of research. Membership is open to all who work in the Humanities, whether independent or in a University post, and the participation of younger colleagues entering the field is especially welcomed.

RESEARCH MONOGRAPHS IN FRENCH STUDIES

The *Research Monographs in French Studies* (RMFS) form a separate series within the Legenda programme and are published in association with the Society for French Studies. Individual members of the Society are entitled to purchase all RMFS titles at a discount.

The series seeks to publish the best new work in all areas of the literature, thought, theory, culture, film and language of the French-speaking world. Its distinctiveness lies in the relative brevity of its publications (50,000–60,000 words). As innovation is a priority of the series, volumes should predominantly consist of new material, although, subject to appropriate modification, previously published research may form up to one third of the whole. Proposals may include critical editions as well as critical studies. They should be sent with one or two sample chapters for consideration to Professor Diana Knight, Department of French and Francophone Studies, University of Nottingham, University Park, Nottingham NG7 2RD.

Editorial Committee
Diana Knight, University of Nottingham (General Editor)
Robert Blackwood (University of Liverpool)
Jane Gilbert, University College London
Shirley Jordan, Newcastle University
Neil Kenny, All Souls College, Oxford
Max Silverman, University of Leeds

Advisory Committee
Wendy Ayres-Bennett, Murray Edwards College, Cambridge
Celia Britton, University College London
Ann Jefferson, New College, Oxford
Sarah Kay, New York University
Michael Moriarty, University of Cambridge
Keith Reader, University of Glasgow

PUBLISHED IN THIS SERIES

www.legendabooks.com

Marie NDiaye

Inhospitable Fictions

SHIRLEY JORDAN

LEGENDA

Research Monographs in French Studies 38
Modern Humanities Research Association
2017

Published by Legenda
an imprint of the Modern Humanities Research Association
Salisbury House, Station Road, Cambridge CB1 2LA

ISBN 978-1-907975-85-1 (HB)
ISBN 978-1-78188-381-5 (PB)

First published 2017

Copy-Editor: Charlotte Brown

CONTENTS

In memory of my mother Avril,
whose door was always open

ACKNOWLEDGEMENTS

The project for this book began in January 2007 with a lecture delivered at the Sorbonne entitled 'La Quête familiale dans les écrits de Marie NDiaye: nomadisme, (in)hospitalité, différence' [The Quest for the Family in the Writings of Marie NDiaye: Nomadism, (In)hospitality, Difference]. Some years later, and in part thanks to conversations following numerous other papers where I tried out ideas on NDiaye in London, Oxford, Cambridge, Durham, Paris, Mannheim, Uppsala, Montreal and St. Louis, the book is finally complete. I owe a debt of gratitude to a great many people: Anne Simon, for the initial invitation to the Sorbonne and for stimulating discussions since I set off en route; Gill Rye, especially for her work on mothers and mothering; Andrew Asibong, with whom I organized the first ever conference on NDiaye and whose dazzling monograph on the author is hard to follow; Micky Sheringham, who alerted me to humour in NDiaye in more ways than one and whose company and friendship were so life-enhancing; Diana Knight, for her interest in the project and her patience as it slowly took shape; and Judith Still, whose work on Derrida and hospitality was a source of inspiration and who knows how to have longer coffee breaks in the Bibliothèque nationale than any of my other friends. I am deeply indebted to her fine and spirited work and grateful to her for reading parts of this book. Thanks to Marie-Claire Barnet for the (optimistically named) 'Genius Pad', which was invaluable for working out many of my ideas. Thanks also to supportive colleagues and friends at Queen Mary University of London, my institutional home for the last ten years, and most especially to Sue Harris whose friendship is a rare gift. Finally, as ever, huge thanks to my husband, Raymond Kuhn, for his encouragement, support and love.

This book is dedicated to my mother, Avril Mattinson, who died while I was in the midst of writing it. Not a day passes that I do not think of her. 'Car on ne peut pas dire que les êtres aimés soient morts tant qu'il reste un vivant pour les aimer.' (Inscription on a gravestone in Montparnasse cemetery, Paris.)

s.j., Oxford, June 2017

LIST OF ABBREVIATIONS

AV	Autoportrait en vert
EF	En famille
G	'La Gourmandise'
L	Ladivine
MCE	Mon cœur à l'étroit
N	La Naufragée
PDM	Papa doit manger
RC	Rosie Carpe
RH	Rien d'humain
S	La Sorcière
SE	Les Serpents
TFP	Trois femmes puissantes
TMA	Tous mes amis
UTS	Un temps de saison

Translations in this book are my own unless otherwise stated.

INTRODUCTION

> The law of hospitality can best be seen in the actions which
> constitute its infringement.[1]
>
> Tout se passe comme si l'hospitalité était l'impossible.
> [It is as though hospitality were the impossible.][2]

This book argues that a profound concern for hospitality is the principal driver of
Marie NDiaye's fictions. If the word 'hospitality' is seldom used in her writing, the
practices and ethics of hospitality are nonetheless perpetually in play, determining
plot and form as well as the intricacies of human interaction across a wide range
of relationships. Such systematic concentration endows the author's extensive
and generically varied corpus — including novels, short stories, plays, children's
literature and textual-visual experiments — with extraordinary consistency of
purpose.[3] All of her works stage opportunities for hospitality that range from
fleeting encounters to elaborate set-piece events and they are frequently structured
around journeying, arriving, the stranger's welcome (or unwelcome) and the
problem of 'home'. She keeps us alert to how outsiderness is constructed and experienced, fills her pages with tropes related to incorporation and expulsion, and has
us linger on any number of real or metaphorical boundaries, constantly inviting
connections between hospitality on interpersonal, national and supranational scales.
Her writing is unusually resonant with the intensive worrying over hospitality
that has characterized French intellectual life over the last thirty or so years, and
the anxiety-ridden testing of hospitality in which her protagonists (and therefore
we) are engaged responds to related discourses and debates with great subtlety and
force.

Two of the factors that make NDiaye's focus on hospitality so compelling are
her minute insistence on intimacy and affect, and her persistent depiction not of
hospitality but of its opposite. It is via the systematic infringement of hospitality's
most basic tenets, from small specific speech acts or gestures on the part of host
or guest to the provision of food or shelter, that the stakes of hospitality are raised
for consideration in her work. Frequently these are heightened by her insistence
on the family, both as a real locus of suffering and unkindness and as a metaphor
for larger social groups. If theorists of hospitality argue that it makes no sense to
apply its laws to family relations given that 'l'hospitalité ne peut s'effectuer qu'en
direction d'étrangers' [hospitality can be extended only to strangers], NDiaye's
imaginative extension of them to this context effectively underscores the existential
strangeness of any self to any Other, and the need for an ethics of hospitality in all

our interactions.[4] The emotional and practical repercussions of inhospitality in her fiction are incalculable, producing interactions whose tenor ranges from mildly apprehensive to paroxysmally fear-soaked. Inhospitality is everywhere in NDiaye, calling into question what it means to be 'mother', 'father', 'sibling', 'neighbour', 'friend' or, more fundamentally, 'human'.[5] The perverse scenarios that she develops perturb and offend our ethical sensibility: we read aghast as the famished little boy from next door joins the Maur family at mealtimes and sits in the corner unfed (*TMA* 81); as an embittered Rudy Descas telephones his neighbour Mme Pulmaire to ask for help but shouts abuse at her instead (*TFP* 115); or as the tourist whose wife shares her water with the parched Lazare and Abel is murdered by the latter with a machete in an unprovoked attack (*RC* 263–64).[6] Many protagonists appear morally anaesthetized; others openly articulate and justify positions of inhospitality. They turn away the needy, break into other's homes, become parasites, steal, abuse, enslave and occasionally murder. NDiaye's fictional world is awash with inhospitable matter and it is this persistent emphasis that makes it such a challenging ethical space. My aim, then, is to respond to a curious critical gap in studies of the author by focusing squarely on her fixation with hospitality and by analyzing her writings as 'inhospitable fictions'.[7]

My purpose in this Introduction is twofold. First, I set NDiayean inhospitality in context by tracing connections between her evolving preoccupations and debates that usefully inform our reading of them. I comment on postcolonial hospitality in a French context, compare NDiaye's approach to that of some contemporaneous literary writers of hospitality, and suggest how her work might be illuminated by the philosophy of hospitality. Second, I seek to demonstrate how the author's use of the fantastic, including her interface with relevant myth and legend, plays a distinctive role in her articulation of inhospitality and how she elaborates what amounts to a 'fantastic anthropology' of inhospitality. I do not follow the usual procedure of providing a sketch of the author at the outset, other than to observe that NDiaye was born in 1967 of a French mother and a Senegalese father, that she was brought up by her mother in provincial France (her father left when she was one year old), and that possible links between her own identity as mixed race and the themes of inhospitality and marginalization in her work — especially as they relate to contemporary France — inevitably filter into our appreciation of it. Readers interested in the figure of the author will find analysis of her reception and construction by the French literary establishment in Chapter 5.

Postcolonial (In)hospitality

French debates about (French) hospitality have been the backdrop to NDiaye's writing from the outset. Her first works were published in the 1980s, the decade in which the Beur novel began powerfully to raise questions of hospitality through largely autobiographical narratives of second-generation North African youngsters struggling to situate themselves on the secular/Muslim fault line that defined their 'bi-cultural condition'.[8] Her novels and plays of the 1990s took shape while the hospitality metaphor was coalescing into a major focus in continental philosophy thanks to extended investigations by thinkers such as Jacques Derrida and Emmanuel Levinas. Simultaneously, hospitality was increasingly harnessed as a powerful tool for a raft of scholarly works across the disciplines and as a key trope for literature and film that set out to explore the themes of immigration and identity. The decade was marked too by powerful indictments of French inhospitality,[9] and by significant studies of how hospitality informed literature, especially literature devoted to understanding identities in a postcolonial framework.[10] What anthropologist Matei Candea refers to as 'hospitality's transformation into a particular kind of rhetorical object in France' is thus underway as NDiaye's project takes shape.[11]

NDiaye's foundational fable concerning French attempts to erase certain categories of individual from the national narrative is the 1990 novel *En famille* [Among Family]. This elusive, oneiric and savage work could scarcely be more different from those analyzed in Mireille Rosello's study of the hospitality theme in 1990s French literature and film.[12] The 'family' in question, implicitly to be equated with a certain idea of France, is rigidly backward-looking towards its ancestry, incapable of envisaging a future with the heroine Fanny who, we intuit, is *métisse*, and intent on negating her sense of legitimacy. The name of the cousin who rebuffs the heroine's romantic interest in him, Eugène (evocative of course of eugenics), is no accident: Fanny's dilution of the stock cannot be admitted. That she continues stubbornly to seek acceptance — even once she has been torn apart by her cousin's dogs and thrown on the dung heap by her aunt (*EF* 186) — is a joke at the expense of France. Fanny simply cannot be erased: she will persist in spite of her apprenticeship in ostracism and, if the dung heap metaphor is to be followed to the letter, she may also enrich the community. A still darker joke is that she is in the end literally assimilated, her particularity eradicated. NDiaye's writing plays frequently on the connection between 'assimilation' (a term long rejected from French political discourse in favour of 'integration', although it is currently being used again by right-wing politicians) and digestion.[13] The resuscitated Fanny, we note, is unlike her original self, less 'singular', paler, indeed almost invisible and sucked dry of her difference in order to conform. *En famille*, then, sets the foundations for NDiaye's sophisticated weaving of contemporary debates about hospitality into fable. One further feature that characterizes this work and that has been much commented upon is its skilful avoidance of the very mention of colour. The reason for Fanny's rejection is hard to pin down precisely because *En famille* systematically replicates the indirectness, euphemism and sometimes hypocrisy that are characteristic of French refusals to admit that colour matters.[14]

NDiaye became especially associated with French inhospitality in the following decade, a decade which saw the riots by sons and daughters of North-African immigrants in 2005, increasingly hard-line policies on immigration, the persecution of groups such as the Roms — legally present on French territory yet forcibly ejected from their encampments — and, at the decade's end, the so-called 'crisis' of French identity which escalated into a national debate. France's cherished traditional values of welcome, hospitality and respect for equal human rights emerged again and again as flattering abstractions which came pitiably unstuck in the face of embodied challenges, before being grudgingly and messily enacted.[15] Famously, NDiaye emigrated to Berlin just after the presidential election in 2007 and shortly before the publication of the novel *Mon cœur à l'étroit* [My Heart Hemmed in], the first part of which depicts a surge of atavistic inhospitality directed at Nadia, its North-African protagonist, by the (white) bourgeois inhabitants of Bordeaux. It seems certain that the backdrop provided by France's increasingly extreme-right domestic agenda, and what NDiaye described as a 'détestable [...] atmosphère de flicage, de vulgarité' [detestable [...] atmosphere of heavy policing and vulgarity] ushered in by Nicolas Sarkozy, along with the prevailing 'refus d'une différence possible' [refusal of possible difference] played into her imagining of this work.[16] The novel also illustrates a clutch of features that sets NDiaye's writing apart in terms of its relation to postcolonial hospitality: the sheer extent to which it is saturated in inhospitable deeds and thoughts, most of them inflected by the residue of colonial power relations; its minute attentiveness to the inexpressible psychic damage resulting from inhospitality of all stripes; its expression of this through fantastic devices; and the overall sense of repression and denial that it conveys, which leaves the horrors of the past and present unspoken and makes of her fictional universe a toxic waste ground.

I argue then that NDiaye's work takes us beyond the emphases and modes of what Rosello calls 'l'âge d'or de l'hospitalité' [the golden age of hospitality] of the 1980s and 1990s to express something more apprehensive and fundamental about the imperative of an ethics of hospitality in a globalizing world.[17] Her writing does not trace the experiences of any specific ethnic minority, but conveys a more generalized sense of individual precariousness and insecurity. We not only follow the expulsion of Nadia from the bourgeois bastion of Bordeaux, we also trace the trajectory, in *Trois femmes puissantes* [Three Strong Women], of the impoverished white French man Rudy Descas, who returns from his teaching job in Senegal to an inhospitable France that affords him scant opportunities; a place in which he seems less materially secure than the families in the gipsy encampment down the road. In the same novel we follow a trail of clandestine migration as the author's diasporic imagination and geographical focus shift to the broader European and global framework in which France is enmeshed and it is this more expansive panorama of (in)hospitality that now affords the context for her writing.[18] It is worth noting too that the emphasis on hospitality in NDiaye's texts gains in resonance as time passes: several years on from the publication of *Trois femmes puissantes*, the razor-wire fence on which the heroine of its final story perishes as she tries to make her way to Europe seems more alarmingly familiar, while the 'moving-on' of refugees, migrants and asylum seekers from camp to camp and country to country within Europe has created a stinging context in which to read her. Meanwhile back in the French metropole, an animated map of the movements of displaced people around Paris displayed for a recent exhibition entitled 'Cartographie du non-accueil' [Cartography of un-welcome] offered an especially sharp example of the tensions that motivate NDiaye's writing.[19]

A final point, and one which too often slips through the net as critics of NDiaye focus on race, is that the author's protagonists are caught up not only in the knotty complexity of postcolonial identities but in the workings of (in)hospitality across class divides. NDiaye's refined class consciousness and her concern for race are frequently intertwined: Malinka's rejection of her mother in *Ladivine* [Ladivine] is generated not only by internalized racial prejudice, but also by the latter's job as a cleaning lady (the daughter refers to her as 'la servante' [the servant], *L* 26); while in *Mon cœur à l'étroit* Nadia abandons her family in order not only to detach herself from her North-African origins but also to escape poverty. Her distaste for her parents' simplicity, her aliveness to the stigma of indigence and her determination to 'better' herself culturally are inextricably bound up with her consciousness of racial discrimination, and it is in fact her class assumptions, prejudices and pretensions that flood the narrative, while the racial dimension of her self-perception remains largely unarticulated.[20]

Hospitality in Thought and Theory

I turn now to some of the core ideas elaborated in philosophical explorations of hospitality which map productively on to NDiaye's project. The author's work is more philosophically-oriented than it has yet been given credit for and seems deliberately to stage interactions that correspond to contemporary thinking on hospitality in all its complexity and slipperiness. My observations here are limited to a small number of key concepts from Jacques Derrida, Emmanuel Levinas, Luce Irigaray — a thinker of hospitality less often cited than Derrida or Levinas, but one whose work is rich in important propositions, not least for thinking about women and hospitality — and Slavoj Žižek.[21] Other readers may trace different routes.

Let us begin with two influential aspects of Derrida's thinking which receive expression in NDiaye. The first is the paradox or aporia at the heart of hospitality. Derrida does not merely concern himself with the laws of hospitality, which are contingent and conditional, but, famously, with the Law: that is, with a form of absolute, unconditional opening to the Other which lets them be on their own terms and asks for nothing in exchange, not even the stranger's name. Such openness is dangerous, even 'unbearable', for it requires, as Derrida says, 'that you give up the mastery of your space, your home, your nation', yet if pure hospitality exists, he continues, 'it should be pushed to this extreme'.[22] There is an irresolvable tension here, since the very condition of providing any kind of welcome in the first place is that the host be master of a home. NDiaye, whose writing incessantly returns to the point of welcome (the threshold in its numerous guises), appears to be mesmerized by similar propositions and paradoxes. Again and again the possibility of welcome and the terms on which a stranger may be 'taken in' are addressed. One work in particular, the play *Rien d'humain* [Nothing Human], seems, as we will see in Chapter 1, deftly to experiment with the problem set by Derrida and to create a (postcolonial) tussle over the question of who can host. Critical here is that NDiaye is conspicuously trying out variants on a complicated spectrum of positions, creating test cases or 'what if's?' rather than a 'story'. This is a most important point. Candea states that Derridean hospitality 'seems to be constantly, breathlessly buffeted from absolute self-annihilating openness to the most virulent xenophobia and back again' precisely because he is working with abstract principles, not concrete, grounded examples.[23] NDiaye does ground her examples of course, but she also conspicuously veers between and tests conceptual extremes so that every incident, from her sketchy vignettes to her major set pieces of (in)hospitality, remains snagged between embodied practice and conceptual exercise, a feature of her writing which is compounded by her use of the fantastic, as I shall shortly go on to discuss. She offers in the same protagonist a stranger and *the* Stranger; an other and *the* Other; a neighbour and *the* Neighbour.[24] And while pure, unconditional hospitality — Derrida's unstinting 'Oui à l'étranger' [Yes to the stranger] — remains a symbolic horizon throughout her writings, her protagonists most often enact the radical failure of the Derridean will to absolute openness, so much so that, as I have already suggested, even family members become hostile, risk-averse and ungenerous strangers to each other.[25] Žižek has protested against Derrida's idealism and countered his configuration of the stranger/Other as 'the abyssal point from which the call to ethical responsibility emanates'[26] with the stranger as something foreboding: the Neighbour-Thing, whose destructive potential and 'radically ambiguous monstrosity' are not to be overlooked.[27] This haunting apprehension of violence lurks within the majority of encounters that NDiaye invites us to contemplate and her protagonists are on the whole more likely to dehumanize and exclude than to welcome the Other.

A second feature of Derridean thinking that is everywhere exemplified in NDiaye concerns the tenuous nature of hospitality in action which the philosopher so deftly captures in the ambivalent portmanteau term 'hostipitalité' [hostipitality].[28] Anthropologists of the gift show how gifts are also poisons due to the debts incurred by the recipient and Derrida's term generalizes such uneasy calibrations, extending them to other forms of human interaction. The word 'hostipitality' buffets us, beginning with the 'host', slipping in a split second into 'hostility', before lurching towards its opposite, ultimately leaving us anxiously undecided and capturing so neatly our sense that the seeds of both hostility and hospitality are latent in any encounter. It opens too on to the idea of the hostage and, in French, recalls that 'hôte' [host] signifies both host and guest, underscoring hospitality's fluidity and reversibility. The term comes to life in NDiaye's writing thanks to her unusual, somewhat cruel curiosity about the quavering lines between welcome and rejection in negotiations of hospitality, her insistence on the complicated structures of feeling that they involve, her teasing into view of the half-formed perceptions, feelings and sensations that might ordinarily be lost but that it is literature's virtue to capture, and her insistence on irresolution. Thus a sense of potential, of anticipation and of dramatic tension suffuses hospitality encounters in NDiaye and while the outcome of these is habitually negative, they are incessantly underwritten with the welcome that might have materialized instead.

NDiaye typically gives us access to a central consciousness which is sharply sensitive to fluctuating hints of welcome and unwelcome. Let us take one tiny example: our apprehension of the young Ladivine's unease as she waves to greet a female sex worker she often sees as she walks through a particular area of Berlin (*L* 177–78). The gesture is teeming with possible meanings that make it teeter on the brink of inhospitality for both women. The sex worker's wary, reluctant response seems to indicate mistrust of the waver's motives while Ladivine, a protagonist alert to hospitality, considers whether her salutation is prompted precisely by a fear of *not* acknowledging the woman on account of her job, thereby defining her by it and constituting a quite inhospitable way of singling her out. Over and again NDiaye alludes to the kinds of delicate, intricate concerns which occupy us so urgently in our everyday lives as we juggle with hospitality's unspoken conditions and with implied degrees of reciprocity which are often tricky to calibrate. We might think here, especially given the everydayness of hospitality encounters in NDiaye, of Levinas's argument for interpersonal ethics. Levinas posits that when faced with the Other we are, as Žižek explains, 'always-already responsible for [them]'[29] and primed to put their needs before our own, a position which constitutes, in Levinas's terms, 'l'un-pour-l'autre lui-même' ('the one-for-the-other in the ego').[30] Further, we feel acutely, and are alert to, their singular presence and vulnerability even in mundane quotidian contact: an act as apparently simple as holding open the door or acknowledging a person in the street is an opportunity ethically to take account of their full humanity. Levinas uses the idea of 'face' to describe the forceful effect of the Other's singular presence and its call to hospitality, and this concept is repeatedly evoked in NDiaye's close-range explorations of how protagonists take account of each other as they teeter between responses. 'Hostipitality' is, then, absolutely central to NDiaye and we might say that her entire *œuvre* lingers around this cusp. Central too in terms of Derrida's thought about the ethics of hospitality is his expanded notion of 'eating well' and what this implies for exchanges that take place at body boundaries and orifices, a set of ideas to which I shall return, especially in Chapter 3.[31]

Irigaray's thought on hospitality also threads through this book. In an article on Irigaray's 2008 work of poetic philosophy *Sharing the World*, Judith Still explores the philosopher's 'hospitality of difference', a creative form of welcome that does not absorb other into same but forges something different, so that 'a true welcome, for Luce Irigaray, implies the possibility of constructing a new and third world as a result of my world's meeting with the other'.[32] The crux of this kind of hospitality is a readiness to change, an idea which removes the term from the ambit of the provisional and the comfortable to re-frame it as much more testing and challenging to the self. Irigarayan hospitality stresses, as Still puts it, 'an intimate sharing in difference, made possible by the cultivation of self-affection by both subjects'.[33] The idea of self-affection, something I also refer to in this book as 'self-welcoming' or 'self-hospitality' arises on a number of occasions in NDiaye, who seems indeed to suggest that it is a precondition of proper hospitality.[34] Thus protagonists who are dogged by shame or self-loathing cannot effectively welcome. There are few instances of self-affection in NDiaye, although a handful of her more recently devised protagonists — such as Nadia of *Mon cœur à l'étroit* who opens progressively to welcome self and therefore other — evoke the idea, and it may precisely be self-affection that accounts for the (otherwise puzzling) *puissance* [strength] of Norah, Fanta and especially Khady Demba, and that allows for new forms of hospitality to begin to emerge in *Trois femmes puissantes*.[35]

Derrida, Irigaray and many other thinkers have approached the question of hospitality through considering our relationships with animals. The dogs, birds and other creatures that play such a major part in NDiaye's work and that are welcomed into her own thinking about hospitality align her fiction with this dimension of contemporary thought and with key concerns in the field of animal studies. NDiaye's animals are integral to the emergent self-understanding of her protagonists and what Irigaray has called 'animal interventions' are important spurs to hospitality in many of her stories.[36] Moving beyond what we might call the 'animal habits' of Western culture, which are constructed around discontinuity and appropriation, NDiaye neither declares animals unknowable nor appropriates them, but keeps them present as familiar strangers from whom we have much to learn. Giorgio Agamben's view that 'L'homme-animal et l'animal-homme sont les deux faces d'une même fracture et d'une même béance, qui ne peut être comblée ni d'un côté ni d'un autre' [Man-animal and animal-man are the two faces of one same fracture and one same breach, which cannot be made whole by either side] is a structuring element in NDiaye, the fractures and breaches being precisely the fertile spaces in which new forms of hospitality may take shape.[37]

Original too in NDiaye is her explicit focus on transactions and patterns of hospitality that involve women. In the traditional literature about hospitality as well as in some recent philosophy such as that of Levinas, women's innumerable roles within circuits of hospitality — not to mention their agency — are little addressed and hospitality is assumed to be fraternal: to be men's business. Social anthropologist Julian Pitt-Rivers's famous comparative essay on the laws of hospitality sets the pattern, for it is entirely confined to hospitality between men.[38] Women are considered neither as hosts nor guests, although they may clearly be adjuncts required to furnish special kinds of openness and receptivity to others and to provide the labour of hospitality, including at its most intimate. Pitt-Rivers mentions women in his essay only as professional beggars (feared for their evil eye) and as chattel, noting that '[t]o attempt to sleep with the host's wife or to refuse to do so may either of them be infractions of a code of hospitality';[39] and of the host, that '[h]is wife's favours are always his to dispose of as he wishes'.[40] Significantly the figure of the traveller in need of hospitality in NDiaye is habitually female and women in her writing are actively involved in a wide range of hospitality transactions which are routinely seen from their perspective.

A related issue is maternal hospitality, which is central to NDiaye's concerns. The most widely read philosophical material on hospitality does not address the maternal, although feminist revisions of hospitality and also of models of maternity (as purely natural-animal-fusional) by thinkers such as Irigaray and Antoinette Fouque have provided theories of uterine or placental hospitality that I shall argue find their way into NDiaye's distinctive emphasis on mothering.[41] The author's investment in mothers is evident not only in her abiding fascination with mother/

child — and often mother/daughter — relationships, as is the case in a great many other women writers, but more fundamentally in her engagement with and fleshing out of the contention that the mother's body is the very origin of welcome. This persistent recourse to the mother figure's potential for hospitality and to her value for thinking about what hospitality might mean is a particularly original feature of the author's interest in mothers. Her closely depicted mother/child dyads appear rooted in Derrida's assertion that mother and child constitute together 'figures par excellence de l'hospitalité' [figures par excellence of hospitality].[42] Consistent with her emphasis on inhospitality however, NDiaye's mothers are repeatedly illustrated as closed off to their children, not just psychically but physically, as maternal body and first home.

NDiaye's fictional world is characterized too by the sheer reach of her probing of (in)hospitality. Every aspect of human behaviour is scrutinized under this particular lens. Areas that are repeatedly held up for our consideration include commensality (often a feature of narrative fiction, but unusually present here and in a range of perversely inhospitable forms); 'gift-giving' of various types, objects and substances, implying diverse degrees of reciprocity; forms of gesture and touch; modes of address, especially naming; and, in varying degrees of intensity from book to book, human–animal relations.

Inhospitality and the Fantastic

One of the most remarked upon traits of NDiaye's writing is its disquieting slippage between sharply observant realism and fantastic modes and tropes.[43] The saturation of her world in fantastic matter has been much analyzed but not, as I do in this book, specifically as it relates to the author's consideration of (in)hospitality. To launch this line of thinking, here are some brief pointers. First, hospitality and the fantastic alike are played out (and conceptualized) on the threshold, an unstable and destabilizing locus of hesitation and suspended understanding which carries the potential for one thing and its opposite.[44] Second, the apprehension or fear aroused in protagonists by encounters wherein welcome, belonging and recognition are at stake can be most urgently conveyed by a lurch beyond the real. NDiaye accordingly draws out the powerful affect latent in such interactions and uses fantasy to access and convey complex emotional truths. Third, the fantastic allows the author to imagine, and hence keep alive in the text, hospitality's unrealizable or undesirable extremes, those that are contemplated by philosophers but fall outside the codified repertoire of everyday practice: Derridean absolute hospitality for example, or an act such as cannibalism.[45] Fourth, the departure from conventional articulations of hospitality is fantastic in both nature and degree in NDiaye: everyday norms of hosting and guesting are routinely raised for consideration by their flouting, as well as by the frequent replacement of recognizable codes with strange ones. Finally (in this list at least) the un-homing associated with the Freudian uncanny, where what is most familiar becomes inhospitably strange, is routine in NDiaye.[46] The author's various observations on her predilection for fantastic devices include her aversion to psychological analysis and abstraction ('ma seule manière de voir les choses abstraites, c'est de les incarner' [the only way I can see abstract things is by embodying them]),[47] and her preference to replace the term 'fantastic' as it applies to her work with 'réalisme exagéré', [exaggerated realism],[48] a significant formulation which plays down any departure from the real in terms of genuinely fantastic events and directs us instead towards a powerfully psychological and affective interpretation of the inextricability of axes.

In a study of experiments with the fantastic by women writers in French since 1990, Margaret-Anne Hutton observes that their work 'escapes the categorization espoused by most theorists of the fantastic' and notes several common functions.[49] These include the exploration of origins and identity; the desire for and interrogation of home; the body as uncanny site; and more generally a desire to communicate, and gloss, the anxieties characteristic of our time. In particular, Hutton describes all the texts studied in her volume as 'diasporic': that is, texts which not only manifest nostalgia for home but deconstruct the very idea of home; which 'have renounced the possibility of their being a 'home', a 'site of origin', or, correlatively, a true state of 'exile'.[50] She also notes the connection between this new fantastic and the emergence of increasingly complex identities, suggesting that the contemporary globalized era has engendered 'a (fantastic) literature of post-national anxiety'.[51] Such reflections are extremely pertinent to NDiaye. So too are the connections one might detect between the fantastic and traumatic experience. Drawing on Cathy Caruth's work on trauma narrative and Suzette Henke's analyses of post-traumatic stress disorder, Deborah Gaensbauer notes how trauma in NDiaye is 'filter[ed] through the conventions of the literary fantastic'[52] and argues persuasively that *En famille*, for example, may be read as an instance of the 'post-traumatic fantastic', with Fanny its heroine as 'shattered subject'.[53] In this reading, the fantastic that surfaces throughout NDiaye derives from a 'posttraumatic symptomology related to abusive families, racial difference and cultural exclusion'.[54] Its function is to betray a disturbing, un-avowed inheritance, either individual or collective, and its deepest roots are frequently connected to a sense of postcolonial disorder. It is, then, the queasily violent eruption of colonialism's multiple inhospitalities that is expressed by the fantastic.

Disavowed matter seeps out into NDiaye's texts in numerous ways, either physical or verbal, which make protagonists abruptly strange to themselves, perhaps newly infantilized or nearly animal. It may also be alluded to via references to visual impairment, blurring or mistiness which suggest half-concealed, unmanageable material. On the first point, Christine Jérusalem notes that bodies in NDiaye are 'saisis par un mouvement de rejet' [seized by an impulse of rejection] and that her texts are saturated in bodily fluids, occasioning disgust, shame and fear.[55] Often voice and speech become unruly, beset by bestial distortions, while the kind of abject matter that is, socially speaking, beyond articulation rises chaotically to the surface in spite of protagonists, calling to mind fantastic tales of possession or exorcism. The new, monstrous voices that erupt in NDiaye are, it is implied, closer to the inner truth of protagonists as well as to a socially reproduced but unspoken (because ethically inadmissible) set of inhospitable values. Again, the fantastic permits especially subtle expression of the stakes of inhospitality: a protagonist may dehumanize others, but in so doing is her-/himself dehumanized. On the question of visual impairment in NDiaye we might consider, for example, how the self-deluding Nadia in *Mon cœur à l'étroit* is not only chronically myopic but disorientated by an implausibly impenetrable fog that descends around her, making the familiar topography of Bordeaux unnavigable (*MCE* 122–26). Blurring implies both a hermeneutic hurdle — a stumbling-block in terms of sense-making — and a problem of denial: as Rosemary Jackson contends, '[t]hat which is not seen, or which threatens to be un-seeable [has] a subversive function in relation to an epistemological and metaphysical system which makes "I see" synonymous with "I understand"'.[56] NDiaye puts blurring to the service of precisely this point. The tendency is reinforced in her textual-visual experiments, all of which are saturated in images whose oneiric haziness suggests unwelcome truths that are present yet unavailable to the conscious mind.[57]

It is worth pausing at this point to consider one telling example: NDiaye's incorporation of details from J. M. W. Turner's marine paintings in *La Naufragée* [The Shipwrecked Woman]. This violent tale about a woman-fish out of her element, to which I return in Chapter 2, is a contemporary myth about difference, indifference, inhospitality and power. It literalizes and hyperbolizes the alterity of all strangers (perhaps too of women to men), asks us to consider the testing of human hospitality by what is other than human, and raises complex issues about welcoming animals and about hosts imprisoning their guests. At first the fantastical creature's yearning for the sea appears to be what connects text and image, but writ small within the book's sumptuous visual matter is a very specific reference to the history of slavery, which we might consider to constitute the narrative's wellspring, in the form of Turner's *Slave Ship (Slavers Throwing Overboard the Dead and Dying, Typhoon Coming On)* (1840).[58] Looking beyond the amber light and silver spume which first dazzle us we pick out — in the foreground yet, tellingly, not immediately visible for all that — evidence of the terrible human drama that the now distant ship has left in its wake. The churning sea is littered with shackled bodies. Everywhere hands are raised out of the water in futile supplication, underscoring the scandal of indifference. It is not so much that NDiaye's story threads its way back through Turner to allude to the history of slavery; more that such histories push their way up to the surface.[59] Fragments of this painting are dispersed throughout *La Naufragée*, appearing on six separate occasions including on the front cover, like dim reminders of partially submerged, atrocious matter. The interweaving of Turner's drowning slaves with a fantastic tale of inhospitality is an exemplary illustration of NDiaye's insistence on all that is hidden and silenced by her protagonists; all that they refuse to articulate or to see. Thus the fantastic, which has a dissociative function, in turn exposes habits of dissociation.

Hospitality in NDiaye is distinguished too by its intermeshing with myth and legend. The author's writing is host to innumerable intertexts and her set-piece scenes often read like contemporary versions of the trials or testing structures of ancient hospitality stories whose significance exceeds the localized and the particular. She experiments explicitly with the challenge of welcoming the Other who comes in non-human or hybrid form (a woman-fish, a woman with cloven hooves, a father-turned-bird),[60] and offers reminders of *theoxeny*, the convention in Greek mythology whereby gods, poised to punish or reward human beings according to the welcome they provide, arrive disguised as humble strangers.[61] It must be noted however that such ethical resolution is unavailable in NDiaye and that inhospitality, while it horrifies the reader, goes unchecked in the world of the text. Most notably, although it has to date escaped critical notice, NDiaye's core intertext is undoubtedly the founding book of Western hospitality, Homer's *Odyssey*. The legend's structuring around a sequence of hospitality scenes and its focus on different kinds and degrees of (in)hospitality shown to the traveller Odysseus and his men seem to offer the very model to which NDiaye repeatedly returns.[62] Further, her persistent underscoring of the vulnerability of travellers and of their reliance on the hospitality of strangers in an increasingly diasporic world is intriguingly underpinned by the scenario in ancient Greece where *xenia* ('guest-friendship') was essential for similar reasons.

As in the Homeric legend then, adventures of (in)hospitality shape NDiaye's stories. Indeed, diegetic developments that seem unaccountable may sometimes precisely be understood as the working out of a new hospitality fable or the re-casting of an existing one. Thus in *Ladivine* Clarisse Rivière's surprising relationship of 'fraternité dépouillée' [bare fraternity] (*L* 128) with the human wreck Freddy Moliger assumes its full meaning when we read it along these lines. Here NDiaye gives expression to Derrida's abstraction of pure hospitality through an extended re-configuration of the myth of Saint Julian the Hospitaller, the repentant hermit who offers to carry travellers from bank to bank of a river on his own back and who helps a leper, nourishing the man, warming him against his own naked body and pressing his mouth to that of his guest so that they become one. The leper turns into a ray of light and Saint Julian, in ecstasy, is transported to heaven. In NDiaye's story Clarisse Rivière, also solitary and repentant (for the (symbolic) killing of her mother, just as the saint killed his parents), welcomes into her home, bed and body the physically unpalatable Moliger who presents on the face of things such a challenge to hospitality and who in the end will murder her. NDiaye's stress on both Moilger's ravaged body and Clarisse's caressing of it without disgust point powerfully towards the myth and the latter's death, while devoid of religious overtones, transports her to a deep forest which promises contentment.[63] Absolute hospitality, in both the biblical story and NDiaye's re-working of it, results in the dissolution and annihilation of self.

This is one of many examples of NDiaye's deliberate updating of classic hospitality myths in order to refresh them and make them newly available. Her stories transpose ancient scenarios to contemporary settings and, largely through their slippage away from realism, seem on occasion to lay claim to the status of myth themselves for they offer complex, concrete instances whose puzzling impact keeps us returning to think with them. Hospitality in NDiaye then is embodied and deeply felt, but it is at the same time unmoored from the continuity of realist narrative the better to experiment with its possible iterations and effects.

Fantastic Anthropology

I turn finally to discuss a further thread that runs through this book: NDiaye's place within the developing field of literature and anthropology studies. I argue that her work represents a significant contribution to the dialogues between literature and anthropology that have multiplied under the impetus of postcolonial studies, and that she shares with anthropologists a number of key questions, perspectives and devices. Indeed, as I show in Chapter 1, she devotes an entire novel, *Un temps de saison* [Seasonable Weather], to the exploration and parody of anthropology, including accounts of the welcome extended to ethnographers in the field and the strain that their presence often places on hospitality. The novel indicates a fine-tuned awareness on the author's part of the political history of anthropology, the notions of (naturalized) inequality that it promulgated as part of the colonial enterprise, and the discipline's evolution towards a reckoning with its own inhospitable assumptions during the emergence of its postmodern forms.

Beyond this isolated exercise, NDiaye's bridging of fiction and anthropology is manifested, for example, in her overt concerns for kin, social structures, collective behaviour, belief and action, ritual, the careful calibration of reciprocity and the intricate ways in which, through a range of codified interactions, groups maintain themselves as bounded entities. Her writing teems with the kind of concrete examples of everyday practice that anthropologists collect as evidence and she has an ethnographer's eye for telling detail, as well as a gift for what Clifford Geertz referred to as 'thick description', a close unpacking of everyday or special events in order to tease out their laws.[64] She has her protagonists voice 'general rules' or maxims, which remain formally similar to, yet slide uneasily away from, our own stock of adages, reminding us as they do so of the controlling function of shared cultural 'knowledge' boiled down to unquestionable nuggets.[65] She also raises for consideration all manner of ambiguous transactions on the taxonomy of exchange, a favourite of anthropologists: gift-giving, lending and borrowing, altruism and favours, purchases and theft may all be rewardingly traced through her fiction. Finally, not only does she create for her work an overarching architecture concerning problems of welcome, marginalization and belonging, but she carries out a kind of obsessive fantasy fieldwork on the subject of hospitality encounters, lingering repeatedly to consider hospitality's manifestations and, critically, showing in each instantiation the violence attendant upon its failure. In short, she encourages us to read about (in)hospitality with ethnographic fascination.

The 'field' for NDiaye has included the ordinary (she would say mediocre) provincial France in which she grew up; a range of French regions, towns and cities; Guadeloupe, where she captures some of the tensions between French expatriates and indigenous people;[66] Senegal, Berlin and a host of imaginary lands which maintain various recognizable as well as fantastic characteristics.[67] Human interaction in all these locations repeatedly takes a fantastic turn so we might say that while anthropologists defamiliarize routine phenomena in order to make their meanings newly available, NDiaye creates double defamiliarizations, devising interactions that are hauntingly bizarre yet, disarmingly, retaining a cool and apparently empirical focus so that invented social behaviour is lent the same status as recognizable social behaviour. In so doing she provides a radical literary twist on the postmodern ethnographic imperative of 'making strange'. My contention is that NDiaye elaborates a fantastic anthropology of inhospitality, both through sustained scrutiny of the non-observance of recognizable rules and customs — which in turn draws attention repeatedly *to* those rules — and through a disorientating process of scrambling whereby what we think we know is dislodged and replaced by strange and impenetrable behaviours. Her particularity is to make hospitality inoperable or unstable, to reveal its horrifying flip side and to invite us into a parallel universe of uncannily opaque rituals and signs. Thus, in *Rosie Carpe* [Rosie Carpe], Titi's insistence that his family may not touch or eat with his mother is a mystery to Lagrand (*RC* 327); thus, the pinning of strips of Ange's skin inside Nadia's coat in *Mon cœur à l'étroit* remains a (horrifying) puzzle (*MCE* 77–78); thus in *Autoportrait en vert* [Self-portrait in Green] the narrator's ritual shredding of philadelphus leaves over the feet of a woman she is conversing with in the street — perhaps a gesture of consolation — remains obscure (*AV* 20).

A further particularity of NDiaye's fantastic anthropology is its insistence on the shaping of inhospitality by one core component of human value systems: disgust. NDiaye's writing shows a pronounced interest in negative affect or 'aversive emotions'[68] such as fear, anxiety, hatred or resentment, and is in tune with the recent emphasis in cultural and literary analysis on 'ugly feelings'.[69] If rituals of hospitality habitually hold such emotions in check, NDiaye systematically unleashes them and her writing is highly charged with disgust reactions on many levels, often mingled with shame.[70] Philosophers of disgust explore it as a violent physical symptom and a key driver of human behaviour that is bent on maintaining the integrity of the self. They note that it is 'contact-sensitive',[71] and observe its 'self-other asymmetry'.[72] In other words disgust is instrumental in policing borders, a factor that comes strongly into play given NDiaye's insistence on proximate enactments of inhospitality which activate the senses — notably touch and smell — as well as on the thresholds of the body. Most significantly for our purposes disgust has been referred to as the 'gatekeeper emotion'.[73] We will encounter numerous instances of and spurs to disgust throughout this book, both aesthetic and ethical, and disgust will be a companion just as it is throughout our reading of NDiaye. The undeniable attractiveness to us of what repels us, and the consequent attraction-repulsion dynamic that helps us to keep in place the boundaries between the self and what disgusts it, account in fact for a deal of our reading pleasure as we navigate her texts. If it is a human characteristic persistently to revisit what is physically or ethically disgusting in order to keep it at bay, then it is precisely this kind of obsessive return that keeps us locked in to NDiaye's world.

We may in addition connect NDiaye's fantastic anthropology to the newly emerging sub-discipline of moral anthropology and, for example, to what Didier

Fassin and Patrice Bourdelais refer to as the 'construction of the intolerable'.[74] The authors note the relative and fluid nature of this term, emphasizing that what is deemed intolerable changes according to culture and time period. There is no 'absolute' intolerable and the intolerable of tomorrow will surely be different from that of today. What, at the start of the twenty-first century do we in Western Europe regard as crossing the threshold of the tolerable? Fassin and Bourdelais note our remarkable tolerance for atrocious inequalities and injustices, including for the assumption that all human life is not equal. What ills are we prepared to accept and in the name of what cause? Such questions are persistently raised for our consideration by NDiaye. We might in fact argue that her corpus contributes in its own right to such an area of study for it calls into question the category of the intolerable, alluding to the numerous examples that saturate public space and itself furnishing a thoroughgoing 'construction of the intolerable'. Our sense of what is tolerable is offended at every turn in a systematic testing of the boundaries whereon the limits of the idea are at stake. What, for NDiaye's protagonists, constitutes crossing this moral threshold? Murders, beatings, mutilation, maternal neglect, theft, the selling or sexual abuse of children (to which the community turns a blind eye) and blatant racial discrimination are just some of the instances of the author's unleashing of unprincipled behaviour around what we might understand to be the threshold. None brings with it any legal or social sanction and the perpetrators are habitually unperturbed by their own actions. The moral threshold is not regulated in this fantastic universe and the results are terrible: 'l'intolérable ne cesse de se déplacer, de s'étendre et de se recomposer' [the intolerable ceaselessly shifts, spreads and reforms] state Fassin and Bourdelais: NDiaye's fantastic fiction responds precisely to this phenomenon.[75]

My last point concerns the overwhelming importance attributed throughout NDiaye's work to thresholds. Postcolonial literature and thought have made much of boundaries and borders, but NDiaye's work stands out for its insistent focus on the threshold as a variant which draws us irrevocably to contemplate the problem of hospitality. Anthropologists have long been interested in the meanings given to and the rituals performed in these select areas of social space. In NDiaye too thresholds are privileged places where belonging and exclusion are negotiated and sharply articulated, where hospitality holds its breath, and where the ethical freight of her writing coalesces. Indeed, the author makes of the threshold an almost mythical contemporary space: one which foregrounds the tenuousness of hospitality while making its urgency keenly felt, and provides a focus for debate about belonging in a postcolonial world. It is perhaps particularly through the trope of the threshold that the fantastic and the anthropological come together in NDiaye's writing. Accordingly the threshold will be a recurring theme in this book's consideration of inhospitality and we will encounter it both as a physical location and as a trope connected, for example, to the body (to touch, skin, membranes and wounds) or to speech, as enacted in the tension between voicing and silence or in acts of naming.

The following chapters trace NDiaye's concern for hospitality through some of its most distinctive articulations. I do not follow a chronological trajectory through her work but instead select powerful examples from across her corpus and organize them thematically, although the evolution in her writing towards more explicit references to race, racism and migration and her growing tendency to endow her darkly pessimistic stories with glimmers of redemptive potential will, of course, surface. Notably, the reader will find close analysis of *Rien d'humain*, *Un temps de saison*, *La Naufragée*, *Rosie Carpe*, *Mon cœur à l'étroit* (the heroine's body is discussed from different perspectives in Chapters 2, 3 and 4), *Trois femmes puissantes* and *Ladivine*. In Chapter 1 I analyze the construction of stranger figures and the problem of hosts and hosting as explored by NDiaye, as well as the ubiquitous trope of the threshold which is seen here in specifically postcolonial perspective. I also interpret the novel *Un temps de saison* as anthropological parody. In Chapter 2 I focus closely on NDiaye's interest in the human/animal borderline and on the potential for hospitality that is latent there. I show how the author uses this particular threshold to address what it means to be human and, in some cases, to offer a way out of the impasse of inhospitality in which her protagonists are locked. Chapters 3 and 4 draw us progressively closer to intimate expressions of (in)hospitality entailing touch, absorption and the opening of bodies. In Chapter 3 I analyze rituals of inhospitable feeding or 'perverse commensality', a major structuring mechanism in NDiaye, as well as the implications for hospitality of the splitting and penetration of bodies through wounding and rape. Chapter 4 concerns the author's persistent anxiety about maternal inhospitality and here I offer a fresh reading of some of her fictional mothers, arguing that she is drawn to maternal bodies as ambivalent places where the opportunity for hospitality begins, where the self is confirmed as stranger and where self–other distinctions are at once challenged and reinforced. In Chapter 5 I apply ideas of (in)hospitality to the construction of the author and the act of reading. I analyze the terms on which NDiaye herself was 'welcomed' as a major French writer, including debates generated by the extraordinary framing of her, at the very moment when she won the Prix Goncourt, as an ungrateful guest who had insulted the hospitality of her hosts. This chapter also turns to the question of what it means to read NDiaye's inhospitable fictions, and perhaps to do so hospitably.

Notes to the Introduction

1. Julian Pitt-Rivers, 'The Stranger, the Guest and the Hostile Host: Introduction to the Study of the Laws of Hospitality', in *Contributions to Mediterranean Sociology*, ed. by J.-G. Peristiany (Paris & The Hague: Mouton & Co., 1968), pp. 13–30 (p. 27).
2. Jacques Derrida and Anne Dufourmantelle, *De l'hospitalité* (Paris: Calman-Lévy, 1997), p. 72; *Of Hospitality*, trans. by Rachel Bowlby (Stanford, CA: Stanford University Press, 2000), p. 75.
3. NDiaye's exploitation of the specificity of genre to decline inhospitality deserves a study in its own right.
4. Aloïs Hahn, 'L'Hospitalité et l'étranger', in *Mythes et representations de l'hospitalité*, ed. by Alain Montandon (Clermont-Ferrand: Presses Universitaires Blaise Pascal, 1999), pp. 9–22 (p. 9).
5. Titles such as *En famille* and *Tous mes amis* (both ironic) as well as *Rien d'humain* highlight NDiaye's problematizing of hospitality along these lines. For abusive friendship in NDiaye see Andrew Asibong, 'Tou(te)s mes ami(e)s: le problème de l'amitié chez Marie NDiaye', in *Marie NDiaye: l'étrangeté à l'œuvre*, ed. by Andrew Asibong and Shirley Jordan (Villeneuve d'Ascq: Presses Universitaires du Septentrion, 2009), pp. 137–52.
6. The protracted build up to the murder, the heat, the problem of responsibility, the racial

dimension of the situation and the description of each plant, leaf and rock in the Guadeloupean forest as 'figée dans une tension inhospitalière' [frozen in an inhospitable tension] (*RC* 257) all evoke the murder of the Arab in Camus's *L'Étranger*.

7. Studies to date concerning hospitality in NDiaye are my own: 'La Quête familiale dans les écrits de Marie NDiaye: nomadisme, (in)hospitalité, différence', in *Nomadismes de romancières contemporaines de langue française*, ed. by Anne Simon (Paris: Presses Sorbonne Nouvelle, 2007), pp. 143–53; and Judith Still's research on hospitality and animals in *Ladivine* referenced in Chapter 2.

8. See Alec G. Hargreaves, *Voices from the North African Immigrant Community in France: Immigration and Identity in Beur Fiction* (New York & Oxford: Berg, 1991), p. 8.

9. For instance, Tahar Ben Jelloun's *Hospitalité française: racisme et immigration maghrébine* (Paris: Seuil, 1997), or *Les Lois de l'inhospitalité: les politiques de l'immigration à l'épreuve des sans papiers*, ed. by Didier Fassin, Alain Morice and Catherine Quiminal (Paris: Éditions La Découverte, 1997).

10. Notably Mireille Rosello, *Postcolonial Hospitality: The Immigrant as Guest* (Stanford, CA: Stanford University Press, 2001); and *Le Livre de l'hospitalité: accueil de l'étranger dans l'histoire et les cultures*, ed. by Alain Montandon (Paris: Bayard, 2004).

11. See 'Derrida en Corse? Hospitality as Scale-Free Abstraction', in *The Return to Hospitality*, ed. by Matei Candea and Giovanni da Col, special issue of *Journal of the Royal Anthropological Institute*, 18 (2012), 534–48 (p. 539).

12. I see three principal differences: first, Rosello's examples in *Postcolonial Hospitality* share an aspirational dimension and hold out some sense of a mutual welcome being possible; second, they highlight the complexity of hospitality practised across specific traditions (e.g. the tea that is not taken with Mme Zineb in François Maspero and Anaik Frantz's *Passagers du Roissy Express*, or the non-sharing of a ritual gift of Eid-time cakes in Yamina Benguigui's *Mémoires d'immigrés*, see Rosello's chapter entitled 'Host(esse)s Granting and Refusing Hospitality Across National and Ethnic Lines', pp. 63–84); third, the aesthetic of her examples is realist while NDiaye's hovers between realist and fantastic modes. I return to this contrast in Chapter 5.

13. 'Assimilation' points towards the disappearance of cultural difference; 'integration' implies that the host society makes some effort to accommodate difference and conveys the idea of 'being with' rather than merely 'being like'.

14. See Andrew Asibong's numerous references to race in *En famille* in his monograph *Marie NDiaye, Blankness and Recognition* (Liverpool: Liverpool University Press, 2013). See too Clarissa Behar, 'Écrire en pays à majorité blanche: *En famille* de Marie NDiaye', in *Une femme puissante: l'œuvre de Marie NDiaye*, ed. by Daniel Bengsch and Cornelia Ruhe (Amsterdam & New York: Rodopi, 2013), pp. 125–39.

15. Patrick Weil notes in a study of diversity in the French Republic since the 1970s that France's recent history is characterized precisely by the conflict of this 'double mouvement de refus et d'acceptation' [double movement of refusal and acceptance]. See *La République et sa diversité: immigration, intégration, discriminations* (Paris: Éditions du Seuil et La République des Idées, 2005), p. 8.

16. See Nelly Kaprièlian, 'Marie NDiaye aux prises avec le monde', *Les Inrockuptibles*, 716 (2009), 28–33 (p. 32). I return to NDiaye's uncustomary intervention into politics in Chapter 5.

17. Mireille Rosello, 'Immigration: discours et contradictions', in *Le Livre de l'hospitalité: accueil de l'étranger dans l'histoire et les cultures*, ed. by Alain Montandon (Paris: Bayard, 2004), pp. 1516–28 (p. 1520). Rosello situates the period between the first and second editions of Ben Jelloun's *Hospitalité française* (1984 and 1997 respectively).

18. See Michael Sheringham, 'Space, Identity and Difference in Contemporary Fiction: Duras, Genêt, NDiaye', in *French Global: A New Approach to Literary History*, ed. by Christie McDonald and Susan Rubin Suleiman (New York: Columbia University Press, 2010), pp. 437–52.

19. The map was exhibited on 11 July 2016 at Point Éphémère in the north-east of Paris.

20. For brief but incisive observations on the depiction of class in NDiaye see Lydie Moudileno, 'L'Excellent Français de Marie NDiaye', in *Marie NDiaye: l'étrangeté à l'œuvre*, ed. by Asibong and Jordan, pp. 25–38.

21. To readers unfamiliar with the key building blocks of thought on hospitality I recommend

Derek Attridge's short introduction to Derrida and Levinas, 'Hospitality', in *The Work of Literature* (Oxford: Oxford University Press, 2015), pp. 280–305.

22. See 'Hospitality, Justice and Responsibility: A Dialogue with Jacques Derrida', in *Questioning Ethics: Contemporary Debates in Philosophy*, ed. by Mark Dooley and Richard Kearney (London: Routledge, 1999), pp. 65–83 (p. 70).

23. Candea, '*Derrida en Corse?*', p. 546.

24. I capitalize 'Other' throughout in order to keep the abstract/embodied dichotomy activated.

25. Jacques Derrida, 'Nombre de Oui', in *Psyché: inventions de l'autre* (Paris: Galilée, 1987), pp. 639–50 (p. 639); 'A Number of Yes', in *Psyche: Inventions of the Other*, ed. by Peggy Kamuf and Elizabeth Rottenberg, 2 vols (Stanford, CA: Stanford University Press, 2007), I, 231–40 (p. 231).

26. Slavoj Žižek, 'Neighbours and Other Monsters: A Plea for Ethical Violence', in Kenneth Reinhard, Eric L. Santer and Slavoj Žižek, *The Neighbour: Three Inquiries in Political Theology* (Chicago: University of Chicago Press, 2005), pp. 134–90 (p. 163).

27. Ibid.

28. See Jacques Derrida, 'Hostipitality', in *Jacques Derrida: Acts of Religion*, ed. by Gil Anidjar (New York: Routledge, 2002), pp. 356–420. I use both 'hostipitality' and (in)hospitality in this book.

29. Žižek, 'Neighbours and Other Monsters', p. 149.

30. Emmanuel Levinas, *Autrement qu'être ou au-delà de l'essence* (Paris: Kluwer Academic, 1996), p. 126; *Otherwise than Being, or Beyond Essence*, trans. by Alphonso Lingis (Pittsburgh, PA: Duquesne University Press, 1998), p. 79.

31. See '"Il faut bien manger" ou le calcul du sujet', interview with Jean-Luc Nancy, in Jacques Derrida, *Points de suspension: entretiens* (Paris: Éditions Galilée, 1992), pp. 269–301; '"Eating Well", or the Calculation of the Subject', in *Points... Interviews, 1974–1994*, ed. by Elisabeth Weber, trans. by Peggy Kamuf (Stanford, CA: Stanford University Press, 1995), pp. 255–87.

32. Judith Still, '*Sharing the World*: Luce Irigaray and the Hospitality of Difference', *L'Esprit Créateur*, 52, (2012), 40–51 (p. 41).

33. Ibid., p. 50.

34. Interestingly, Daisy Connon characterizes NDiaye's willed vulnerability in her autofiction as an ethically-oriented gesture of 'self-hospitality'. See 'Marie NDiaye's Haunted House: Uncanny Autofiction in *Autoportrait en vert*', in *Redefining the Real: The Fantastic in Contemporary French and Francophone Women's Writing*, ed. by Margaret-Anne Hutton (Oxford: Peter Lang 2009), pp. 245–60 (p. 259).

35. I shall return to debates about the meaning of *puissance* in this novel. NDiaye explained to Pascal Casanova during the radio programme *L'Atelier littéraire* (France Culture, 4 October 2009) that before settling on this term she considered 'grâce' [grace] but decided against it for fear of religious interpretations. See too Lucie Clair, 'Dossier Marie NDiaye', *Le Matricule des anges: le mensuel de la littérature contemporaine*, 107 (2009), 20–29 (p. 29). Interestingly for our purposes, 'grace' as manifested in un-calculatingly generous interaction leans towards Irigaray's and Derrida's observations on pure hospitality as an unexpected, almost divine, gift that exceeds any sense of transaction and recalls Pitt-Rivers's discussion in 'The Place of Grace in Anthropology', in *Honour and Grace in Anthropology*, ed. by J. G. Peristiany and J. Pitt-Rivers (Cambridge: Cambridge University Press, 1992), pp. 215–46.

36. See Luce Irigaray, 'Animal Compassion', in *Animal Philosophy*, ed. by Matthew Calarco and Peter Atterton (London: Continuum, 2004), pp. 195–201 (p. 200).

37. Giorgio Agamben, *L'Ouvert: de l'homme et de l'animal*, trans. by Joël Gayraud (Paris: Bibliothèque Rivages, 2002), p. 58.

38. Pitt-Rivers, 'The Stranger, the Guest and the Hostile Host'. Pitt-Rivers's study spans various regions and periods and aims to draw out hospitality's '"natural law"', deriving from 'sociological necessity' (p. 27).

39. Ibid., p. 28.

40. Ibid.

41. Luce Irigaray, *Sharing the World* (London: Continuum, 2008); Antoinette Fouque, *Génésique. Féminologie III* (Paris: Des femmes, 2012).

42. In an unpublished seminar quoted in Ginette Michaud, '"Un acte d'hospitalité ne peut être que

poétique": Seuils et delimitations de l'hospitalité derridienne', in *Le Dire de l'hospitalité*, ed. by Lise Gauvin, Pierre L'Hérault and Alain Montandon (Clermont-Ferrand: Presses Universitaires Blaise Pascal, 2004), pp. 33–60 (p. 52).

43. See my 'Fantastic Spaces in Marie NDiaye', *Dalhousie French Studies*, 93 (2010), 97–108.

44. See Tzvetan Todorov, *The Fantastic: A Structural Approach to a Literary Genre*, trans. by Richard Howard (Ithaca, NY: Cornell University Press, 1975), p. 33.

45. Montandon makes a similar point concerning myth, which 'permet de réfléchir sur les limites et ce qui excède les limites' [allows us to reflect on limits and what exceeds limits]. See *Mythes et représentations de l'hospitalité*, ed. by Montandon, p. 20.

46. See Daisy Connon, *Subjects Not-at-home: Forms of the Uncanny in the Contemporary French Novel: Emmanuel Carrère, Marie NDiaye, Eugène Savitzkaya* (Amsterdam & New York: Rodopi, 2010).

47. Marie NDiaye, interview with Alain Nicolas, 'Le Cœur dans le labyrinthe', *L'Humanité*, 1 February 2007, <http://www.humanité.fr/2007–02–01_Cultures_Le-cœur-dans-le-labyrinthe> [accessed 9 February 2007].

48. Marie NDiaye, 'Maudits soient-ils...', *Télérama*, 2979, 14 February 2007, p. 54.

49. Margaret-Anne Hutton, 'Introduction', in *Redefining the Real*, ed. by Hutton, pp. 1–12 (p. 10).

50. Ibid., p. 12.

51. Ibid., p. 2.

52. See Deborah Gaensbauer, 'Further Outside the Bounds: Mobilization of the Fantastic as Trauma Narrative in Marie NDiaye's *En famille*', in *Redefining the Real*, ed. by Hutton, pp. 207–24 (p. 208).

53. Ibid., p. 214.

54. Ibid., p. 209.

55. Christine Jérusalem, 'Des larmes de sang au sang épuisé dans l'œuvre de Marie NDiaye (*hoc est enim corpus meum*)', in *Marie NDiaye: l'étrangeté à l'œuvre*, ed. by Asibong and Jordan, pp. 83–91 (p. 84).

56. Rosemary Jackson, *Fantasy: The Literature of Subversion* (London & New York: Methuen, 1981), p. 45.

57. The visual matter in *La Naufragée, Autoportrait en vert* and *Y penser sans cesse* troubles and interrupts the text in unexpected ways, the aesthetic of paintings and photographs alike underscoring NDiaye's persistent suggestions that her work harbours more than it reveals.

58. Captains of slave ships threw slaves overboard in order to collect insurance payments. Turner's painting represents a notorious episode of 1780 when 132 Africans — men, women and children — were thrown overboard, in shackles, from a British slave ship in the Caribbean. Importantly, the painting does not merely represent slavery but is integrally bound up with the history of its abolition, for it was inspired by Thomas Clarkson's *The History and Abolition of the Slave Trade* and its exhibition at London's Royal Academy was timed to coincide with the June 1840 World Anti-Slavery Convention. My thanks to Pauline Eaton for a subtle politico-aesthetic reading of the dialogue between text and paintings in *La Naufragée* at the conference *Marie NDiaye's Tales of Power* (University of Kent, Paris, March 2013).

59. The graphic depiction of slave torture in the exhibition visited by Ladivine and her family during their African holiday (*L* 236–39) is also worth studying in this light.

60. In *La Naufragée, Providence* and *Trois femmes puissantes* respectively.

61. See René Schérer, *Zeus hospitalier* (Paris: Armand Colin, 1993).

62. Jordan, 'La Quête familiale dans les écrits de Marie NDiaye', takes some initial steps down this path, drawing on Steve Reece's *The Stranger's Welcome: Oral Theory and the Aesthetics of the Homeric Hospitality Scene* (Ann Arbor: University of Michigan Press, 1993).

63. Other connections include magic hospitality from the animal world (St Julian is assisted by a stag in a forest, replaced in *Ladivine* by a dog). The myth as recast in one of Flaubert's *Trois contes* would seem to be a further intertext, given the high-pitched timbre of the leper's voice in the tale, which NDiaye also bestows upon Freddy Moliger.

64. Clifford Geertz, *The Interpretation of Cultures* (New York: Basic Books, 1973), pp. 3–32.

65. Examples include: 'La fragilité est provocante' [Fragility is provocative] (*RH* 39); 'La femme riche, même une fois ravagée, est haïssable' [The rich woman, even once ravaged, is detestable]

(*RH* 34); 'Pas de contrat entre amies' [Friends need no contract] (*RH* 16); 'Ce qui n'est jamais exprimé ne peut exister pour personne' [What is never expressed cannot exist for anybody] (*LGP* 38); 'un Noir [...] n'est pas responsable de ses actes' [a Black man [...] is not responsible for his acts] (*PDM* 65); 'On peut prêter à plus riche que soi' [One may lend to a person richer than oneself] (*SE* 13).

66. Embittered and disdainful observations on French settlers are proffered in *Rosie Carpe* (*RC* 15; 22; 38; 40).

67. Senegal in *Trois femmes puissantes*; Berlin in *Ladivine* and *Y penser sans cesse* [To Think of it Ceaselessly].

68. Aurel Kolnai, 'The Standard Modes of Aversion: Fear, Disgust, and Hatred', in *On Disgust*, ed. by Carolyn Korsmeyer and Barry Smith (Chicago & La Salle, IL: Open Court, 2004), pp. 93–108.

69. Sianne Ngai, *Ugly Feelings* (Cambridge, MA: Harvard University Press, 2005).

70. My emphasis on disgust represents a very different approach to NDiaye from that explored by Asibong in *Marie NDiaye: Blankness and Recognition*. Asibong's psychoanalytic account stresses traumatized numbness, disavowal, negation and 'flights into blankness' (p. 14). In parts of this book, especially Chapters 2 and 3, I am interested in how NDiaye conveys not blankness but the operative presence and intensity of affect.

71. Colin McGinn, *The Meaning of Disgust* (Oxford: Oxford University Press, 2011), p. 41.

72. Ibid., p. 50.

73. Susan B. Miller, *Disgust: The Gatekeeper Emotion* (London: Routledge, 2004), especially Chapter 9, 'Group Identities and Hostility across Borders' (pp. 153–70).

74. *Les Constructions de l'intolérable: études d'anthropologie et d'histoire sur les frontières de l'espace moral*, ed. by Didier Fassin and Patrice Bourdelais (Paris: Éditions la Découverte, 2005).

75. See 'Introduction', in *Les Constructions de l'intolérable*, ed. by Fassin and Bourdelais, pp. 7–15 (p. 7).

CHAPTER 1

Configuring the Stranger: Repulsion, Assimilation and Thresholds

Tout le monde peut *devenir* étranger, parce qu'il l'*est* déjà
d'une certaine manière, et qu'il le *restera*.[1]

[Everybody can *become* a stranger, because everybody *is* a stranger
already in a certain sense, and will *remain* a stranger.]

NDiaye's works typically entail the unrelenting configuration of a central protagonist as 'stranger'. Her outsider figures take shape on the innumerable thresholds
which provide her fictional world with its spatial, political and ethical logic and to
which she returns with nervous obsessiveness. Ambivalent places of 'hostipitality'
and hinges between modes of being (together), these spaces are associated with
potential contamination, forced entry, failed (re)union and disputed belonging.
Threshold scenes and the meanings they harbour insistently detain us, problematizing categories of insider and outsider, host and guest and the terms of their
engagement. Significantly, several of NDiaye's texts begin with a threshold confrontation, privileging the protracted tension of arrival over the drama of departure
with which journey narratives are perhaps more habitually propelled into motion
and plunging without preamble into densely ethical terrain. What, we are required
to ask, is at stake interpretatively when Fanny is confronted by the iron gates
and maddened dogs that guard the family's ancestral home (*EF* 7–10); when Papa
wedges his foot in the door and pleads with his daughter Mina to open it (*PDM*
9–16); or when Norah confronts her diminished father on the threshold of his
'maison arrogante' [arrogant house] (*TFP* 11–15)? On what terms are individuals
welcomed or repulsed? And when is a welcome not a welcome — as in, for instance,
forms of assimilation motivated by the eradication of difference?

A glance at the opening of the play *Providence* [Providence] will serve as an initial
example of the moral complexity of NDiaye's threshold scenes, as well as their
intimacy and fable-like quality. *Providence* begins with a threshold conversation
between two hoteliers and the eponymous heroine who has come in search of her
child. The hoteliers argue about the duties of hosting and the dangers of receiving a
stranger who arrives on a dark night, clearly reprising the repeated testing of human
hospitality that characterizes NDiaye's key Homeric intertext, not least because
Providence, with her cloven feet and dangerously captivating hair, fuels fears that
the stranger (*xenios*) may be borderline human, a god or a monster. Unresponsive

to the promise embedded in Providence's name, the husband counsels prudence, holds the door partially closed, regrets that the hotel's bright lights mark it out as prosperous (thus attractive to strangers) and reveals his reluctance to host. The wife conversely articulates fully, insistently and in impassioned terms an ethos of absolute hospitality that is seldom voiced and even less acted upon in NDiaye:

> HÔTELIÈRE: Ouvre, efface-toi. Est-ce à la douleur de supplier, de se justifier et de présenter... quelles preuves, quelles garanties? Humiliée sur le seuil, devant nous. Nous sommes florissants — nous sommes comblés. J'en ai trop de honte. Ouvre, recule. Qu'elle fasse tout ce qu'elle désire, qu'elle boive et mange et dorme meme dans notre lit.

> [HOTEL OWNER: Open up, step aside. Must pain beg, justify itself and present... what proof, what guarantees? It stands humiliated on the threshold, before us. We are flourishing — we have all we need. I am too ashamed of this. Open up, back away. Let pain do anything it wants, let it drink and eat and even sleep in our bed] (*P* 15–16).

This vignette is consistent with NDiaye's keen interest in domestic thresholds for the productive to-and-fro that they encourage between contexts: doorstep encounters keep us uncomfortably alert to the ways in which interpersonal practices of hospitality are harnessed in political discourse to allude (often disingenuously) to practices at a national level, as well as prodding us to consider whether the apparently benign homeliness of domestic doorsteps may be belied by much that goes on there. Threshold transactions between individuals unfurl within a global and national context of which they are a part, and dialogues are set up in NDiaye between numerous challenges to rights at places of potential access, so that the barred threshold at the start of *En famille* and the barbed-wire border fence from which the would-be migrant Khady Demba falls to her death at the end of *Trois femmes puissantes* are on a continuum, both alerting us with equal force to domestic and global politics.[2] Further, the unusual insistence on the threshold in NDiaye serves as a reminder of the permanent tension and irresolution between host and guest in any context, and of the fact that hospitality is never definitively settled but always requires to be renewed and reconfirmed.

This chapter traces the configuration of stranger figures in two of NDiaye's less frequently analyzed texts, *Rien d'humain* and *Un temps de saison*. Both are organized around threshold negotiations, both evoke persistently France's colonial past, and both are directly concerned with the laws of hospitality. The first, an elaborately violent threshold encounter determined by colonialism's pernicious legacies, shares *Providence*'s concern with the Law of hospitality. The second satirizes ideas of hospitality and practices of othering inherent in classic anthropological field relations. The chapter concludes with some thoughts on the fantastic hyperboles of outsiders beyond the threshold that haunt the author's world.

Rien d'humain

Rien d'humain is a concise and clear-sighted play that stands in telling relation to the postcolonial resurgence of interest in the human.[3] NDiaye's threshold negotiations usually unfurl against unspoken back stories of inhospitality, but the explicitness of *Rien d'humain* in this regard sets it apart. Here the back story — as well as the complicated calibrations of class difference and postcolonial 'hostipitality' that ensue — is articulated with tremendous impact, raising for consideration what it means to be friend, neighbour or family, what constitutes the human, and what are the limits of virtues such as kindness, fidelity, generosity, philanthropy and love. Here too the (inherently dramatic) trope of the domestic threshold is foregrounded especially forcefully, for the play disturbs our tacit understanding of how long we should be held or hold others there. Threshold negotiations, however complex, need ideally to be rapidly resolved and a decision made about inviting a person in or not. But if *Providence* shows the supplicant rapidly turning away from the hoteliers' doorstep, the protagonists of *Rien d'humain* struggle around the same contested threshold for the play's entire duration.

Rien d'humain plays out in miniature postcolonial anxieties about resources, territory, power, appropriation, belonging, assimilation and agency. It interrogates the idea of home and asks who is entitled to one; it raises issues of hosting, the power of the host and the right to host; and it alludes to parasitism, dependency and the burden of indebtedness.[4] Its three protagonists are Bella, Djamila and Ignace. The two women are marked by a shared history that re-enacts the grotesque intimate underside of France's *mission civilisatrice* [civilizing mission].[5] Bella, sole daughter in an affluent French family, 'befriended' Djamila, the daughter of the family's handyman, who was adopted, educated to share the family's values and violently abused. The play is set years later when Bella returns to France with her young children after a five-year spell in America and a divorce from her violent husband, uttering a classic NDiayean phrase: 'J'arrive de loin et je suis écœurée. J'ai besoin d'un toit' [I have come from far and I am sickened. I need a home] (*RH* 18). She intends to reclaim the luxurious apartment that she lent to Djamila during her absence, but Djamila refuses to relinquish it, knotting the pair into transactions whose power play and ironic combination of violence and courtesy are worthy of Jean Genet's *Les Bonnes* [The Maids]. Ignace, a neighbour who is in love with Djamila, acts as mediator and sounding board for two people incapable of moving beyond the corrosive and perverse logic of colonial power relations. The play enacts one of the many reversals of fortune that mark NDiaye's unstable universe, as the insider abruptly learns what it is like to be outside, and the arrival home brings with it a permanent unravelling of the very idea of home, marking it out as definitively fragile.

Most of the play concerns Bella's disingenuous reflections on her asymmetrical relationship with Djamila, beginning with a consideration of friendship and its conditions. The possessives and mirroring structure of the play's opening sentences, 'C'est mon amie. C'est mon appartement' [This is my friend. This is my flat] (*RH* 13) equate person and property and confuse friendship with ownership. Repeatedly

Bella emphasizes Djamila's 'friend value', with the assistance of various epithets such as 'fidèle et adorable' [faithful and adorable] and 'plus vieille' [longest-standing] (*RH* 13), but the friendship is entirely of her construction and Djamila, now an independent woman with her own career, neither welcomes nor indeed recognizes Bella (another nod from NDiaye to the terms of Odysseus's homecoming).[6] For Bella, lending between friends is an act of faith: 'Pas de contrat entre amies' [Friends need no contract] (*RH* 16) she states, yet she does impose tacit contractual expectations, notably that Djamila remain overwhelmed with gratitude. Bella clings less to Djamila than to the process of making Djamila, to Djamila as evidence of her own beneficence. But Djamila is also Bella's ingrained bad conscience. Her family's hospitality in fact amounted to a horrifying contract of abuse, entailing repeated rape by Bella's father and brothers. Surfacing in spite of Bella, this competing narrative dislodges her control over speech and erupts in sporadic glimpses of the entire colonial enterprise as a frenzy of violent appropriation: 'Ma famille a beaucoup donné à Djamila. Ils ont usé et usé d'elle [...] Nous l'avons formée et cultivée. Baisée, baisée, baisée' [My family gave a lot to Djamila. They used her and used her [...] We trained and cultivated her. Screwed her, screwed her, screwed her] (*RH* 18). The relationship of Bella's family to Djamila is the relationship in miniature of France to a (feminized) North-Africa 'baisée à mort' [screwed to death] (*RH* 15). Bella's involuntary acknowledgement of this repressed past redoubles her latent self-disgust: certain words erupt from her mouth, she complains, like 'des bestioles un peu répugnantes dont la bave tache le devant de mes vêtements, l'intérieur de mon âme' [slightly repugnant creatures whose slime stains the front of my clothes, my inner soul] (*RH* 17). Here we notice a further iteration of the threshold as marker of the fractured and porous space between silence and speech, disavowal and avowal.[7]

Schisms abound in Bella's references to Djamila, so that degrading characterization cascades into respect and affection or vice versa as in the following: 'Elle s'allonge dans une passivité méprisable au premier claquement des doigts. C'est mon amie' [At the slightest click of one's fingers she lies down in pathetic passivity. She is my friend] (*RH* 17). The syntax makes it hard to ascertain whether this dog-like behaviour is in fact a condition of friendship. Equally, in Bella's allusions to Djamila's violation it is difficult to tease out the measure of anger, desire, cruelty, fear and (possibly) excitement. What Bella needs is a Djamila who is simultaneously same (like me) and different (lesser, abased, uncultivated).[8] The conflicting physical and psychic uses to which Djamila is put emerge subtly and violently on the threshold, where the new terms of the women's relationship are in the process of being determined.

Rien d'humain raises, then, questions about colonial violence and its tangled inheritance specifically as experienced by women. As I observed in the Introduction, women's place within circuits of hospitality is a recurring consideration in NDiaye who explores the expectations placed upon them to create openings for hospitality, including sexual ones. Her work demonstrates concern about the vulnerability to sexual violence of all marginal women: protagonists such as Fanny, Providence, Rosie Carpe and Khady Demba are related to Djamila in that all suffer sexual abuse.[9] During her interrogation of friendship, Bella fleetingly shifts the terrain to women's common susceptibility to invasion: 'Tu es mon amie, ils t'ont prise pour se préserver de me prendre, baisée pour éviter de me baiser' [You are my friend, they took you so as not to take me, screwed you to avoid screwing me] (*RH* 41). Djamila, Bella's dark double, is thus a sacrificial figure — one of many in NDiaye — within a layered economy of abuse. Her own reading of the host family's arrogant drive to assimilation and of her value to them as evidence of the rightness of their principles is unerringly clear-sighted: she serves as walking guarantor of the precept that 'tout prolétaire est perfectible, toute femme, une illustration indéfiniment modelable' [all proletarians are perfectible, all women an infinitely plastic illustration of this] (*RH* 24). Although she concedes that without Bella's family 'Je serais mes sœurs, je serais ma mère, je serais une misérable' [I would be my sisters, I would be my mother, I would be a wretch] (*RH* 25), Djamila delivers a magnificent diatribe on the terms and consequences of their hospitality. She also announces her intention to retain the flat, not as a gift from Bella which would leave her indebted, but on revised terms in which gift-giving has no place: 'Tu ne me donnes rien du tout. C'est moi qui prends et qui possède' [You are giving me nothing at all. It is I who take and possess] (*RH* 42).

Bella's eventual entry into the flat is almost comically marked by schizophrenic slippage between self-positioning as host and guest, and by agonies of contrition that coalesce around the question of aesthetic taste. Djamila plans to undo the bourgeois refinement of the flat's interior by painting over the delicate ivory colour with yellow: 'Oh non!' regrets Bella, 'C'était un ivoire si ingénieux, si difficile à... Pardon, asseyez-vous, mettez-vous à l'aise' [Oh no! It was such an ingenious ivory, so difficult to... Sorry, sit down, make yourself comfortable] (*RH* 39). By the play's denouement a set of new power relations is forged as colonial/class logic recycles itself in reverse: Bella becomes Djamila's cleaner and will henceforth visit her former apartment merely in that capacity, while Ignace, 'un étranger, le voisin [...] le seul à m'accueillir' [a foreigner, the neighbour [...] the only one to welcome me] (*RH* 19) is ousted by Bella from his own flat which she in turn appropriates. The play ends as it began, with a newly disorientated figure made homeless and reduced to pleading for access on revised terms to a place he once considered his own. It is as if NDiaye were asking how hospitality could possibly take place, how home could be inviolable against such a backdrop. In a rapidly shifting global panorama of uprooting and migration, 'outsider' status seems to be relative: of Bella and Djamila, which is now the outsider? And what of Bella's nomadic little American children 'mécontents de quitter leur pays pour arriver ici où ils ne comprennent personne' [unhappy to leave their country to fetch up here where they understand nobody] (*RH* 19)?

(In)hospitable Naming

Naming in *Rien d'humain* clamours for our attention. It is worth pausing, then, to consider how NDiaye's rather unusual practice in terms of the distribution and articulation of names is enmeshed with her concern for hospitality. If the contributors to an intriguing volume entitled *Le Dire de l'hospitalité* pay surprisingly little attention to naming as a speech act that can demonstrate or create the conditions for hospitality, it is nonetheless the case that names are in themselves thresholds, places of potential crossing wherein self-other relations are keenly at stake, and strategies of naming suggest the often tense alertness of protagonists to one another.[10] An original feature of NDiaye's writing is her persistent highlighting of names and naming along precisely these lines. If, as Derrida remarks after Lévinas, 'le langage *est* hospitalité' [language *is* hospitality], one of the most important interpersonal instances of this is speaking the proper name (hospitably).[11] NDiaye's world is instead full of subtle instances of aversive naming, refusals to name, un-naming and other tactics which repeatedly activate the strangeness of Others in order to keep them at bay — or indeed which render the self newly strange, since protagonists puzzle too over their own names which become the locus of estrangement and unease as if, comments Dominique Rabaté, 'jamais aucun de ses personnages ne pouvait coincider avec son marqueur d'identité' [none of her protagonists could ever coincide with their identity marker].[12]

The repetition of names in NDiaye's work is deliberately troubling. Texts may be surprisingly dense with a particular name which clamours for our attention, becoming incongruous and fascinating. In our own lived practice the insistent reiteration of names, particularly of given names, is most habitually associated with expressions of love or a desire to comfort, but NDiaye gives an inhospitable twist to the intimacy of speaking another's name — an act which entails taking in (the idea of) the other, giving it space to inhabit and traverse the self, and making the sounds that designate it — so that it becomes associated with fear, distaste or disgust. As we will see in Chapter 3, her writing frequently makes us aware of mouths, mouthing, chewing, swallowing and spitting, an emphasis which surfaces with regard not only to eating but also to speaking a name, to processing another in one's mouth. Aversive naming reaches its height in *Mon cœur à l'étroit* with Nadia's refusal to speak her granddaughter's name 'Souhar', a name experienced as a pollutant and a personal affront, its un-French sonority striking the protagonist as 'une provocation, ricanement ou indécence ou même injure fielleuse' [a provocation, sniggering or indecency or even a venomous insult] (*MCE* 232). Here the act of naming is physical and visceral, a 'coup de pied au ventre' [kick in the stomach] (*MCE* 107) although at last, in a scene where naming uncharacteristically provides a route to hospitality, the infant's name is sung out loud by Nadia creatively, with pleasure and as a gift to the child herself (*MCE* 297). This instance of naming in love is rare indeed in NDiaye.

Rien d'humain is dominated, even overwhelmed by 'Djamila', a name belonging to NDiaye's pointedly ethnic register.[13] It is seldom far from the lips of either Bella or the hapless mediator Ignace who is caught up in the postcolonial wash of the women's affairs yet who is, as his name suggests, supremely ignorant of what is at stake. The distinctly North-African sonority of 'Djamila' dominates the play, rooting it in a Franco-Algerian context, the density of its utterance suggesting irresolution. Significantly, while Djamila scarcely ever mouths 'Bella', her own name is articulated so frequently and with such extraordinary range of nuance from caressing to bruising that the play progressively coalesces around her as an object of fascination, a puzzle which needs processing. To speak 'Djamila' is to enact or recall all manner of appropriation, dubious affection, cajoling, violent desire, resentment and need for expiation. Ultimately, as uttered by Bella in a paroxysm of desire and self-hatred, the name is a vector for the entirety of France's colonial enterprise in Algeria, as well as its legacy. Bella's surprise at Djamila's lack of kindness and her comment 'Djamila vit pourtant chez moi' [And yet Djamila lives in my house] (*RH* 14) is thus far more complex and laden a statement than it seems on the surface. *Rien d'humain*, then, provides one of the clearest examples of NDiaye's recourse to names and naming as a litmus test of hospitality. In her study of hospitality in Derrida, Judith Still observes the trickiness of 'trying to disentangle different kinds of calling by name' and the observation applies nicely to this play.[14] NDiaye's determination to engage us in the delicate issue of naming is one of the ways in which she ensures our close engagement with her protagonists and, more than this, our reflection on how the smallest instance of calling by name can point to hidden chasms of inhospitality.

I conclude with a note concerning the play's title. '*Rien d'humain*' nods to post-colonial debates about re-establishing humanism and the human while highlighting at the same time its own provocative negativity. The apparently insurmountable situation of inherited inhospitality worked out on this play's thresholds affords no glimmer of reconciliation and nothing emancipatory. Instead there lurks at the play's heart, inside the apartment, a most inhuman (posthuman?) legacy: Djamila's spectral daughter. A 'présence hostile et polaire' [hostile and polar presence] (*RH* 34), she is most likely the product of union with Bella's father and is conceptualized not as a flesh-and-blood child but a malefic, elemental force. If Djamila describes herself as dehumanized to the point of becoming inanimate matter, not woman but stone (*RH* 42), her daughter is an icy blast, an indistinct, inhospitable force.[15] In the final act, filled with horror at his one glimpse of the abominable entity which he once fondly hoped was his own daughter, Ignace takes refuge in denial: 'Il suffit de ne pas y croire' [It is enough not to believe in it] (*RH* 44). I shall return to this unspeakable phantom and some of its cousins at the end of the chapter.

What we have seen so far is NDiaye's finely-tuned sense of the threshold as a dramatic location and a charged conceptual meeting point, where thought on hospitality across politics, literature, philosophy and anthropology converges, and where practice and imagined potential put one another to the test. We have seen that the threshold is the author's preferred setting for addressing in concentrated form what Jane Hiddleston, discussing humanism and the human in postcolonial thought, refers to as 'the legacy of imperialism and its persistent aftershocks';[16] and that it engages us with one of the author's most frequently recurring motifs: 'l'étranger qu'on ne veut pas recevoir mais qu'on ne peut plus renvoyer' [the stranger one does not want to admit, but can no longer turn away].[17]

(In)hospitality in the Field: *Un temps de saison*

What happens when we try to make sense of NDiaye's puzzling fifth novel *Un temps de saison* by reading it as anthropological parody? Here I pursue precisely such a reading in order to unlock some of the text's as yet unexplored meanings and to show how in this instance NDiaye's focus on (in)hospitality centres around the two-way construction of the Other as produced in the field. I suggest that although it has not yet been read as such, *Un temps de saison* sustains intensive dialogue with classic anthropological situations and accounts and engages deliberately and knowingly with what Graham Huggan refers to as the 'postcolonial exotic'.[18] The novel rehearses the tensions of field relations, explores the many levels on which (in)hospitality inheres both in participant observation and in the (reductive) writing of ethnography and redoubles NDiaye's trademark interest in multiplying the interfaces where hospitality is negotiated.

Several uncharacteristic aspects of NDiaye's fictional apparatus in *Un temps de saison* such as the intensive confinement to and probing of one bounded location; the way in which an entire cultural and social system becomes the central focus of the text; or the unusual choice of a male rather than a female traveller (the colonial-era anthropologist was habitually male), justify a reading along anthropological lines. Herman, this novel's 'professional stranger', is devised as a vehicle for considering a range of self–other relations.[19] Cast at first as a holiday-maker, he is jolted into a new position vis-à-vis the host culture when his wife and son disappear just before the family is due to return to Paris at the end of August. Motivated by his need to find them, he becomes a solitary investigator (= anthropologist) intent on understanding the culture from an insider viewpoint once the tourist season is over. His assumptions of authority and superiority, connected to his 'privileged' status as Parisian in the provinces and to his academic profession — a teacher of mathematics, he is introduced to us as 'le professeur' [the teacher] (*UTS* 9) — are rapidly deflated as he struggles to adapt.[20]

This anthropological gloss on the question of the outsider is characterized by a series of skilful transpositions and slippages, whereby the 'welcome' extended to the stranger anthropologist begs to be read on several levels at once: for instance, at times it is implicitly compared with the often harsh reality of the reception of non-indigenous Others in metropolitan France. It is also used to evoke, with deliciously bathetic irony, episodes of the *Odyssey* which see the hero–wanderer in a state of entrapment. I shall refer to the interweaving of these diverse outsider positions as my analysis progresses, along with NDiaye's scrutiny of mind-sets associated with anthropology. Throughout, the author invites us to focus less on the foreign culture itself than on how Herman comes to terms with it: his resistance, incomprehension, arrogance, frustration, disgust and fascination offer plenty of reminders that anthropology grew out of/was in the service of colonialism, while his occasional self-reflexivity fleetingly alludes to the self-conscious stance of postmodern anthropology.[21] What stands out too is that, unusually for NDiaye, this is an immensely funny book about (in)hospitality and outsiders. The joke is on Herman and all he represents, but also on us in as much as we sometimes recognize ourselves in him.

From Tourist Gaze to Anthropological Gaze

Herman's abrupt fall into alienation at the start of the novel at first draws attention to the specificities of what Huggan refers to as 'the tourist gaze', a particular version of the drive to objectify and instrumentalize other people and cultures.[22] NDiaye's works frequently allude to the tourist industry, showing a keenness to expose not its structures of hospitality but its exploitative, damaging dimensions and insisting particularly on enclaves within former colonies such as holiday villages designed for affluent Westerners.[23] Accordingly in *Un temps de saison* we learn that during the summer months Parisians on vacation habitually group together in a 'hill station' away from the village centre, interacting only superficially with the locals and consuming on their own terms what *le pays* — a strategically unnamed yet uncannily familiar location with many features reminiscent of northern, rural France — has to offer. Herman confesses that in as much as they considered the matter, he and his wife imagined that the place 'entrait en hibernation' [went into hibernation] (*UTS* 18) when they deserted it each 31 August: that is, they conceptualized it as somehow ahistorical, outside the march of time and remained entirely ignorant of the laws and customs structuring 'l'existence post-estivale' [post-summer existence] (*UTS* 28), as well as of the prevailing climate. A policeman explains to Herman that the cold and wet arrive punctually on 1 September with the departure of the tourists, and the fog and mist that descend on the text's first page are a satirical variant of NDiaye's customary use of atmospheric conditions to indicate her protagonists' loss of cultural and/or ethical bearings. In this instance the technique is redoubled by sudden darkness, mitigated only by the weakest of moonlight as Herman picks out his way towards a local farmstead, the entire scene constituting a heavy-handed blinding of the protagonist which may be read as a *reductio ad absurdum* of the uninitiated 'stranger' suddenly finding himself in a dark continent.

The opening of *Un temps de saison* is marked by a threshold scene at the farm where Herman has gone to seek help, an impenetrable encounter of disguised inhospitality, cultural insensitivity and mixed messages. The farmer's wife seems attentive and courteous in manner, but rather than invite Herman indoors she keeps him on the wrong side of the threshold in the rain, blocking the entrance with her sturdy body, smiling yet refusing to budge as he makes a move to seek shelter (*UTS* 11). It seems that as the tourist season comes to an end, so too does a particular dynamic of hospitality: the superficial, commercially-driven cordiality that prevails during the summer. When Herman assumes rights of access beyond this, he gets nowhere. The new mores are puzzlingly indecipherable to him. If the policeman — as superficially empathetic but substantively unhelpful as the farmer's wife — reassures him that outstaying his welcome into the autumn will not be a problem and that hospitality is, for many of the villagers 'une véritable manie' [a veritable obsession] (*UTS* 23), this boasting of a long tradition of welcome does not appear to extend beyond a corporate image. The 'vieux devoir de courtoisie envers les visiteurs' [ancient duty of courtesy towards visitors] (*UTS* 13), readily demonstrated in manner and facial expression, is not accompanied by proactive aid now that the tourist season and its own particular contracts of hospitality are over.

Herman's exasperation at 'cette paysanne' [this peasant woman] (*UTS* 13) gives rise to a scene that is a classic of its kind: the 'authoritative' Westerner attempting to make himself understood by speaking more loudly. He repeats his demand 'en accentuant soigneusement chaque mot [...] comme il faisait aux élèves à la tête dure' [emphasizing each word carefully [...] as he did for blockheaded children] (*UTS* 12–13), certain of his superiority not only as a teacher but, as I have already mentioned and as the novel very frequently reminds us, as a Parisian. By parodying relations between the West and the developing world through the lens provided by a Paris/province axis, NDiaye achieves a multi-directional satire of ingrained inhospitality and mutual ignorance. The implied relationship between the village and Paris has a colonial flavour too: Paris is patently the village's powerful and resented 'other' place and the two are conceptually and spatially inaccessible to each other. Villagers express resentment towards and fascination for the metropole. Young Alfred, for instance, who is determined to get there, seeks to enter into exchanges with Herman that might guarantee that result. At the same time Parisians are conceptualized as 'cette race détestée' [that detested race] (*UTS* 41), the word 'race' here being far from incidental.[24]

Following Herman's initial attempt to gain entry on other than tourist terms, NDiaye begins to configure what Huggan refers to as the 'conventional (if by now somewhat dated) anthropological distinction between the foreign "participant-observer", possessor of analytical expertise, and the local "native informant", owner-guardian of cultural knowledge'.[25] Motivated by the desire to find his family, the protagonist proceeds to negotiate gatekeepers (beginning with 'big men' such as the mayor), to seek access to reliable informants, to elicit information about the culture, to make 'field notes' and ultimately to learn enough humility to understand the culture in its own terms. Passages wherein the chairman of the Tourist Board, Herman's chief informant and himself a (former) Parisian, imparts advice about undertaking immersive ethnography (be patient and discreet; learn to listen; leave your assumptions behind; become unremarkable) and proffers nuggets of information corresponding to anthropological categories (economic and political organization, values and beliefs, etiquette, exchange and reciprocity) constitute textbook stuff. Amusingly, other clichés of field research such as the idea of 'going native' are also part of Herman's trajectory for he becomes progressively embedded in the new culture, all but forgetting the quest for his wife and son.

The messy 'hostipitality' of anthropological field relations is drawn methodically into NDiaye's account: is the target culture made up of hosts or hostages? And what peculiar kind of guest (perhaps sometimes hostage) is the anthropologist? The typical vexations and dilemmas of the anthropologist are systematically inflicted upon Herman. His physical discomfort, disarray and unpreparedness for the rainy season are heavily underscored and his doubts, frustration, sense of inadequacy and sometimes anger are all reminiscent of iconic fieldwork accounts. He is obliged to overcome his 'répugnance' [repugnance] (*UTS* 50) and accept an offer of primitive accommodation in the village square; his love affair with the foreign culture gives way to disgust and frustration and his attempts to understand the people and their ways are punctuated with moments of despair. Herman's cry: 'Quelle région haïssable!' [What a hateful region!] (*UTS* 39) typifies the cathartic exclamations scribbled in the field diary of many an exasperated ethnographer.

The Heart of Darkness

NDiaye's supple and creative topographies which merge real and imaginary environments to allude to the tensions between the global, the national and the local receive particularly sustained expression in *Un temps de saison*. I have already mentioned the confinement of the action to one bounded space. *Le pays*, a variant on the equally vague *là-bas* also used by NDiaye to designate former colonies, is hermetically cut off from the rest of the world like some exotic, anachronistically autonomous location; it is as if Herman were Evans-Pritchard among the Nuer or Lévi-Strauss among the people of the Amazon Rainforest. However, while his enquiry is modelled on fieldwork in remote parts of the globe, the actual field is a first world setting reminiscent of Normandy: it is agricultural, wet and chilly, and has recognizable features such as *pensions*, squares, a town hall, a Co-op and a tennis court. A dialogue is consequently set up in the text between contemporary urban ethnography which self-reflexively makes the familiar strange, and classic ethnographic accounts which are interested in unfamiliar, traditional, small–scale and technologically simple rural societies. I select below some instances, laced with humour, wherein ideas of the 'dark' and 'primitive' generate considerations about hospitality across settings and situations.

The cliché of a 'dark continent', satirically underscored by the inhospitable darkness of this text's opening pages, is turned on its head by NDiaye so that we imagine an outsider acclimatizing to the unfamiliar rigours of a Western locale. In climatic terms, the tropes of extreme heat or debilitating humidity that are familiar from colonial accounts are exchanged for unrelenting coldness and distinctly un-tropical rain. Herman's difficulty in adapting to the climate is frequently highlighted (*UTS* 112; 113; 118) and he becomes exhausted and physically weakened. In terms of the inhabitants of *le pays*, the colonialist's confrontation with darkness is exchanged for its opposite: fair skin and a 'blond blanchâtre' [whitish-blondness] (*UTS* 48) which constitute a hyperbolic non–pigmentation 'comparable à rien qui existât dans la nature' [comparable to nothing that existed in nature] (*UTS* 21).[26] The marked difference in appearance between the indigenous people and Herman, with his 'figure de Parisien' [Parisian face] (*UTS* 38) clearly evokes that between races, countries or continents, while the attribution of physical specificities to Parisians serves once more to satirize their sense of themselves as a 'group' in some coherent way.

If darkness is associated with backwardness, then *le pays*, like many other supposedly primitive societies, holds some surprises. David Richards points out that colonial ethnography emphasized 'the timeless and unchanging nature of a primitive Africa', and so too Herman mentally situates the village outside time and progress.[27] Yet while it may play self-consciously on its traditionalism as it markets itself to tourists, it nonetheless has highly developed infrastructures and technologies that are quite at odds with Herman's reductive assumptions. He is amazed to see the women shopkeepers not wearing aprons and participating as powerful business partners in a protracted and complicated 'assemblée hébdomadaire' [weekly assembly] (*UTS* 34); but it is especially the village's impressive administrative apparatus that enthrals him and he discovers with astonishment the complex architecture of the village centre, all the buildings of which extend deep into the hillside. This labyrinthine spatial infrastructure peopled by sleek, modern women in high heels and sharp suits accommodates a sophisticated bureaucracy, by far outstripping the metropole in terms of technology and efficiency. Similarly the astonishing town hall makes Herman think ruefully of the run-down fabric of the town hall in his *quartier* of Paris with its blackened parquet and 'rares méchantes chaises' [few, sorry-looking chairs] (*UTS* 29).

It is significant that NDiaye endows *le pays* with such an advanced bureaucratic system. First, bureaucracy betokens impersonal relations and a social organization that is far removed from the smaller face-to-face societies cherished by anthropologists and imagined by Herman. Second, French bureaucracy frequently figures as a fearsomely inhospitable obstacle to arriving immigrants and indeed as Herman becomes increasingly destabilized, baffled and defeated he slips precisely into the position of the immigrant attempting to get to grips with an opaque and impenetrable system. Not only must he negotiate the rigid 'insider/outsider' division and the defensive mistrust of the villagers, but he is obliged to navigate the baffling warren of the town hall, which is surely a parody of the French bureaucratic system. Uncertain of where to turn for help so as to find his wife and son, he is repeatedly rebuffed by officials who pay no heed to the seriousness of his case or to his mental distress: in response to his 'Je viens pour une affaire grave' [I am here for a serious matter], the gendarme replies: 'Demain. Le bureau est fermé maintenant' [Tomorrow. The office is closed now] (*UTS* 19), while the receptionist at the Town Hall merely greets him with: 'Avez-vous pris rendez-vous?' [Have you made an appointment?] (*UTS* 29).

NDiaye's text alludes too to the gendered dimension of anthropology, not only by staging a confrontation between a foreign culture and a male authority figure but also by foregrounding the sexual availability of indigenous women. Sexual 'hospitality' in the field frequently figured in anthropologists' field diaries, if not in their published accounts, and Herman is not impervious to such comforts. His first overtly anthropological observation shows him fascinated by a custom linked to the women's blouses, which combine the recognizably homely — an apple blossom motif — and the anthropologically exotic, for not only do they indicate the wearer's marital status, but the various gaily coloured laces which fasten them at the sides provide information on the year in which she took a husband.[28] Such observations on symbolic systems are meat and drink to the anthropologist and Herman begins to congratulate himself on his ability to interpret the coding. He notes too, the system of legitimized sexual exploitation at work in the village: Charlotte, for instance, is an integral part of the hospitality that her mother, owner of the boarding house, offers to paying guests. Such transactions are consistent with NDiaye's preoccupation, played out elsewhere in her writing, with economies of coercive 'hospitality' played out in sexual tourism, the porn industry, and most disturbingly, paedophilia.[29]

While Herman initially rejects the prevailing sexual mores as '[des] rites antédiluviens!' [antediluvian rituals!] (*UTS* 45), he is nonetheless seduced. NDiaye endows the villagers not only with a high-tech environment and hard-headed commercial expertise, but by contrast, and playing on another stereotypical trope characterizing 'primitive' peoples, with great sensuality and a 'langueur caressante' [caressing languor] (*UTS* 32) that imbues their every gesture and gaze. The overt sexualization of human contact in the novel and NDiaye's stress on the 'exotic' allure of the other are clearly integral to her anthropological parody. In a further scarcely concealed joke, the author allows her recurring Homeric intertext to surface by setting up deliberate connections between the contagious, sensuous apathy of the villagers — especially Charlotte — and that of the Lotus-eaters or of the nymph Calypso. Like Odysseus's men soporifically stuck on their North-African island, like Odysseus held captive for seven years thanks to Calypso's charms, Herman experiences a strong sense of entrapment: 'Ce peuple est si courtois', he notes, 'qu'il me tient prisonnier plus sûrement que par des ordres et des interdictions' [These people are so courteous [...] that they hold me captive more firmly than by orders and proscriptions] (*UTS* 31). Ultimately Herman succumbs to entropy and leaves off caring about home, about telling his story (= writing his ethnographic account) or even about his wife and son.

Going Native?

The second part of *Un temps de saison* is less concerned to allude to the pursuit of anthropology and its (in)hospitalities, becoming more fantastical and ghostly. Nonetheless, a conclusion to our reading of the text along anthropological lines is available for the novel enacts a further anthropological cliché: that of the outsider who 'goes native' and never returns. Throughout the narrative, the possibility is alluded to of Herman's adapting to the cultural norms of *le pays* and staying there permanently like his chief informant. He develops a degree of cultural relativism, begins to understand the villagers in their terms and even acquires certain of their mannerisms and gestures (*UTS* 105). Progressively he becomes so absorbed by the village, so attuned to its listlessness, so acculturated that he is terrified of leaving. In the end, return (to the West) is no longer an option.

I have already suggested that *Un temps de saison* is deliberately capacious enough to allude to several categories of people 'out of place': Parisians in the provinces, Westerners in other (anthropologically interesting) continents and immigrants from former French colonies who come to metropolitan France all intermingle in our minds as the text implicitly invites us to consider the situations of (in)hospitality in which they become involved. Thus the President's advice to Herman about disappearing into the local culture may be interestingly and ironically read as advice to the immigrant trying to settle in metropolitan France:

> Il vous faudra une grande patience, beaucoup de doigté et tâcher de vous glisser
> discrètement dans la vie du village, de devenir villageois vous-même, invisible,
> insignificant, et faire oublier surtout que vous êtes un Parisien hors l'été, c'est-
> à-dire un intrus. (*UTS 39*)

> [You will need great patience and lots of skill and you must try to slip discretely
> into village life, to become a villager yourself, invisible, insignificant, and make
> people forget that you are a Parisian here off season, that is to say an intruder.]

Seen in this light the advice is politically dubious: ideas of mutual hospitality between anthropologist and host culture are exchanged for a more imperious requirement for the outsider to be so utterly available as to disappear into the homogeneous fabric of society without creating a disturbance. Thus the chance for mutual change — hospitality's most positive dynamic — is lost. Perhaps Herman's fate constitutes a cautionary tale. By the novel's final pages he is so integrally part of this rain-soaked country, so divorced from his original self that he is literally dissolving, as his father-in-law observes with horror: 'vous êtes fondu, littéralement fondu' [you have melted, literally melted] (*UTS* 135). Such liquefaction is consistent with the recurring motif of digestion in NDiaye. This village, defined by its hyperbolic moistness, is the ultimate digestive environment reducing everything to spongy sameness and producing in Herman's case a *reductio ad absurdum* of assimilation, that most complete form of absorption that consists in breaking down the 'foreign' body for the benefit of a larger organism.

The denouement of *Un temps de saison* has puzzled critics. While NDiaye's denouements are seldom resolutions, this one is especially inconclusive and unusually abrupt. The text is allowed to hit a brick wall, ending on a random interruption which in my view simply indicates that the author's anthropological exercise has attained its goal and exhausted itself. After a brief trip beyond the village perimeter, Herman seeks to return. His taxi breaks down, the journey ends and both story and protagonist are suitably stranded as the conceits, metaphors and allusions to hospitality in the field that have been the motor of the narrative run out of fuel.[30]

Conclusion: Beyond the Threshold

We have seen in this first chapter a sample of engagements with strangers on various thresholds and noted that the threshold in NDiaye is a place where difference is confirmed and welcome hard to come by. The author's fictional world is also structured by peripheral figures destined to wander perpetually on the outer edges of community and presenting insiders with especially complex ethical challenges: the idiot boy Edo in 'La Gourmandise', the undomesticated dogs in *Ladivine* and the hybrid woman-fish in *La Naufragée*, all fulfil such a function. NDiaye's suggestive marking of the periphery with entities that are less than, other than or perhaps differently human confirms her interest in the mechanisms by which strangers are configured and the tension between the need to keep sight of them and to hold them at bay. I conclude with some thoughts on a range of still more hyperbolic outsiders or 'things' that lurk within NDiaye's signifying system and that are so radically foreign that they are inadmissible, resistant to conceptualization and irreducible to language: 'figure[s] particulière[s], paroxystique[s] et paradoxale[s] de l'étranger' [particular, paroxystic and paradoxical figures of the stranger], such things are simply beyond welcome.[31]

NDiaye's things throw the very idea of hospitality into crisis. It is significant that they come not only from without, such as a darting black shape which terrifies the community in *Autoportrait en vert*, but also lurk within, such as Djamila's insubstantial daughter in *Rien d'humain* or the eel-like creature in *Mon cœur à l'étroit* which emerges from Nadia's body and slithers out of the house.[32] All are indeterminate, slippery and connected obscurely to any number of terrors that jeopardize what is closest to home. The thing in *Autoportrait en vert* is spotted near the school playground; a search is organized to flush it out; a woman fears that it may penetrate her body; and at the text's end it darts through a cluster of playing children like a small, malefic tornado inducing a definitive wedge between the world of the child witnesses (who have seen it) and the mother narrator (who has not).[33] It is, like other of NDiaye's things, doubly unspeakable: not only are there literally no words to designate it, but the horror it inspires generates its own proscriptions on articulation, for to articulate is, in a sense, to admit it. Things cannot be described, only denied. The children and mother narrator rapidly cease trying to speak of it; in *Mon cœur à l'étroit* Nadia scrubs away its traces; in *Rien d'humain* Ignace purports to eradicate it through determined disbelief. The emphatic expression of conceptual and communicative defeat that characterizes NDiaye's resort to the trope is all the more remarkable since in each case the call for language is strong. In *Autoportrait en vert* the narrator asserts that the thing has no name *in French* (implying curiously that it may do in some other language/conceptual system) and her children's silence is emphasized; in *Mon cœur à l'étroit* Nadia's reluctant attempts to speak the thing do not take her beyond 'cette chose noire, luisante, fugitive' [this black, sheeny, fugitive thing] (*MCE* 295); while Ignace's endeavours to conceptualize Djamila's daughter collapse in frenzied failure. In her texts as in the consciousness of her protagonists, NDiaye's ultimate pollutants are given the most rapid of depictions, just enough to keep them on the radar as abiding threats, either at large 'out there' or couched within homes or wombs. As Žižek notes, 'beneath the neighbour as my *semblant*, my mirror image, there always lurks the unfathomable abyss of radical Otherness, of a monstrous Thing that cannot be "gentrified"'.[34]

That the thing in NDiaye may come from within as well as without is not at all paradoxical for, as her treatment of it so powerfully suggests, it is of our own making. It instantiates (and at the same time critiques) the exaggeration of difference, the making monstrous of what is outside, and the paroxysms of rejection that all too frequently appear to be a condition of the maintenance of bounded groups on whatever scale, from village to nation. Since suggestions that the stranger is like us carry with them the possibility of acceptance and incorporation, it is less threatening to harbour and protect a sense of others as things. Outsiders inspire a fear which we 'justify' by distancing them so radically that we are able to imagine them as lesser and alien, and to remain closed to their appeal. The thing in NDiaye is in essence a pointer to an all too common propensity to dehumanize inconvenient people, to push them out beyond our horizon and to put out of question our will to welcome by making welcome inconceivable. Things are one illustration of NDiaye's powerful recourse to the fantastic in order to put us in touch with something very real about (in)hospitality. My next chapter turns to explore how the urgency connected to belonging and rejection is given expression in NDiaye through the author's numerous evocations of the human/animal divide.

Notes to Chapter 1

1. Hahn, 'L'Hospitalité et l'étranger', p. 12.
2. Rewarding companions in terms of thinking through connections between thresholds in NDiaye's fiction and in the context of immigration in contemporary France are found in *Les Nouvelles Frontières de la société française*, ed. by Didier Fassin (Paris: Éditions de la découverte, 2010); *Les Lois de l'inhospitalité*, ed. by Fassin, Morice and Quiminal; and Anne Gottman, *Le Sens de l'hospitalité: essai sur les fondements sociaux de l'accueil de l'autre* (Paris: Presses Universitaires de France, 2001).
3. See *The Postcolonial Human*, ed. by Jane Hiddleston, special issue of *International Journal of Francophone Studies*, 15 (2012).
4. Referring to the immigrant as 'l'éternel invité' [the eternal guest], Rosello questions whether his (*sic*) status as outsider is confirmed by making it impossible for him to host, see 'Immigration: discours et contradictions', ed. by Montandon, p. 1526.
5. The location of their early relationship, while unspecified, is alluded to in Bella's 'là-bas' (*RH* 14), which suggests a North-African context.
6. Odysseus, returning to Ithaca to find his home and family possessed by suitors, is not recognized. Failure of recognition (visual and other) is a recurring aspect of NDiaye's arrival and reunion scenes.
7. In *Ladivine* Malinka/Clarisse rolls ethically unpalatable words around in her mouth like fetid balls of bread that can be neither spat out nor swallowed (*L* 72); throughout *Mon cœur à l'étroit* such words percolate up (in italics) within Nadia's interior monologue.
8. The very names, meaning 'beautiful' in Arabic and Italian respectively, mirror each other.
9. Fanny is abused by her uncle; Providence is raped; Rosie Carpe is coerced into participating in pornographic videos; Khady Demba is prostituted.
10. *Le Dire de l'hospitalité*, ed. by Gauvin, L'Hérault and Montandon.
11. Derrida and Dufourmantelle, *De l'hospitalité*, p. 119; *Of Hospitality*, p. 124.
12. Dominique Rabaté, 'Exercice de la cruauté', in *Marie NDiaye's Worlds/Mondes de Marie NDiaye*, ed. by Warren Motte and Lydie Moudileno, special issue of *L'Esprit créateur*, 53 (2013), 90–96 (p. 92). Self-naming is especially intensive in *Trois femmes puissantes*: in Khady Demba's story it constitutes an unusual instance of Irigarayan self-affection; in that of Rudy Descas, to which I return in Chapter 5, it is part of a stark existential reckoning. For Khady Demba's self-naming see my 'Marie NDiaye: la puissance de Khady Demba', in *Une femme puissante*, ed. by Bengsch and Ruhe, pp. 263–83.
13. Names in NDiaye can be divided along axes of familiarity (to the French ear) and distance. Traditional names such as Georges, Sophie, Valérie or Robert, as well as 'popular' names such as Priscilla or Rudy, jostle with others which splinter the hermetic French name-map, most significantly North-African and African names — Djamilla, Djibril, Sony, Khady — each working hard in its respective context as a pointer to often unspoken inhospitalities.
14. Judith Still, *Derrida and Hospitality: Theory and Practice* (Edinburgh: Edinburgh University Press, 2010), p. 147.
15. NDiaye's unwelcomed and objectified protagonists often live out the ultimate terms of their dehumanization by dissolving, liquefying or metamorphosing into inanimate matter.

16. See 'Introduction', in *The Postcolonial Human*, ed. by Hiddleston, p. 372.

17. Abdoulaye Sylla, 'La Négoce de la distance', in *Une femme puissante*, ed. by Bengsch and Ruhe, pp. 201–15 (p. 205).

18. It invites what Huggan calls 'anthropological readings', readings which incorporate an awareness of the connection between a text and ideas/practices of anthropology, usually intended ironically, see *The Postcolonial Exotic: Marketing the Margins* (London & New York: Routledge, 2001), p. 37.

19. The reference is to Michael H. Agar's classic *The Professional Stranger: An Informal Introduction to Ethnography* (New York: Emerald Group Publishing, 1996).

20. For NDiaye's creation and excoriation of numerous teacher protagonists, all of them self-satisfied repositories of French Republican values which they fail to enact in practice, see Michael Sheringham, 'La Figure de l'enseignant chez Marie NDiaye', in *Marie NDiaye's Worlds/ Mondes de Marie NDiaye*, ed. by Mott and Moudileno, pp. 97–110. Teacher figures analyzed in the current study who are brought to acknowledge their inhospitality towards certain pupils include Nadia (*MCE*) and Rudy Descas (*TFP*), but there are many others in NDiaye.

21. On the shifting mind-sets of anthropology since its imperial origin see David Richards, 'Postcolonial Anthropology in the French-Speaking World', in *Postcolonial Thought in the French-Speaking World*, ed. by Charles Forsdick and David Murphy (Liverpool: Liverpool University Press, 2009), pp. 173–84.

22. Huggan, 'Transformations of the Tourist Gaze', in *The Postcolonial Exotic*, pp. 177–208.

23. In *Trois femmes puissantes* the unpalatable fathers of Norah and of Rudy Descas both made their money out of holiday villages. In *Rosie Carpe* NDiaye targets the grotesque, lycra-clad French holiday makers whose disregard for Guadeloupe and its people is flagrant, as well as the Carpe family's involvement in sex tourism. A sustained and more variable exploration of tourism's (in) hospitalities is available in the second part of *Ladivine* where Ladivine the younger and her family take a vacation in Africa and where genuine hospitality on the part of tourists enters the mix. See Judith Still, 'Being a Guest: From Uneasy Tourism to Welcoming Dogs in Marie NDiaye's *Ladivine*', in *Hospitalities: Bodies and Texts, Transitions and Transgressions*, ed. by Merle A. Williams and Russell West-Pavlov (Berlin: de Gruyter, forthcoming in 2017).

24. For comments on Paris-Province tensions in the novel see Nora Cotille-Foley, 'Permanence et métamorphose: l'évolution du lieu de mémoire Paris-Province de J.-K. Huysmans à Marie NDiaye', *Essays in French Literature*, 43 (2006), 47–63.

25. Huggan, *The Postcolonial Exotic*, p. 49.

26. This represents the polar opposite of Papa's hyperbolized blackness in *Papa doit manger*.

27. See Richards, 'Postcolonial Anthropology in the French-speaking World', p. 181.

28. NDiaye's clever invention, which calls into question the very categories of the 'exotic' and the 'homely', might well allude to the brightly-patterned *madras*, a head-tie whose language of knots signalled the wearer's availability. The madras derived from south-eastern India and was worn by the freed women slaves who came to work as indentured labourers in the Antilles following abolition. Such half-buried allusions to colonial history abound in NDiaye and here we sense, in spite of the dead-pan narrative voice, her almost palpable enjoyment in what appears to be a melding of the Normand and the Antillean.

29. One of NDiaye's most painful threshold scenes entails an organized ritual of repentance in the play *Les Grandes Personnes* where an abusive (French) schoolmaster kneels before Karim, the boy he has violated, on the doorstep of the latter's home (*GP* 52).

30. I suggest one final level of meaning at work in *Un temps de saison* in Chapter 5.

31. Bernadette Bertrandias refers here to ghosts, see 'Le Fantôme: hostilité d'une inquiétante étrangeté', in *Le Livre de l'hospitalité*, ed. by Alain Montandon, pp. 1122–41 (p. 1125).

32. I discuss this uncanny 'birth' in Chapter 4.

33. NDiaye thus re-enlists the horror of H. P. Lovecraft's *Thing* which, as Deleuze and Guattari observe, 'arrives and passes at the edge, "teeming, seething, swelling, foaming, spreading like an infectious disease"', see *A Thousand Plateaus: Capitalism and Schizophrenia*, trans. by Brian Massumi (Minneapolis: University of Minnesota Press, 1987), p. 245.

34. Žižek, 'Neighbours and Other Monsters', p. 143.

CHAPTER 2

Less than Human? (In)hospitality and the Human–Animal Border

We are strangely composed of animals who flesh out our being,
a diverse zoology of the self.[1]

Increasingly NDiaye has drawn upon our relationship to animals' worlds in order to approach the question of what it is to be human, and especially to explore human (in)hospitality. One key articulation of the threshold in her work is therefore the human-animal borderline. She repeatedly draws our attention to the openings made available by this ambivalent space and in so doing she strains against philosophy's traditional construction of hospitality and inhospitality as uniquely human propensities. Animals and the idea of (our) animality are woven throughout her fiction, and beasts — a veritable menagerie from donkey, ox, cat, jelly fish or octopus to fantastical animals, but most notably birds and dogs — shadow or mingle with humans, companionably or otherwise, or serve as metaphors for them.[2] With a very few exceptions, animals in NDiaye are not domesticated but unassimilable, differently co-present, and interfacing in more troubling ways with the human realm as constant reference points that generate curiosity, fear, disgust or desire.[3] Throughout, protagonists in the throes of ontological and ethical crises use animals to think with and to address the aporia of their, or others', strangeness. We note too that animal noises, habitually fearful in NDiaye, are seldom made by animals (excepting the cattle's unabated chorus of fear which gives *Rosie Carpe* its ethical sound track)[4] but instead find human utterance, dislodging the intentionality of 'rational' speech. In an essay on animal thinking, Frédéric Boyer describes the human being as 'un animal avec un animal dans la tête' [an animal with an animal in mind].[5] Accordingly, to read NDiaye is to focus not first and foremost on the ethics of our treatment of animals — although beating, hunting, trading, sacrificing, eating and general cruelty are more habitually foregrounded than respect or love and this too concerns us — but on how animals constitute our mental landscape, how we are inhabited by them and how, if we let them, they might transform the ethics of human-human hospitality.

In this chapter I evaluate some significant examples of thinking and being with animals in NDiaye on thresholds of hospitality. The first two parts show how ideas of the animal are central to the construction of Otherness and to dominant patterns of affect which characterize transactions of (in)hospitality, namely a combination of anxiety and disgust. Here I analyze NDiaye's most frequent kind of recourse to animals as the unwelcome, 'abject', disavowed part of the human.[6] I also take a fresh look at the complexities of her mythical tale of hybridity *La Naufragée*, the first and one of the most elaborate of the author's sustained examinations of (in)hospitality on the human–animal threshold. The chapter's third part explores a recent evolution in NDiaye's writing which admits animals as agents of change in more subtle and far-reaching ways than, for example, her early recourse to thereanthropy or fantastic metamorphoses resulting from witchcraft.[7] In *Trois femmes puissantes* and *Ladivine* human–animal merging becomes still more probing, central to the architecture of the text and instrumental in affording her bleak narratives with a comparatively redemptive structuring.[8] Here animals impose themselves more compellingly, test our conveniently restricted concepts of them and intervene in the impasse of human inhospitality. These stories take us closer to plumage, to pelt, to another warmth and odour; they go beyond the uneasy flashes of species blurring that punctuate all of the author's texts to explore the possibility of hosting between species and to suggest human–animal continuity not division.

The questions that are prompted by animals in NDiaye do not conform to any single theory or position, but tap experimentally into the span of ontological and ethical issues that have taken centre stage in the vast emerging field of animal studies. Within a given work a range of human–animal relations typically co-exists, from conscious analogies and identification to involuntary 'animal' behaviour on the part of humans, deep fascination with the animal world, animal avatars, metamorphoses and, especially in more recent writings, what might be construed as a Deleuzo-Guattarian emphasis on the openness and fluidity of human–animal thresholds, on 'becoming-animal' (although it is important to note that NDiaye is in no way seeking to illustrate such theory and the interest in becoming-animal is for her confined to an exploration of the ethics of hospitality).[9] In her study on hospitality in Derrida, Judith Still looks at what the animal provokes in us and gives four reasons for drawing our relationships with animals into any questioning of hospitality:

1. To allow for this relationship between humans and other animals as a possibility.
2. To encourage this as an ethical relation between humans and (all) animals.
3. To open up the question of the boundaries within and between species, which particularly haunts philosophy and maybe also fiction, as the definition (or 'end') of man.
4. To reflect back on human–human hospitality after this detour via other species.[10]

The reader of NDiaye is encouraged to consider all four and, as we shall see, is brought to think again about elements that have historically been used to divide humanity from the animal world, such as language, rationality, gazing, suffering, empathy, compassion and hosting.

(In)hospitality and Animal-Becoming

Outsider figures in NDiaye are 'made' animal in order to justify their expulsion. We are of course familiar with such recourse to the animal world in the dehumanizing rhetoric of, say, racism or misogyny which seeks to naturalize disgust towards certain categories of people, but NDiaye's animal-becoming revisits such commonplace strategies with remarkable subtlety. In two of the author's most sustained explorations of how outsiders are constructed, involving Fanny of *En famille* and Nadia of *Mon cœur à l'étroit*, the work of exclusion is accomplished in part through thinking with dogs. The human appropriation of dogs affects Fanny's destiny in a number of complex ways, not least because she is identified (and self-identifies) with them as 'other' and 'less than'. *En famille*'s foundational inhospitality scene evokes the dog as both domestic pet and instrument of human aggression: the puppies that Fanny played with as a child now snarl at her from inside the ancestral enclave, producing a compact vignette of exclusion that evokes in miniature France's intolerance to outsiders and implicitly associates the family seat/village with a nation whose borders are robustly guarded against 'difference'. Later, Fanny hides in a kennel in the family home and is fed left-over scraps by her mother. When she emerges from her hiding place, she is set upon and ripped to pieces by her cousin's dogs (although, as already mentioned in the Introduction to this book, she survives). Fanny's multiple connections with dogs offer tacit reminders of how rejections of otherness are effected — discursively, cognitively and behaviourally — through appropriation of the animal world. She is in fact a scapegoat, 'the narrative animal par excellence' and a recurrent figure in NDiaye, bearing the weight of her 'community's' repressed repugnance for racial Others and cast out with its sins on her shoulders.[11]

In *Mon cœur à l'étroit* Nadia's abrupt expulsion from her elected community is also explored via the human-animal divide, although less critical attention has been paid to Nadia's canine-becoming than to Fanny's. It is worth pausing to assess the surfacing of dogs in three failed hospitality scenes that shape both the protagonist's initial ostracizing and her arrival in a new place. My interest here is less in zoomorphic analogies — the way in which, for example, Nadia has split-second perceptions of herself as a lizard (*MCE* 228) or a mollusc out of its shell (*MCE* 229) — than in NDiaye's deliberate re-casting and destabilizing of rituals of hospitality so that they too become animal, further heightening the sharply ethical sense of thresholds in her writing as well as the presence upon them of disgust, the 'gatekeeper' emotion that regulates many of her encounters. Here we note in particular the attribution of disgust properties to animals; the disgust that characterizes human-animal thresholds; the urgency, potency and physicality of disgust reactions such that '[e]verything seems at risk in the experience of disgust';[12] the way in which disgust lingers between 'conscious patterns of conduct and unconscious impulses' and also perhaps the powerful pleasure of disgust.[13] This novel, the story of a woman's struggle to ignore the emotional costs incurred by her 'jumping ship' in terms of class and ethnic origin (we slowly piece together a back-story which sees her abandoning her little son and husband, declaring her working-class North-African parents to be dead and re-marrying into the Bordeaux bourgeoisie) is riddled with disgust responses — those she prompts in her community and also her own.

In the opening stages of *Mon cœur à l'étroit* the everyday interactions in which Nadia is involved start to slither between human and animal frames, making hospitality especially unstable. Stripped of the codes that habitually regulate vulnerabilities on the threshold and that contain or diffuse disturbing emotions, interactions become fantastically unrecognizable and an opportunity to acknowledge a stranger in the street, or a simple commercial/social transaction in a local shop, become specifically dog-like. It is Nadia who begins thinking with dogs, fleetingly self-identifying with them as she gropes for an analogy to convey how she and her husband are treated (as 'des chiens fouineurs'; 'de vilains chiens' [snooping dogs; nasty dogs], *MCE* 13). These negative projections of the dog are carried through into encounters wherein both parties seem to take on animal traits.

In response to a young man who approaches her in the street Nadia instinctively offers a smile of acknowledgement. What ensues is perplexing and terrifying. With an unaccountable gesture which sidesteps the canon of legible responses, the man comes to a halt before her, rubs his hands on his thighs and challenges her with an 'aboiement' [barking]: 'Alors quoi ? Quoi donc ?' [Well? What is it then?] (*MCE* 14). Such unanticipated aggression hurls the encounter into the realms of unpredictability, reminding the reader rather of a sudden confrontation between two dogs. The unusual proxemics at work are also dog-like and disrupt the codes that regulate social distance. NDiaye describes in graphic terms a phenomenologically sharp succession of sensations: the young man's breath on Nadia's face; his spittle in her fringe (saliva and warm sour breath are common elements in the scenarios I touch on here); her close-up view of his chest heaving beneath his sweater (it seems that he too is afraid); her urgent need to urinate. The couple form a knot of dread until, as Nadia observes, '[l]a poitrine recule lentement, puis elle s'éloigne et sort de mon champ de vision' [the chest backs off slowly then moves away out of my field of vision] (*MCE* 14), this latter detail reminding us that, like a submissive dog, Nadia has ceased to look people in the eye and removed herself from the circuit of the human gaze. This detail is especially significant in light of Levinas's view, discussed in the Introduction, of how even the apparently casual automaticity of daily courtesies exchanged between strangers is profoundly enmeshed with ethics, obligation and awareness of the other's vulnerability and even mortality. The ethical shock of Nadia's street encounter lies precisely in its failure to recognize the other in this way. Instead the anxiety that is dominant in NDiaye's fiction, and that is especially in play on the threshold, is given heightened expression through recourse to the animal world: the tremulousness and vulnerability of animals — 'être[s]-aux aguets' [watchful beings] — is suggestive of our own.[14] This street encounter might of course be re-familiarized by reading it as a set-piece performance of unprovoked urban aggression motivated by racism, but although such a reading lurks within the vignette, it cannot entirely account for its complexity.

In the chapter entitled 'Pirouettes d'une pharmacienne' [Pirouettes of a pharmacist] (*MCE* 20–30) not only do we see Nadia being further dehumanized, further written out of the social body by touch, gesture, word and gaze, but this very writing out is the topic of conversation. Nadia has come to the local shop, where she knows the pharmacist, to buy compresses for the wound that her husband has sustained in an unprovoked attack. She is a customer, but the encounter is more than commercial and the pharmacist dances inconclusively around the challenge of diagnosing the social disorder that has led to the couple's ostracizing, as well as around her own excited position with regard to it.[15] Hers is a faltering speech that refuses to name the fault, suggesting it is unspeakable and referring merely to the couple as, for example, 'différents', 'disproportionnés' [different, disproportionate] (MCE 28). What is inadvertently highlighted by this spokeswoman for the (French) body is the gulf between a shared fantasy of the collective as principled, fair, ethical and hospitable and the dark reality of readily-stoked prejudice which in Mon cœur à l'étroit takes on fantastic and frenzied forms.

The codes of this encounter slip perturbingly between the respectful gestures and standardized speech of face-saving civility, even apparent compassion — Nadia is addressed as 'Madame' (MCE 26); the pharmacist considers taking her hand (MCE 27) — to hyperbolic expressions of disgust consistent with the 'allégorie de la répulsion' [allegory of repulsion] (MCE 24) that Nadia reads on the face of a passer-by. At the end, the exchange becomes animal. The women are close enough for Nadia to note the pharmacist's sour breath, the white deposit on her lips and the way in which her nervously ferocious laugh 'retrousse les lèvres, découvre la gencive' [curls back her lips and uncovers her gums] (MCE 29), a recurring human-dog slippage in NDiaye.[16] Nadia takes leave as a cowed dog, 'les yeux baissés [...] entendant sourdre de ma gorge un grognement qui me surprend et me fait honte' [eyes lowered [...] hearing a growling well up from my throat which surprises and shames me] (MCE 30). The dislocation of human speech by animal noises such as growling, yelping and whimpering occurs throughout NDiaye, taking us aback and suggesting an emergent hybridity or convergence of voice. In the Introduction I observed that human speech often goes awry in NDiaye due to grotesque, guilty material percolating its way to the surface of a speaker's consciousness against their will. Here the interruption of speech by involuntary sounds instead challenges established definitions of humanity: since language is frequently pointed to as the primary feature distinguishing man from beast, to dislodge it is to undermine the Cartesian logocentrism that elevates the human subject.[17]

The third animal encounter belongs within an extended (in)hospitality sequence in which Nadia is 'welcomed' to the home of her estranged son Ralph and his partner Wilma. Here, in a form of self-disgust which melds her own repressed shame with her consciousness of Ralph's embittered dislike of her, Nadia begins reluctantly to associate herself with Arno, the couple's ungainly mastiff, her self-awareness sharpened through co-presence with the dog in unfathomable ways that go beyond passing analogies. When it springs up close behind her in Ralph's car, she is repelled but soon realizes that she and the dog are breathing at the same rhythm: the idea is set up that the margin between them might be slight. Beginning to accommodate the perception, Nadia tries to make her breath felt upon her son's neck as a way of asserting her presence. There follows a notable subversion of human threshold rituals upon arrival at the homestead, when the anticipated welcome for Nadia as mother-guest is replaced by an ostentatious display of mutual affection between the dog and its owners, the excess of which underscores her exclusion and marks her, not the dog, as Other. Crouching to join Arno, the couple offer their faces to be licked at length, jostling for position in what Nadia refers to ironically as a 'bénédiction' [benediction] (*MCE* 240) and emerging shining and sticky with canine saliva. The ritual, in more moderate forms an accepted expression of human-dog relations, underscores the physical proximity of hospitality and its aim to incorporate. Montandon has described how certain North Australian Aborigine groups would 'collect' their sweat to daub it on the bodies of arriving guests: 'bel exemple de proxémique où le don de l'odeur corporelle est signe de partage et d'identification à la personne, au groupe' [a fine example of proxemics wherein the gift of bodily odour is a sign of sharing and identification with the person, the group].[18] There are in addition ironic maternal allusions in the inter-species ritual that Nadia is obliged to watch, combining an animal's welcoming of a new-born and a human mother's use of her own spittle to clean her child's face, both tender gestures of incorporation.[19] Although by and large Nadia appropriates the dog within a human frame of reference, subtle shifts in her awareness of animals progressively indicate a greater reach of empathy. For instance, as she eats the rich dishes made from animals hunted by Ralph, she intuits the terror of his quarry and wonders with pity whether it is fear that lends the flesh its potent flavour (*MCE* 244).

The brief scenes that I have described from *Mon cœur à l'étroit* where the presence of dogs is felt on thresholds of human (in)hospitality prompt us to consider the instability of any line separating the animal and the human, and highlight what is at stake for an individual's sense of self even in momentary encounters. They show Nadia being inhabited by animals, tentatively identifying with them in spite of her repulsion, then opening in empathy to their imagined world. This is a form of hosting and an agent of change. We will see in the latter part of this chapter that NDiaye begins to focus more insistently upon animal interventions in hospitality scenarios and explores the ideas of animal hosts and animal compassion. First, however, I consider how an earlier text might be read for hospitality across the human–animal fault line.

La Naufragée

La Naufragée concerns a woman-fish incongruously washed up beside the Seine in nineteenth-century Paris. She is brutalized, puzzled over and kept against her will in freshwater holding places: first, a reptile tank in the Jardin des Plantes and then a tub specially devised by an English painter (Turner) who, captivated by her song, purchases her and confines her in his London studio as 'muse' or, less lyrically, slave. An unusual physical characteristic of the text is its saturation in reproductions of Turner's paintings, which are mentioned briefly in the Introduction and to which I return somewhat differently here. Like all NDiaye's *contes* [tales] *La Naufragée* exceeds any one line of interpretation. I read it as an exercise in thinking on and around the human-animal divide and, more than this, on complicating the very idea of binaries and hierarchies and straining to think instead, hospitably, with continuity.

The tale reprises NDiaye's incessant concern about welcoming strangers in need. Its title — *La Naufragée* [the shipwrecked woman] as opposed to *la sirène* [the mermaid] — directs us away from the mythical creature and towards the all too familiar human drama of arriving bereft and desperate for hospitality on foreign shores. Further, it is as a beggar woman, hobbling on makeshift crutches and wrapped in rags, by definition a supplicant that the protagonist appears among humans (N 23). A postcolonial cousin of Baudelaire's city-stranded swan, she advances 'pesamment et gauchement' [heavily and gauchely] (N 25), dragging her inert tail through the hot, dusty streets.[20] Her story is densely packed with overlapping questions related to inhospitality and the human-animal divide which find sharp articulation particularly given her permanent hybridity as 'femme-poisson' [woman-fish] (N 29), a status used to blur distinctions more effectively than if she were fully animal: can animals reason? How do they think? Do they have a developed language? How do their sensory experiences differ from those of humans? Can they feel empathy and compassion? Can they suffer (a question that humans frequently ask apropos of fish)? The concept of a *sirène*, one of many human fantasies that stoke anxiety about the co-mingling of species, is not admitted by the woman-fish herself who has never heard the word 'n'ayant jamais été qu'une femme-poisson' [having only ever been a woman-fish] (N 35). The text's insistence on her preferred self-definition asks us to address the meanings of 'woman', of 'fish' and of the hyphen.

What does NDiaye gain by approaching the ethics of human-animal hospitality via the woman-fish? First, the strategy allows her to redouble hyperbolically the threshold or divide between human and animal, while at the same time calling it into question, even denying it, since the protagonist seamlessly conjoins both, and the hyphenated term *femme-poisson* is matched by her divided, yet single body. There is much focus on her body's two parts as if to keep them distinct, and also on the point of divide, as well as on the conflicting feelings that arise when we are called upon to acknowledge the animal (as like us) and to recognize the animal part of ourselves. Out of her element she loses the value of hybridity: 'Hors de l'eau je ne suis qu'un poisson' [out of the water I am but a fish] (N 17); humans see only the scaly marker of difference, although it does not define her completely. They cannot admit of a hybridity that so disturbs the dualistic view of two realms. They therefore do not take proper account of her 'moitié d'humanité' [human half] (N 19).

In this text of borderlines, splits and forays into both animal and human experience, the narrative focalization is cleverly divided. The first half of the story is a vivid first-person, present-tense account of the traumatized protagonist, allowing us access to her quite other (animal?) consciousness up to the point where she is purchased; the second is a third-person, past-historic account given from the painter's perspective. The accounts overlap slightly so that we get two versions of the moment when the woman-fish sings near the wet fish stalls in the vast food market, Les Halles. The first part of the story is the sole instance in NDiaye where a non-human animal is explored from the inside and in a sustained way. Here non-human perceptions flood the text, inviting us to engage with them. The woman-fish's account might interestingly be read alongside other animal-alert experimental works such as, for example, Marie Darrieussecq's *Truismes* or Ananda Devi's *Moi, l'interdite* which take us inside animal experience via animal-human hybrids, showing us the world — and the human animal since all hybrids comment on the society in which they are enmeshed — from a new perspective.[21] It shares too, to an extent, their feminist concern with the connections between woman and animal, again an unusual emphasis in NDiaye.

What knowledge do we glean from the woman-fish's own account? It offers a take on the world which is removed from, yet overlapping with our own; one which notably thinks across species, responds to what we recognize as essentializing discourse about the animal, and arouses empathy. One of the first things we learn about her, her instinctive rather than reasoned responses to situations, raises the Cartesian view of the 'animal machine': 'La reflexion, le calcul sont difficiles aux femmes-poissons' [reflection, calculation are difficult for women-fish] (*N* 13), yet the observation itself demonstrates fine self-awareness. She is sharply alert to danger and able to project forward, knowing that the bottom part of her body — the disputed, abject, ill-adapted part — will dry rapidly and painfully in the sun. We learn that this part is the more sensitive and dream with her of the sensual/sensory memory of using her undulating tail to propel herself through the sea. Our attention is drawn to her senses: her vision, for instance, is adapted to navigating a marine environment, whereas on land it is blurred, objects are indistinct and she is largely aware of light. She cannot focus on or look at humans and meet their gaze. We feel her painful awareness that her speaking voice is not audible out of water; in spite of her intensive efforts she cannot be heard — except of course in her song, a communication so powerfully attractive that it provokes violence in the crowd. A leitmotif of the text is therefore the silently opening and closing fish mouth which moves to no avail: 'ma bouche clapote' [my lips plash together] (*N* 25).[22] We learn that she has a clear place within her social group and that the group has shared values including respect for mature women-fish. Above all, what is clear is not only that she suffers but that she recognizes the suffering of others. Her ethical sensibility is developed (we note her ill-founded hypothesis that 'on a pitié de ce qu'on trouve échoué et mal à sa place' [one pities what one finds washed up and out of place], *N* 15) and she is capable of compassion and empathy: it is she, not humans, who observes that all are 'constituée de la même chair souffrante et des mêmes pensées affolées' [made of the same suffering flesh and the same panic-stricken thoughts] (*N* 41).

From the outset of the story the question of hospitality arises. The very figure of alterity, the woman-fish cannot be incorporated. It is possible neither to welcome (or desire) her as a woman nor to eat her as a fish, although there are strong calls to both and the latter question is raised by her fetching up in the fish market as well as by the (now alarming) details from Turner's paintings of lifeless gutted fish. Her reference to her 'chair de poisson' and 'chair de femme' [fish flesh and woman flesh] (*N* 7) keep the edible-sexually desirable tension hard at work. The first humans to see her on the river bank set upon her and poke a sharp object between her scales, express surprise when she bleeds, and are interested not in whether she may be suffering but in whether she would taste of fish or meat, raising the spectre of cannibalism. Their 'Saloperie de Léviathan!' [Dirty Leviathan!] and 'putain de sirène' [bloody mermaid] (*N* 19) equate the despised female with the animal — not least since the French invective is related to *putain* [whore] and *salope* [tart] — and bring together the question of fish suffering with sexual violation. A later equally penetrative attack also seems sexualized: at the place where her fish skin and woman skin meet 'on a tâché d'introduire un doigt, un ongle, comme pour séparer les deux chairs' [somebody tried to insert a finger, a fingernail, as if to separate the two kinds of flesh] (*N* 39). The hyphenated opening of one part to the other and the continuity it represents cannot be conceptualized or admitted; anxiety about the woman-fish's lack of orifice reads like a re-casting of the much-theorized male responses to the opening of female genitalia.

As for the painter, he first touches her woman skin by accident in the bustling market and is sexually stirred then disgusted by his response. Later, on the sea voyage when he is at leisure to examine her closely, he eroticizes her upper body but is filled with repulsion by the lack of clear demarcation between this and her lower part which merges 'sans ligne apparente' [without any visible line], seeming a 'prolongement naturel' [natural prolongation] (*N* 63) of her woman skin. He too imagines eating her, even boasting about it with no risk of condemnation 'car personne ne pourrait affirmer qu'elle avait plus de conscience qu'un poulpe' [for nobody could affirm that she had more awareness than an octopus] (*N* 71).[23] The question of animal mental capacity is raised as the painter gazes into her eyes and sees only a look 'parfaitement vide d'intelligence' [perfectly empty of intelligence] (*N* 55), militating against his compassion. He ponders over what the woman-fish is to him. She is certainly not an 'animal de compagnie' [pet] (*N* 61) although she spends the sea voyage to Portsmouth in a wicker casket of the kind used for domestic animals. He admits of no possibility of friendship or confidence with her but insists on ownership: he is specific that this creature he keeps locked away in secret is his and that she must labour for him. He has, nonetheless, been transformed by something that she can offer and that is not known in the human world.

The painter (like Ulysses) is transported but not killed by the woman-fish's song. He is also notably feminized as his senses are modified, giving rise to a radically new and disturbingly powerful kind of openness to the world: 'il se dilatait de haut en bas, lui qui était un homme' [he, a man, dilated from top to bottom] (*N* 53), becoming a 'vaste cavité accueillante, heureuse receptacle de plaisir et de soumission' [vast, welcoming cavity, a happy receptacle of pleasure and submission] (*N* 53). He is completely seduced and fecundated (perhaps by the woman-fish's *queue* — French for both 'tail' and 'penis'). A communicative correspondence is conveyed throughout the book between the genius of both woman-fish and painter, for *La Naufragée* is suffused in something beyond the logos: a hazy, light-flooded, indistinct but captivating form of expression. The woman-fish sees as the painter aspires to see, something that is abundantly clear from her account of her impression of the on-shore world and her sensitivity to light rather than to form. The limitations of human perception and the question of what we might gain by seeing through animal eyes are raised, as it is the painter's obsession with vision that leads him to enslave the woman-fish.[24] It is worth adding that in spite of what we know to have been Turner's anti-slavery stance, his fictional avatar is unable to make the ethical leap required either to see his captive as human or to consider her animal right to freedom.[25]

La Naufragée asks how far species can open to each other. It invites a porousness to the animal other and consideration of the animal part that is inseparable from our humanity: we too are, as the French expression (which remains unspoken in this fable) has it, *ni chair ni poisson*: neither one thing nor the other but both. Diegetically, however, while we see the boundary and assumed hierarchy between human and animal being probed, no dislodging of human assumptions is effected; no ability to welcome the animal is evident, only to exploit it. Unlike the works by Darrieussecq and Devi mentioned earlier, this fable is not emancipatory. The protagonist is not a woman who expands her being through attaining familiarity with the animal realm and, to an extent, becoming animal; she is familiar already with the animal, becoming instead more acquainted with humanity, which has nothing to offer her and much to deprive her of. Learning in this direction is unedifying. In the end, only the painter knows the centrality of animal perception to his art, but at the conclusion of the tale he is dead, the woman-fish has disappeared from her prison and those humans who puzzle over the large tub do so only briefly because, the last words of the tale, 'c'était sans importance' [it was unimportant] (*N* 81). Binary thinking has not been dislodged; only the astonishing light-filled paintings, the vestiges of some kind of human-animal awareness remain, but they are not legible as such and are attributed only to human genius.

Trois femmes puissantes: Birds and Meeting Places

NDiaye's three-part novel *Trois femmes puissantes* is saturated with allusions to birds — crows, buzzards and chickens — and to the 'bird-becoming' of humans. Thematically birds seem consistent with this novel's emphasis on journeying between Africa and France and with the depiction of migration in the final story, where people traffickers converge terrifyingly with crows and would-be migrants huddle like a desperate, grounded flock.[26] Their meanings however are typically fluid and unresolved, reaching beyond this more obvious reading as well as resisting any overly close connection one might be tempted to make with ideas of deterritorialization or liberating lines of flight.[27] Here I focus on birds and hospitality in the first story, that of Norah and her father, and in particular on the spaces of hosting and the substitution of a domestic threshold with an alternative place of meeting not customarily associated with human hospitality.

Wherever he crops up in her work, NDiaye's 'fantasy' African father figure is unerringly depicted as a domineering patriarch and a dangerous host.[28] The quality of hospitality he affords to the numerous guests and sometimes bewilderingly extended kin who fill his large house is unpredictable, but always on the decline, and his daughter is never made welcome. This particular story, in which the guests have gone, is shaped as a sequence of failed hospitality scenes between father and daughter in and around his house. It begins, characteristically for NDiaye, with a tense and troubling reunion on a threshold. Norah, a lawyer, has made the journey from France to Dakar to comply with her father's imperious demand that she help him. Although she is not yet aware of the nature of his need (she will learn only later that he has strangled his wife, persuaded Sony, his son and Norah's brother, to take the blame and now wants Norah to defend Sony) she still arrives in trepidation: accepting an invitation to her father's house entails the risk of undoing her carefully controlled world since 'tout ce qui venait de cette maison n'était que ravage et déshonneur' [nothing came from that house but ravage and dishonour] (*TFP* 73).

From the outset, Norah's father appears part bird. His arrival on the threshold is unusually complex for it entails crossing from the animal to the human domain: he does not come forth from the house to greet his daughter, but seems instead to have descended abruptly from the branches of a nearby tree. Dishevelled, stinking and pitiful, hands crossed over his stomach and head cocked to one side, he stands and eyes her in the dusk. His descent explodes the spatial grammar of welcome and his hybridity throws its very possibility into question, for wild birds — perhaps birds of prey — do not welcome humans. The flame tree whose canopy arches over his empty house has become the 'sombre asile' [dark refuge] (*TFP* 87) to which he escapes, perching in self-imposed exile from his own kind. How are we to read the father's disconcerting hybridity? Since the narrative is focalized through Norah, one reading would be that his becoming animal is a projection, her device for coping with the trauma of his presence and with the disgust aroused by his unpalatable claims on her. Thus the fleeting mid-sentence allusion to 'son père aux ailes repliées sous sa chemise' [her father, wings folded under his shirt] (*TFP* 30) keeps us focused on the danger that he represents and renders with great impact her distrust, distaste, incomprehension and anxiety. This species shift literalizes the father's inability to observe the fundamental norms of hospitality which are part of being human, and perhaps also humane. It also confirms his inability to self-welcome: even he no longer feels at home as the master of his house, but must perch somewhere outside it, in a tree. Yet the exploration of this bird-father is not solely negative: it is powerfully ambivalent and productively slippery, petrifying neither man nor bird in readily understood meanings and opening the door to Norah's new conceptualization and acceptance of her father. For much of the narrative the feelings that he arouses in her oscillate between anger and pity, but a resolution and a welcome of sorts — the first indication of father-daughter welcome in NDiaye's entire *œuvre* — is at last attained.

Key in this regard is the father's elective perch. The flame tree persistently competes with the human dwelling, its branches scratching the corrugated iron roof in an unrelenting reminder of its presence as an alternative, transformational and more hospitable space. The idea of 'flamboyance' that it brings to the text (the French for flame tree is *flamboyant*) connects with the uncanny glow that Norah notices emanating from her father's own body and that introduces a further layer of meaning to his hybridity: not only is he an old man and a squat and fleshy bird, he is also an angel of sorts, shining with a 'froide luminescence' [cold luminescence] (*TFP* 41), a detail which allows NDiaye overtly to activate the theoxenic framework that frequently injects something of the divine into her hospitality scenarios: could Norah be engaging unawares with a conduit to the divine?[29] Once again hospitality is played out on the fault line between realism and the fantastic as the challenge is faced of offering it to a being who is on the borders of the human, and the transaction is elevated to the status of (contemporary) myth. The father's luminosity represents not any inherent goodness in him, but rather the opportunity that he represents for generosity, perhaps for enlightenment, or for becoming more human. When Norah looks up at the tree to pick out her father's form she detects his laboured breathing, muffled tears and groans of distress. Critically, she has no language to cross the gulf between them: 'Brisée d'émotion, elle voulut l'appeler. | Mais par quel mot?' [Broken with emotion, she wanted to call out to him. | But with what word?] (*TFP* 41). Here the protagonists are no longer speaking subjects: the father has no bird call and the daughter has no voice.

Ultimately, a space of possible compassion begins to be opened up by the father's sidestep into the animal realm. At this point it is useful to recall the English philosopher Jeremy Bentham's re-focusing of the very question of human knowledge about animals, which challenged the dominance of the Cartesian conundrum about whether animals think by asking instead whether they suffer, a more humane — and enduringly influential — iteration of the key point of connection between human and animal worlds. Bentham's emphasis is particularly relevant to NDiaye's universe where suffering is explored unrelentingly and where it constitutes in fact the chief human/animal meeting point.[30] Significantly, and ironically, humans are not cast in Cartesian perspective either for they are characterized much less by their ability to reason (NDiaye's protagonists are seldom effective thinkers) than by their vulnerability, incomprehension and propensity for experiencing incommunicable, incommensurate pain.

If the conclusion of human-animal tales frequently involves the re-establishment of a familiar hierarchy of values between realms, there is no such resolution in Norah's story. The coda unfurls in an animal place and it is, we suspect, as bird-human hybrids that Norah and her father finally come together, if not in harmony at least in tolerance of each other. It is not that the father becomes hospitable in a human sense: instead Norah accommodates him, overcomes 'l'horreur de partager un secret avec cet homme' [the horror of sharing a secret with this man] (*TFP* 80), opens to him as bird (not as man) and rises to the tree:

> Il percevait près de lui un autre souffle que le sien, une autre présence dans les branches. Depuis quelques semaines il savait qu'il n'était plus seul dans son repaire et il attendait sans hâte ni courroux que l'étranger se révélât bien qu'il sut déjà de qui il s'agissait. (*TFP* 93)

[He perceived nearby another's breathing, another's presence among the branches. For some weeks he had known that he was not alone in his lair and he waited, without hatred or resentment, for the other to reveal herself while all the time knowing who it was.]

Luce Irigaray has insisted on silence rather than on verbal exchange as a precondition for hospitality: it is silence, she contends, that betokens welcome by showing one's preparedness to 'leave the circle of one's own discourse — or usual house of language' in order to listen.[31] She speaks of silence as a precursor to good listening and dialogue and argues that it is thanks to silence that 'another world can manifest itself and take place'.[32] In NDiaye's story the regime of unarticulated mutual respect lasts for weeks as the presences, breathing together in quiet co-acceptance, practise a kind of patient, bare hospitality. In joining her father on a non-human threshold, Norah opens the couple's potential for new kinds of access to each other and for bypassing the codes (based on the father's misogyny and violation and the daughter's fear) that have governed their poisonous relations to date. Whereas in the house Norah felt hostage and the father could not host, in the tree the two begin a muted, tentative form of co-hosting. In the end Norah accommodates to the branches, the leaves, the odours and sensations of a quite new dimension to find ways to say 'yes' to her father, to open to and support him.[33]

The flame tree is, then, a special kind of meeting place, differently transitional from the human threshold with which it is constantly juxtaposed in this narrative. On the latter are staged multiple negotiations of passages between inside and outside and self and stranger through familiar ritual and brief transition. The tree is instead a liminal stopping place, straddling human and animal worlds (after all trees can be climbed by people as well as perched and nested in by birds), where hours are spent outside the routine organization of human hospitality. There is no food to offer here, no conversation, no touching and no inviting in. The space is in-between but also transcendental, a third place. It cannot be policed by the father as it is open to the elements and has innumerable points of access. He does not invite his daughter to sit in the branches with him, and here the burdens of reciprocity are irrelevant. What is achieved is a bare co-existence: a *being* together. Norah progressively drops her vengeful bitterness towards her father, extending compassion *without* focusing unrelentingly on his defects and insisting that he change. Towards the end of the story comes the serene and lucid repetition of her reconciliatory mantra: 'Car c'était ainsi' [For it was thus] (*TFP* 93). It is such hospitality to the idea of Other, however challenging, that accounts, at least in part, for the much-debated strength with which NDiaye invests the key female protagonists of *Trois femmes puissantes*, each of whom wavers conspicuously at points of their respective narratives between human and bird. What matters here is not any particular inherent virtue of 'birdness' or any desire to *be* a bird: when Khady Demba flies away off the razor wire fence that debars her from access to Europe, she is henceforth inaccessible to the narrative, perhaps now as species-bound and stuck within her own frame of reference as are we. Key to hospitality is rather what we can gain from (imagining) the wavering threshold between human and animal.

Writing on the ambivalence of animality in NDiaye, Sheringham notes the capacity of the human–animal interface, as it wavers between the realist and the fantastic, to communicate with tremendous impact a range of experiences and perceptions, and to do so outside habitual analogical schema so that both human and animal are renewed and made productively strange.[34] I have suggested that *Trois femmes puissantes* offers some rich instances of this. Derrida's 'fantasmes de participation, de fusionnement, de libération' ('fantasies of participation, fusion, liberation') of which Sheringham speaks are perhaps still more central to the inter-species relations envisaged in our next text, *Ladivine*.[35]

Ladivine: Gazing and Hosting

In *L'Animal que donc je suis* Derrida famously posits that thinking begins with an animal–human gaze: 'L'animal nous regarde et nous sommes nus devant lui. Et penser commence peut-être là' ('The animal looks at us and we are naked before it. And thought perhaps begins there').[36] The gaze throws us back self-consciously onto ourselves, insisting at the same time that we extend ourselves in order to imagine something other than human consciousness. NDiaye frequently seems concerned with what is at stake in human–human looking, especially in a context of hospitality, and habitually shows the welcoming function of the gaze as defective. We might indeed speak of a crisis of the gaze in NDiaye, a kind of visual aphasia or faulty ocular grammar: her protagonists do not issue invitations or lay themselves open through gazing; they seldom look at each other in mutually affirmative ways; they fail to recognize each other; and gazing in love is an aspect of human interaction that scarcely figures at all in the author's work. Instead gazes are blank, furtive, malicious or, like the sideways glance of Norah's father-bird, obliquely inscrutable. Under the entry for 'Regard' [Look] in an ABC of human–animal relations, Elisabeth de Fontenay observes: 'Aucun animal n'aurait du regard... Les bêtes ne feraient jamais que scruter, épier, guetter' [no animal, it seems, 'looks'... Beasts are said only to scrutinize, to spy, to watch out]; she continues: 'Les chiens, eux, baissent les yeux devant le regard des hommes' [As for dogs, they lower their eyes before the human gaze].[37] We saw this to be the case with Nadia. We saw too that the woman-fish of *La Naufragée* was unable to engage with humans through her gaze. *Ladivine* however explores what are the most profoundly meaningful and hospitable gaze-exchanges in NDiaye, and these take place between humans and dogs.

Dogs thread their way through *Ladivine* on revised, more curious terms and there is a great deal to be said about (thinking with) dogs and hospitality in the novel.[38] Here not only are protagonists gauged, by themselves and others, via canine com-parisons — some more searching than others[39] — but ethical questions related to care, love, self-sacrifice, and also to violence and murder are raised through focusing on dog, as much as on human, behaviour. As with *Trois femmes puissantes* we are asked to consider the possibility that animals are capable of resolving, or helping to resolve, the consequences of human inhospitality, but *Ladivine* opens much more fully to the richness of animal intelligence, both cognitive and emotional. Here the dog that follows (leads?) Ladivine is an ethical actor, almost a protagonist in its own right, and referred to indeed on one occasion as an 'individu' [individual] (*L* 221), with its own elaborately beneficent designs in interacting with the human world. Dogs enact what Irigaray in a philosophical and poetic essay refers to as 'animal compassion', an unsolicited comfort or even empathy that can be deeply nurturing.[40] Further, dogs can be impeccable guests and even loving hosts. The novel, then, quietly dismantles any prior assumptions about the poverty of an animal's inner life. Constant (cognitive) companions for the reader, NDiaye's dogs evoke a range of canine cousins who have troubled the human–animal threshold: they keep company with Cixous's Fips,[41] Lévinas's Bobby,[42] Kafka's richly intellectual dog anthropologist[43] and many others besides.[44]

Ladivine concerns a family destiny spanning four generations of women. It begins with the young Malinka's rejection of her origins (like Nadia in *Mon cœur à l'étroit* she is working class, mixed race and ashamed of both) and with her establishment of fiercely impermeable personal boundaries as she attempts to pass as white, renames herself 'Clarisse' and blanks out the African mother, Ladivine Sylla, who brought her up. The narrative explores the enduring impact of Malinka's original offence through the generations. Its first part follows her becoming Clarisse, her marriage to and separation from Richard Rivière (a life she keeps scrupulously secret from her mother) and her murder by Freddy Moliger, an unsavoury 'stray' she has taken in. Its central section concerns Clarisse's daughter Ladivine and her family. We see too that Clarisse ultimately withdraws from her own daughter, manifesting a kind of numb unavailability even in the midst of her fierce love. Most of the section concerning the young Ladivine is set during a holiday to an unnamed African country which is, unbeknown to her, the birthplace of her grandmother. Here she is followed by, and ultimately merges with a large brown dog. The novel's final part concludes with the trial of Freddy Moliger and, we are led to believe, the miraculous return of daughter and granddaughter to Ladivine Sylla, carried in the body of the dog.

The most protracted gazes and the most remarkable for the privileged quality of communication that they suggest are experienced by the young Ladivine, first as a baby with an Alsatian dog which climbs into her cradle to lie beside her, and later on her African trip with a mangy dog chained up outside a shop. In each case the gaze is described as magnetic and as giving uninterrupted access to another form of consciousness: 'plonger' [to dive] and 'noyer' [to drown] (*L* 224) are the immersive verbs of choice here for human engagement with the animal look and what it harbours. In the second of these incidents Ladivine withholds her hand from the dog's proffered head, not touching its 'poil crasseux' [filthy coat] (*L* 224) for fear of vermin, but extrapolates from the creature's steady gaze, even as she keeps her distance, something of a lesson in hospitality: 'Elle noya son regard dans le regard calmement éploré, calmement suppliant, et toute l'humanité et l'inconditionnelle bonté de l'animal docile lui remplirent les yeux de larmes' [She looked deep into the calmly imploring, calmly supplicating gaze and her eyes welled up with tears at all the humanity and unconditional goodness of the docile animal] (*L* 224). Derrida's observations on the ontological unsettling that comes from being gazed upon by an animal Other (in his case a cat) are perhaps deliberately referenced in the above scenario, but where in *L'Animal que donc je suis* the abyss of the animal gaze first throws the philosopher back onto himself, provoking a sequence of thoughts on what is proper to the human (dress, nakedness, awareness of nakedness, language, reason, laughter, mourning, gift-giving and so on), the animal look in the fictional world of *Ladivine* is immediately interpreted in relational and ethical terms.[45] It is presented as deeply reciprocal. It suggests a strong desire on the part of the animal for something that the human can satisfy, as well as a range of moral qualities proper to animals. It indicates, curiously that the dog has more 'humanity' than its human counterparts and the unconditional nature of its welcome alludes to the hyperbolic Law of hospitality, the black hole of absolute unconditional openness around which thinking on hospitality continues to dance. The gaze is comfortable and fraternal, devoid of the awkwardness of what Derrida, deftly melding *malséance* [impropriety] with *animal* to allude to a specific cross-species phenomenon, dubs 'animalséance'.[46] Instead it gives rise to a new kind of human desire — not only desire for the animal, but desire *to be* the animal (Ladivine 'désira ardemment être lui' [ardently desired to be him], *L* 224) — a philosophically and ethically driven urge that is far removed from the magical shape-shifting of the witch twins in NDiaye's *La Sorcière* [The Witch].[47] In addition, the profound mutuality of acknowledgement in this ethical, post-anthropocentric gaze runs sharply and firmly counter to Lévinas's assertion that the animal does not have 'face'.[48]

Towards the end of *Ladivine* the threshold between species is crossed and there is a merging of bodies, of human into animal, which ultimately permits a reunion of the narrative's three women outside the poisonous parameters of race, class and poverty and, in the case of Ladivine the younger, away from the postcolonial violence with which her husband and children appear to be alarmingly contaminated part way into the family's African holiday. Not only does this transformation bypass the fact that the animal body is precisely what we disavow as we accede to culture, it also literalizes the idea that the animal and the human are embedded in each other. It is the case too that no human-human exchange in NDiaye takes place in such confidence, friendship — friendship is rare in NDiaye but here Ladivine refers to the dog as 'son ami' [her friend] (*L* 326) — and love.[49] The dog that has almost exhausted itself in its determined shepherding and protection of Ladivine throughout her stay in Africa comes to rest beside her in a forest, stinking of humus, sweat and effort. He is embraced unconditionally, merges with or absorbs the woman and in so doing provides a liberation in which she both sorrows and delights. In her canine incarnation she is a delicate guest, visiting Ladivine Sylla at the novel's end and bringing back the child and the grandchild who, in human form, were unavailable for welcome. At once a fairy-tale helper animal, a *deus ex machina* and a philosophical spur, the dog in *Ladivine* evokes cliché ('man's best friend'), defies cliché (perhaps rather a 'best mother', a compassionate maternal surrogate who becomes womb and carries back the lost child) and suggests, by providing a fantasy version of the idea, that another species may serve as effective intermediary in order to bypass our chronic inability to open to each other.[50] Critically too the dog's unconditional offering of its skin, of its body, is one way of imagining what the utopian Law of absolute hospitality might mean. In *Ladivine* as in *Trois femmes puissantes* then, an incipient resolution to the human inheritance of inhospitality is at last effected, but only via passage through the animal realm.

Conclusion

NDiaye's compelling depiction of how the animal 'breaches the human subject' both fascinates and shames us.[51] I have argued in this chapter that the author makes a powerful contribution to postcolonial questioning of the human-animal border by drawing animals in to her consideration of the ethics of hospitality. In her work the distinction between human and animal is made conspicuously to fray, informing the ways in which protagonists take account of each other and bringing us to focus sharply on the stakes of rituals and embodied manifestations of hospitality by defamiliarizing them. The idea of animals can be used by protagonists to dehumanize others but real animals can, it is implied, provide opportunities for change by dislodging anthropocentric ontology and by offering friendship and compassion. Significantly, it is animals that bring about or provide some of the most thought-provoking instances of hospitality in NDiaye's entire *œuvre*. Especially in *Trois femmes puissantes* and *Ladivine*, it is through being with animals that giving, hosting, forgiving, opening to the other and understanding the self are brought within reach. With great concision and lucidity NDiaye asks us to imagine being in the world in unfamiliar ways; to question reflexively our stock of 'knowledge' about the animal world; to attend to other possibilities concerning, for example, animal communication, emotions and culture; in short, to think outside human inhospitality with the help of animals rather than use them as reference points to bolster it.

Notes to Chapter 2

1. Paul Shepard, *The Others: How Animals Made Us Human* (Washington, DC: Shearwater Books, 1996), p. 80.
2. See Michael Sheringham, 'Ambivalences de l'animalité chez Marie NDiaye', in *Une femme puissante*, ed. by Bengsch and Ruhe, pp. 51–70. Relationships dependent on dogs and their meanings are found in the novels *En Famille*, *Rosie Carpe*, *Mon cœur à l'étroit* and *Ladivine* as well as the story 'Une journée de Brulard' [A Day in the Life of Brulard] (*TMA* 111–66). Birds take over in *Trois femmes puissantes* and the play *Les Grandes Personnes* [The Grown-ups].
3. An unusual early case is the pet kept by Stéphane Ventru in *La Femme changée en bûche* [The Woman Who Turned into a Log], 'une sorte d'animal, une boule de poils bruns et jaunâtres d'où sortaient quatre pattes d'égale longueur' [a kind of animal, a ball of brown and yellowish hair from which emerged four feet of equal length] (*FCB* 92).
4. I return to this soundtrack in Chapter 4.
5. Frédéric Boyer, 'Un animal dans la tête', in *Qui sont les animaux?*, ed. by Jean Birnbaum (Paris: Gallimard, 2010), pp. 11–25.
6. On NDiaye's animals as 'bestial pseudo-kin' from whom protagonists seek to dissociate themselves, see Andrew Asibong, '*Moja sestra*: Marie NDiaye and the Transmission of Horrific

Kinship', in *Transmissions: Essays in French Literature, Thought and Cinema*, ed. by Isabelle McNeill and Bradley Stephens (Oxford: Peter Lang, 2007), pp. 95–112 (p. 101).

7. As in *La Sorcière*.

8. Redemptive elements have gradually taken greater prominence in NDiaye's fiction: in *Mon cœur à l'étroit* the protagonist ultimately acknowledges her inhospitable impulses; in *Trois femmes puissantes* each story is given a positive, more hospitable coda; and in *Ladivine* animal intervention, even 'grace', is healing.

9. NDiaye's metamorphoses overlap with but do not map onto the idea of 'becoming-animal' as elaborated by Deleuze and Guattari. For them, to become animal is 'to stake out the path of escape'; 'to cross a threshold' (*Kafka: Toward a Minor Literature*, trans. by Dana Polan (Minneapolis: The University of Minnesota Press, 1986), p. 13), which suggests something more voluntary and clear-cut than we see in NDiaye, although the 'zones of liberated intensities' (p. 13) provided by human-animal merging are relevant. In this chapter I replace 'becoming-animal' with 'animal-becoming' to avoid too close an association.

10. Still, 'Animals and what is Human', in *Derrida and Hospitality*, pp. 219–54 (p. 220).

11. Chris Danta, ' "Like a Dog, Like a Lamb": Becoming Sacrificial Animal in Kafka and Coetzee', *New Literary History: A Journal of Theory and Interpretation*, 38 (2006), 721–37 (p. 722). As we will see in Chapter 4, Titi in *Rosie Carpe* also has a sacrificial function.

12. Winfried Menninghaus, *Disgust: Theory and History of a Strong Sensation*, trans. by Howard Eiland and Joel Golb (Albany: State University of New York Press, 2003), p. 1.

13. Martha C. Nussbaum, *Hiding from Humanity: Disgust, Shame and the Law* (Princeton, NJ, & Oxford: Princeton University Press, 2004), p. 110.

14. Gilles Deleuze, 'A comme animal', in *Abécédaire* (DVD: Éditions Montparnasse, 2004).

15. The pharmacist's speech is a counterpart to, and worth comparing with, the circuitous, 'colour-free' explanation for Fanny's exclusion given by Tante Colette in 'Les Accusations de Tante Colette' [The Accusations of Aunt Colette] (*EF* 149–57).

16. See for instance Bella's passing reference to 'mes frères aux babines retroussées' [my brothers with curled-back lips] (*RH* 44), where 'babines' may be either zoological or human.

17. See for example Agamben, *L'Ouvert*, p. 57. Twists on inter-species thinking via human-animal sounds work in both directions in NDiaye: Ladivine hears Marko 'sangloter comme un chien' [sob like a dog] (*L* 259); in *Rosie Carpe* 'hurler' [to scream] is used for cattle and 'meugler' [to low] for the little boy Titi (*RC* 32); Lazare whinnies in his sleep (*RC* 135); while the starving herd issue a 'gémissement humain' [human groaning] (*RC* 160).

18. Montandon, 'Le Toucher de l'hospitalité: Gustave Flaubert', in *Désirs d'hospitalité: de Homère à Kafka* (Paris: Presses Universitaires de France, 2002), pp. 127–51 (p. 126). Saliva is more ambivalent than sweat given its digestive function. I have already suggested that saliva in NDiaye is routinely connected both to expulsion (there is a deal of spitting in her work) and assimilation or digesting of the Other.

19. See Chapter 4 for Nadia as inhospitable mother.

20. The themes of exile, captivity, displacement, the need for water, human cruelty as well as the nineteenth-century urban context make 'Le Cygne' an intricate intertext.

21. Marie Darrieussecq, *Truismes* (Paris: P.O.L., 1996); Ananda Devi, *Moi, l'interdite* (Paris: Dapper, 2000). For a study that follows through a specifically Deleuzian becoming-animal in both writers see Amaleena Damlé, *The Becoming of the Body: Contemporary Women's Writing in French* (Edinburgh: Edinburgh University Press, 2014).

22. The leitmotif of the fish mouth also works quietly behind the scenes in *Rosie Carpe* whose eponymous heroine is characterized by inexpressible bewilderment, and surfaces in *Papa doit manger* with Papa's cruel remark than his daughter Mina 'parle et parle dans la langue des carpes' [talks and talks in the language of carps] (*PDM* 25).

23. NDiaye intensifies the irony here by having the painter refer to one of the most intelligent and behaviourally diverse of invertebrates.

24. We may equate him to the Cyclops. Unlike Ulysses, the woman-fish is unable to blind him and escape to the open sea. Given the reproduction of Turner's *Ulysses Deriding Polyphemus* (1829) in *La Naufragée*, we may deduce that the reference is intended.

25. See the Introduction for allusions to slavery in *La Naufragée*.

26. For birds in this story see my 'Marie NDiaye: la puissance de Khady Demba'.

27. Positive theoretical models of nomadism and productive mobility such as those explored by Deleuze and Guattarri, Rosi Braidotti, Caren Kaplan and others do not map convincingly on to experiences of displacement in NDiaye's fictional world.

28. The father migrates from *En famille* to *Papa doit manger*, *Autoportrait en vert* and the first story of *Trois femmes puissantes*. I return in Chapter 3 to discuss feasting with the father.

29. We might think specifically of the biblical episode where the three Angels of the Lord appear to Abraham (who offers them hospitality) in a tree, the Oak of Mamre. The Oak thus becomes a place of epiphany and the symbol of a link between earth and heaven. The flame tree is perhaps a secular version.

30. Sheringham, too, focuses on suffering in 'Ambivalences de l'animalité chez Marie NDiaye'.

31. Irigaray, *Sharing the World*, p. 43.

32. Ibid., p. 5.

33. Asibong describes this meeting as the 'weird climax' of a 'perverse relationship' which signifies the daughter's corruption (see *Marie NDiaye: Blankness and Recognition*, p. 105). To me it makes more sense to read the conclusion through the lens of hospitality.

34. Sheringham, 'Ambivalences de l'animalité chez Marie NDiaye'.

35. Ibid., p. 54.

36. Jacques Derrida, *L'Animal que donc je suis* (Paris: Galilée, 2006), p. 50; 'The Animal That Therefore I Am (More to Follow)', trans. by David Willis, *Critical Inquiry*, 28 (2002), 369–418 (p. 397).

37. Elisabeth de Fontenay, *Le Silence des bêtes: la philosophie à l'épreuve de l'animalité* (Paris: Fayard, 1998), p. 43.

38. For further accounts of hospitality and NDiaye's dogs see Still's 'Love and Money in Marie NDiaye's *Ladivine*', in *Derrida and Other Animals: The Boundaries of the Human* (Edinburgh: Edinburgh University Press, 2015), pp. 337–45; '"Welcoming animals bei Derrida und Irigaray — unter besonderer Berücksichtigung des Hundes in Marie NDiaye's Roman *Ladivine*"', in *Perspektiven europäischer Gastlichkeit: Geschichte — Kulturelle Praktiken — Kritik*, ed. by Michael Staudigl and Burkhard Liebsch (Weilerswist-Metternich: Velbrück Wissenschaft: 2016), pp. 374–94; and 'Being a Guest'.

39. For instance, the younger Ladivine's fascinating assessment: 'comme un chat, comme un oiseau [Clarisse Rivière] n'avait pas de discernement' [like a cat, like a bird [Clarisse Rivière] had no discernment] (*L* 177). Presumably dogs *are* discerning.

40. Irigaray, 'Animal Compassion'.

41. Cixous imagines her dog's complex story, aligns his suffering with her own as a Jew in post-WWII Algeria and affirms his desire to cross borders. See Michelle B. Slater, 'Rethinking Human-Animal Ontological Differences: Derrida's "Animot" and Cixous' "Fips"', in *Human-Animal*, ed. by Roger Célestin, Eliane Dalmolin and Anne Simon, special issue of *Contemporary French and Francophone Studies*, 16 (2012), 685–93.

42. By welcoming them, 'Bobby' confirms the humanity of the Jewish prisoners in the Nazi camp where Levinas was held, see *Difficult Freedom: Essays on Judaism*, trans. by Seán Hand (Baltimore, MD: Johns Hopkins University Press, 1990), pp. 152–53.

43. Hero of Kafka's 'Investigations of a Dog', in *The Great Wall of China and Other Short Works* (London: Penguin, 1991) pp. 141–77.

44. NDiaye also acknowledges David Garnett's 1922 story of metamorphosis *Lady into Fox* as an early influence on her writing. See Andrew Asibong and Shirley Jordan, 'Rencontre avec Marie NDiaye', in *Marie NDiaye: l'étrangeté à l'œuvre*, pp. 187–99 (p. 189).

45. For a lucid account of Derrida's sequence of thoughts, see Gerald L. Bruns, 'Derrida's Cat (Who Am I?)', *Research in Phenomenology*, 38 (2008), 404–23.

46. Derrida, *L'Animal que donc je suis*, p. 18; 'The Animal That Therefore I Am (More to Follow)', p. 372.

47. Maud and Lise turn into crows in a move that captures the otherness of adolescence and, for their mother Lucie, the sharp sense of maternal loss that this can bring. See my 'Telling Tales:

Marie NDiaye's Mythopoeic Imagination', in *Contemporary French Women's Writing: Women's Visions, Women's Voices, Women's Lives* (Oxford: Peter Lang, 2004), pp. 164–67.

48. On the face as discussed by Levinas and Derrida see Still, *Derrida and Hospitality*, pp. 224–25.

49. Further discursive shifts that bring about human-animal rapprochement include Ladivine's conviction that she has already 'met' the dog and recognizes its 'voice', and her grandmother's instinctive knowledge of 'who' scratches to be let in at the end of the novel (*L* 402): like the title of Jean Birnbaum's *Qui sont les animaux?* [Who are Animals?] (Paris: Gallimard, 2010) such small slippages have the power to disturb the bedrock of an entire philosophical tradition.

50. Variants on human-dog merging elsewhere in NDiaye are less thoroughly hospitable. In *Rosie Carpe* Lagrand believes that an unpleasant yellow dog has returned to him in the form of Lazare (note once more the reversibility in human-animal merging here) and towards the novel's end both describe their relationship in terms of dog and master (*RC* 227–309). In *Y penser sans cesse* the narrator notes that as a child she believed a large black and white dog to be her father coming to watch over her (*YPSC* 44–45), a vain wish since it emerges that she had no place in her father's consciousness or conscience.

51. Still, *Derrida and Hospitality*, p. 220.

CHAPTER 3

Intimate Invasions:
Feeding, Eating and Wounds

Allons dîner. Papa est revenu. Je veux tous vous voir, grâce à moi, vous amuser et vous empiffrer jusqu'à ce que la nourriture vous ressorte par les yeux. *(PDM 37)*

[Let's go for dinner. Papa's back. I want to see you all, thanks to me, have fun and stuff your bellies until the food comes out of your eyes.]

La plaie n'est désormais qu'une plaie —
et tout le corps n'est qu'une plaie.[1]

[The wound is henceforth only a wound —
and the whole body is nothing but a wound.]

NDiaye's universe is intensely physical. We engage with her beleaguered protagonists through fine-grained accounts of embodied experience and sensation more than through tracing their processes of reasoning, and it is in large part via their propensity to blush, to perspire, to be overtaken by the symptoms of anxiety or panic, or to remain conscious of their bodies as disagreeable encumbrances that we gain a sense of their being in the world. The author draws us to contemplate bodies on several levels: as awkward burdens; as metaphors for things beyond themselves; and as sites where the emotional economies of hospitality and inhospitality receive intricately personal expression. Hospitality as it is enacted at body boundaries requires us to juggle with sharply-felt fears of invasion, contamination and assimilation, notably where self and other touch or, as with the examples discussed in this chapter, where they interpenetrate.

The first part of this chapter explores some of the ambiguities expressed via food in NDiaye and argues that the author's numerous references to eating and eating events are an important mechanism in her work for highlighting inhospitality. Dramatizing what I refer to as 'perverse commensality', they perform the tensions analyzed by anthropologists between gifts and poisons,[2] probe the power-play and subtle meanings that inhere in the preparation and sharing of food and demonstrate how hospitality is 'mediated through substances'.[3] The chapter's second part turns to the breaching of bodies in NDiaye through wounding and rape and shows how the author dwells on painful apertures as markers of 'hostipitality', striving to keep them literally and semantically open. Both parts of the chapter in fact show bodies caught up in what we might call a phenomenology of 'hostipitality' in NDiaye. Both relate too to Derrida's imperative of 'bien manger' [eating well],[4] a capacious idea that incorporates but exceeds issues of appetite or dietetics and extends metonymically to all manner of exchanges 'au bord des orifices' [at the edge of orifices] where what he refers to as 'la conception-appropriation-assimilation de l'autre' [the conception-appropriation-assimilation of the other] is calibrated and enacted.[5]

Perverse Commensality

The sharing of food is especially central to hospitality, and activity organized around food is typically rule-bound and teeming with codified meanings. Food is instrumental in creating, maintaining and transforming relationships and in making manifest affective structures and shared values. To prepare and offer food ideally expresses a will to the well-being of guests, although any number of more slippery meanings may be at work, such as a will to valorize the self by expressing power, prestige or good taste. Accepting food implies trust and a readiness to open to, and to some extent to be like, the host, who is embodied in the offering and symbolically incorporated or absorbed. Host and guest thus 'feed' each other, both of them nourished by the reciprocities entailed. In literature as in life meals are often important occasions and readers as well as protagonists are invited to table. Detailed, sometimes sumptuous descriptions of foodstuffs make guests of us as well as analysts, and most of us enjoy reading about food and eating events, not least for the sometimes theatrical opportunity they provide for the consolidation or transformation of relationships and their depiction of shared cultural knowledge at work. In short, the sharing of food constitutes an important part of our cultural imaginary.

The reader will not be surprised to learn that NDiaye's meals tend to be challenging affairs. Pleasurable feasting is seldom on the menu and if eating is charged with a heightened sense of the connection between food and hospitality, this is precisely because the codes of commensality are conspicuously derailed. What happens around food is ethically, aesthetically and sometimes hermeneutically indigestible, and eating together typically involves inhospitable gestures and affect, concretizing family or social dysfunction. Food is not equitably distributed and protagonists are either stuffed or starved. They are admitted to table grudgingly like Fanny who gate-crashes the extended family feast at the start of *En famille* (*EF* 10), or banned from it altogether like Rosie Carpe (*RC* 328). Some are fed like animals, either on meagre scraps or, as we shall see later in this chapter, mysteriously fattened. Foodstuff itself is often obscenely, inhospitably, attractive or repellent. Finally, the very spaces of commensality may be spoiled: when Rudy Descas botches the installation of Mme Menotti's fitted kitchen, she can no longer hold the kitchen launch party that was intended perhaps less to entertain loved neighbours than to boost her self-image and social standing (*TFP* 192).

Decisions about taking foodstuff into the body are far from simple. In *Ladivine*, Clarisse Rivière's disavowal of her ethnic origin makes her loath to touch, let alone eat, food prepared by the black cleaning lady that is her mother. Moreover, the mother's love is conceptualized as a stinking morsel of bread that must, like a particularly repellent Sisyphean challenge, be eternally chewed but never swallowed (*L* 72). A leitmotif of bitterness and indigestibility comes to characterize this mother–daughter relationship, surfacing in the punitive 'gruau d'infamie' [gruel of infamy] (*L* 73) that Clarisse must eat, the 'pain amer' [bitter bread] (*L* 98) that she has made of her mother's life and the sense of her own mouth as a 'puits de honte' [well of shame] (*L* 72). In the same novel eating as invasive of the self is illustrated by the bond that begins to form between the vulgar and materialistic Cagnac family and Ladivine's children and husband thanks to the 'nourriture révoltante avalée en commun' [revolting food swallowed in common] (*L* 302) at the Cagnac's opulent dinner. Commensality here is felt obscurely by Ladivine to be a celebration of the rush of postcolonial violence that was unleashed in her family after her husband Marko struggled with the local guide Wellington and threw him from the hotel balcony. The fact that Wellington — resuscitated but henceforth even more laden with memories of violation — is now helping to serve the meal only compounds Ladivine's horror. In short, eating in NDiaye is deeply ambivalent, often an ordeal rather than a pleasure and redolent with darker scenarios of consumption in which, as Rosello has pointed out, 'the host can always devour the guest, the guest can always devour the host'.[6] It should be no surprise given the author's fascination with ideas of assimilation, absorption and annihilation that cannibalism, according to Jean Baudrillard hospitality in its most radically ambivalent form, lingers menacingly around certain of her meals, or that her exploration of power relations sometimes centres on this idea, either in fantastically literalized form — as in *Les Serpents* [The Snakes] where Mme Diss fantasizes about her son eating his little boy Jacky and imagines the bulge made in his stomach as the child is digested (*SE* 49–50) — or expressed through plots whose ultimate logic is the feeding of the powerful on the weak.[7]

Two fleeting and unusual instances of a will to 'eat well' stand out in NDiaye. Both involve accepting rather than offering food and in both the protagonists demonstrate a desire to open absolutely and unconditionally to the Other. In the first, a hungry Nadia is given a half-eaten boiled egg by a stranger and, as a token of deep gratitude, seeks to bite into it in such a way as scrupulously to match the teeth marks already left in the white and yolk (*MCE* 198). In the second, the younger Ladivine buys a glass of mango juice in an African market and is careful to place her lips on precisely that part of the rim that has been left sticky and soiled by a previous drinker, noting that she feels not disgust but satisfaction in doing so (*L* 156). Any revulsion aroused in the reader by such unusual gestures cleverly underscores the stakes involved in taking things foreign and unknown into the body, while the readiness to open unquestioningly to others that is expressed by Nadia and Ladivine seems to suggest that NDiaye devises the gestures precisely with the tensions of Derridean hospitality in mind. These rapid vignettes concern simple foodstuffs and frugal consumption. By contrast, the remainder of this chapter studies the meanings of excess in NDiaye's depictions of food and eating, beginning with inhospitable feasting as orchestrated by the author's composite father figure, then turning to solitary gorging and to different categories of foodstuff in *Mon cœur à l'étroit* and a much earlier story, 'La Gourmandise' [Gluttony].[8]

The Father's Feast

I have already suggested elsewhere in this book that NDiaye's composite father figure is a quixotic, immoderate and manipulative host. It is therefore ironic that he is connected structurally, materially and economically to hosting, not only through a sense of patriarchal largesse that situates him as former provider for an extended family and numerous guests, but also through his involvement in the hospitality industry (we learn in *Autoportrait en vert* that he was a restaurateur in Paris, then owner of a holiday village in Ouagadougou, both failed ventures). He hosts meals whose meanings are ambivalent and which tend not to cement but further to trouble the bonds between diners. The title of the first work to focus intensively on his meaning, *Papa doit manger* [Papa Must Eat], alludes to the urgency of his appetite without configuring him as host or guest, simply as one who demands to be 'fed' — in this case, as the first epigraph to this chapter suggests, by the admiration and indebtedness of his guests. Here I explore how NDiaye pursues her interest in inhospitable eating through the father and suggest how we might make sense of the structures of feeling and the broken-down relations that coalesce around his feasts.

The feast that is prepared for Norah's arrival in *Trois femmes puissantes* is at once an absorbing fictional vignette and an anthropological exercise in underscoring the meanings of commensality. It is one of NDiaye's most lavish meals yet, dispro-portionately, it is intended for only two people and Norah is overwhelmed even before it begins by the disconcerting overabundance of dishes. She notes too, with great distaste, the 'invisible' labour that has gone into its making, empathizing with her father's intimidated manservant Masseck and with the kitchen maid Khady Demba, stuck behind the scenes in an inhospitably minuscule kitchen and struggling to wash large pots in an inadequate sink. The uneasy rituals and unstated implications of what turns out to be a sordid eating event soon prove to be both repellent and harrowing. After rushing his daughter unceremoniously to table, the father falls at once to devouring ravenously, 'la figure presque au ras de la nourriture' [his face almost level with the food] (*TFP* 23), with no regard for his daughter except to cast the occasional glance in her direction to check the respective size of their portions. The feast is one-sided, solitary and unsociable, 'entièrement dénuée de discours et de faux-semblants' [utterly devoid of talk and pretence] (*TFP* 23), and entailing none of the offerings of conversations, jokes or stories that confirm tables as places of exchange. Neither father nor daughter takes pleasure in it, or indeed in each other. Dish after dish is produced at a rhythm that defeats Norah while her father gobbles, 'respirant à peine entre bouchées, se gavant sans joie' [scarcely drawing breath between mouthfuls, stuffing himself joylessly] (*TFP* 23). His response to food is portrayed first as 'animal-like' and then, by the end of the meal, as that of a pre-socialized child:[9]

Pour finir, Masseck lui présenta une mangue coupée en morceaux.

Il fourra un morceau dans sa bouche, puis un autre, et Norah le vit mastiquer avec difficulté et tenter d'avaler mais en vain.

Il cracha la bouillie de mangue dans son assiette. Ses joues ruisselaient de larmes. (*TFP* 24)

[To finish, Masseck presented him with a mango cut into pieces.

He stuffed a piece in his mouth, then another, and Norah saw him chew with difficulty and attempt to swallow but in vain.

He spat the chewed mango onto his plate.

His cheeks were running with tears.]

The chopped fruit, spat-out purée and tears bring this particular cycle of perverse commensality to a close with the father-host's removal from the adult sphere of hospitality, increasing rather than reducing the distance between his daughter and himself, as well as hinting at what will soon emerge to be his helplessness and reliance upon her.[10] Commensality fails here in both horizontal and vertical terms, since it neither produces cohesion nor reinforces respect for hierarchy.

This baffling feast bursts with invitations to anthropological, and diegetic, interpretation. While Norah seeks an empathetic rationale for her father's inhospitality, connecting it to the torment of hunger that he experienced in childhood which now leaves him 'résolu [...] à se gorger' [resolved [...] to gorge himself] (*TFP* 50), she nonetheless intuits that such conspicuous overabundance translates more dubious desires: namely, a will to confirm his power as host — somewhat in the spirit of the potlatch — and a determination to create a heavy burden of obligation by overwhelming his guest. Hosting here entails a form of deferred reciprocity that is unspeakable (literally so for a while) and the extravagant meal is commensurate with the enormity of the request. That the father eats most of it himself is perhaps an expression of self-loathing, perhaps a compensatory gesture. Whatever the case, Norah's overriding sense is one of invasion. Anthropologists argue that via the material exchanges of hospitality, especially the sharing of substances that enter the body, hosts are extended and dispersed, their potency deployed. Norah's conceptualization of her father as an ineradicable parasite, entering his children uninvited and 'installé en chacun d'eux en toute impunité' [installed in each one of them with complete impunity] (*TFP* 65) is consistent with such ideas: the contamination of heredity that the father's children note elsewhere in NDiaye is made live in this story through sharing his food.[11]

Other meals over which the father presides show him lurching between models of inhospitable hosting. In *Autoportrait en vert*, to take one example, the narrator and her son are given a ceremonious welcome at his restaurant in the twentieth arrondissement of Paris, but eat alone and are seated, and treated, like clients. Indeed the restaurant, 'Ledada', has little to do with hospitality but is a platform for the father's prestige, boasting murals of animals which he has painted and an exhibition of black-and-white photographs which show him as slender, elegant and young. When the narrator is next received, this time in her father's rambling house in Ouagadougou, he is reduced to a maddened, dirty, half-blind old man who throws his plate of semolina and chick peas out of the window at each sitting and has starved himself to the point of emaciation. The father figure, then, performs both feast and famine, gorging and starving, equally perverse enactments of power that write him out of the circuits of commensality. As his young wife observes: '[o]n ne peut pas continuer d'aimer quelqu'un qui ne se nourrit plus' [one cannot continue to love a person who no longer feeds themself] (*AV* 91).

It is evident, not least because he migrates from book to book and because we are invited not to access him on the level of individual psychology but to read something more into his creation, that NDiaye's African father figure requires careful decoding. His meals may be read as vignettes that exemplify in concentrated (and in negative) form the social and ethical meanings of eating. But eating with the father also invites one of the scalar shifts that NDiaye's fiction — and indeed the theme of hospitality itself — frequently encourages, and asks us to interpret the micro detail of interpersonal interaction according to broader, geo-political lines related to postcolonial energies and relationships. This is not to say of course that any one model of host-guest relationship involving the father and food maps in some simple or transparent fashion on to Franco-African relations, just as the figure of the father himself cannot be said simply to represent 'Africa' or, as Asibong puts it, some 'allegorical figure of Third World suffering'.[12] Rather, the total spectrum of models of feeding and eating, and the ethics and politics they entail, indicate an unhealthy and unstable entanglement that cannot find hospitable equilibrium but expresses itself in aggressive and damaging modes of exchange.

NDiaye insists on the father's African-ness, portrays him as at once haunting and haunted, has him slip into a range of roles on the spectrum of (in)hospitality from parasite to host in both Africa and France and explores his embroilment in legacies of the falsely familial, paternalistic 'hospitality' of colonial relations which troubles the categories of host and guest. This reading is especially invited in *Papa doit manger* where a hyperbolically black African Papa returns, after twenty years of separation, to a white French Maman, whom he explicitly regards as symbolizing France, for the two to work out the new terms of a relationship which veers between violent desire and violent rejection and which stages almost to the point of parody Frantz Fanon's analyses in *Peau noire, masques blancs*.[13] In terms of the paradigm of hospitality, it is above all the father's reluctance to concede to the status of guest, his insistence on hosting and his ability and authority to host that NDiaye raises for consideration. Materially impoverished, alert to slights and humiliation, the father repeatedly sets himself up as host in a conspicuous effort to negotiate status. His mobility as trope rather than as protagonist, combined with his frankly psychotic enactments of 'hostipitality' are clearly intended to raise questions about how, both materially and imaginatively, Africa and France 'feed' each other and the meals I have described are all to be refracted to some extent through a postcolonial lens. What are also served up at the father's feasts are a number of postcolonial leftovers — namely ideas of Africa as unruly, violently unpredictable and alien — that NDiaye lets the reader chew over at will. The title *Papa doit manger* contains ideas of irrepressible hunger and implicit responsibility and asks to be glossed simultaneously in two ways: as an expression of authority and as one of nagging dependency.

Eating Well: Fat, Meat, Grain

There are further cases in NDiaye of solitary gorging. In 'La Gourmandise' a housewife, Antoinette, makes an art of binge eating. The fable conjures up the sensory and ethical tensions between a wide range of factors that inhere in the consumption of food, from pleasure to disgust, order to disorder, belonging to rejection, as well as touching upon gendered relationships to eating and offering as sharply perceptive a depiction of bulimic experience as the author has provided elsewhere of anorexia.[14] Laden with bags of rich fare bought with money stolen from her husband, Antoinette walks beyond the outskirts of her village, away from society and family, to indulge in long, dream-like orgies of eating, interrupted only by the mute village idiot Edo who begins to follow her. As if to provide her with moral lessons about her transgressive behaviour, Edo puts on a grotesque mumming display outside a shop in which she is selecting her delicacies:

> Il collait son nez à la vitrine et lui adressait des gestes obscènes, il fourrait ses doigts dans sa bouche et les suçait avec une feinte délectation, parfois essayait d'avaler son poing entier, en suffoquant et grimacant, puis le ressortait gluant de bave qu'il entreprenait de lécher, les yeux mi-clos. (G 60)

> [He pressed his nose to the shop window making obscene gestures at her, he stuffed his fingers in his mouth and sucked them with feigned delectation, sometimes trying to swallow his entire fist, suffocating and grimacing, then withdrawing it sticky with spit which he began to lick, his eyes half-closed.]

Edo's mime encapsulates the drama taking place in this tale at body boundaries. It is eloquent on the excessively sensual, almost erotic delectation of Antoinette's eating as well as its potentially self-destructive nature, for in social terms she is in fact eliminating herself, eating herself obsessively out of her community and its circuits of hospitality. Edo begins to sit close to her as she gorges, forcing upon her a minimal sociability and furthering his edifying mime by starving himself until his cheeks are hollow. At the end of the tale, after rumours in the village about the nature of her relationship with Edo, Antoinette puts an end to the intense pleasures of her solitary eating, remains within the village boundary and retains a vague, ambivalent memory of Edo either saving her from, or depriving her of, something.[15]

Antoinette's *gourmandise* is carried over by NDiaye into the novel *Mon cœur à l'étroit*, which is even more unusually focused on the preparation and sharing of food and which offers a different menu of grotesque surplus, along with all manner of uneasily indeterminate relations between hosts and guests. Here Antoinette's sister in greed, Nadia, lives out her own troubled story of belonging which is articulated in part through food. While Antoinette reluctantly plans meals for her family, Nadia is never engaged in feeding others; instead she is fed in ways which probe the question of what it means to 'eat well', precisely in the expanded sense of the term intended by Derrida. Ethical considerations raised by eating are highlighted in chapter titles such as: 'La Nourriture nous console; grave erreur de notre part' [Food consoles us; a serious error on our part] (*MCE* 60–67); 'Tout le monde aime la viande' [Everybody likes meat] (*MCE* 77–91); or 'On se nourrit mal chez mon fils' [They eat badly at my son's house] (*MCE* 251–59); and the text is remarkably insistent on the nature and provenance of foodstuffs and on dietetics as a marker of culture. Nadia's entire (un-avowed) story of the rejection of her working-class, North-African origins and family is played out through tropes related to appetite, digestion and (in)hospitable feeding. She is fed in three distinct phases, each involving food with specific characteristics that is prepared by and thus externalizes a rejected protagonist: her neighbour, her son and her mother. What are some of the meanings attached to food in this, NDiaye's most gastronomically challenging portrayal of disorderly eating?

When Nadia's despised neighbour Noget turns up uninvited with an offering of home-made food and proceeds authoritatively to take over her kitchen, there begins an ungainly dance of 'hostipitality' between the pair which raises for explicit consideration the terms and terminology of hospitality and the nature and limits of given roles. Their ambivalent acts and discourses flag up explicitly and prod at the meanings of neighbourliness, friendship and hosting, while Nadia also conceptualizes Noget as servant, beggar and parasite as she attempts to fix his meaning to suit her own purposes and perspective. We ponder on the bizarre transactions and exchange practices emerging between the two: can the intruder offer hospitality to the home owner? How rapidly might a host be turned into a guest? There is exaggerated play here on the part of NDiaye with the transgression of norms: Noget may tap politely on the door, but he also hammers as if to break it down; he may deploy the discourses of hospitality, but he does so with an unctuousness and 'intimité détestable' [detestable intimacy] (*MCE* 63) that make their intention dubiously undecidable; he may present himself as neighbour and friend but he challenges Nadia and Ange for sovereignty; he may protest that he is feeding Nadia 'par affection' [out of affection] (*MCE* 100) yet he serves her with an insolent 'déférence exagérée' [exaggerated deference] (*MCE* 64), prepares her food with 'doigts malpropres' [dirty fingers] (*MCE* 91) and his regime puts her health at risk. We are reminded sharply by NDiaye's fantastic manoeuvres that subject positions in relations of hospitality are always provisional and fragile. The relationship between Noget and Nadia is one small instance of the fantastic anthropology of (in)hospitality that I discuss in my introductory chapter as a particularity of NDiaye's work and is worth reading in those terms, as well as for its suggestions of Noget as Žižek's frightful Neighbour-Thing, the intruder who disturbs from within.[16] My primary interests here, however, are in how the stakes of this relationship are heightened by their expression through food and how NDiaye underscores what Jean-Jacques Boutaud refers to as 'l'ingestion des valeurs liées aux aliments' [the ingestion of values connected to foodstuff].[17]

Almost at once, Noget the usurping host begins intensively to feed Nadia with a 'lourde nourriture équivoque' [heavy, dubious food] (*MCE* 147) in an orgy of fatty excess which sees the text bathing in oozing croissants, triple croque monsieur with béchamel, and succulent meats hand-reared by his cousin in the Périgord. Nadia feasts under the neighbour's gaze in a confused mixture of desire, suspicion and guilt. Noget's oily creations and the discourses in which they are enrobed constitute a grotesque parody of French bourgeois cooking, the values it enshrines and the shared metadiscursive delectation, the naming and describing of dishes that is part and parcel of special eating events. What is being taken into Nadia's body via the butter, cream, bone marrow, cheeses, sauces and pastries, not to mention the dietary/national lynchpin, bread (it is this that brings tears to her eyes), is not just something of Noget, the shunned neighbour who kneads the very dough she eats and to whom she therefore opens in the most intimate of ways, but a superabundance of Frenchness itself.

NDiaye's genius in this particular episode of perverted commensality is its unspoken reliance on the connection between Noget's feeding of Nadia, who is gorged to excess, and the *gavage* [stuffing] of geese or ducks to make the distinctively French 'delicacy' that is foie gras. Nadia who, as we have seen elsewhere in this book, has ruthlessly cut off all ties with her family in her determination to be assimilated in the bastion of Bordeaux bourgeoisie, is being stuffed like a goose by her own aspirations, her heart (which we know from the book's title to be at stake and which is better than the liver for NDiaye's purposes since it conjoins the physiological and the affective) becoming encased in fat, and her flesh — like that of Antoinette — beginning to resemble what she eats.[18] Nadia is thus thoroughly incorporated in, and ultimately a product of, a specifically national alimentary circuit, her body itself an organic index of (the unhealthy terms of) her belonging. At the same time, singling out this contested aspect of national food production as the very index of Frenchness allows NDiaye to take an enjoyable glancing swipe at the dubious ethics of certain French cultural values.

A second sequence of inhospitable feeding again raises the values associated with particular foods. At the home of her estranged son Ralph and his astonishingly carnivorous partner Wilma, the emphasis is no longer on the French provenance of ingredients and recipes but on 'chair sauvage' [wild flesh] (*MCE* 261) and blood sport. The hare, rabbit and boar served up here are hunted, killed and prepared by the hosts. Portions are once more over-abundant and the meats and sauces are complicated, cloying and rich. Even the chocolate mousse has the colour of cooked blood. Nadia's body is traversed by indigestible food that is an edible correlative of the moral mess between those at table. She eats without appetite, in disgust and suspicion, although she manages to play the good guest and emit the occasional noise of delectation to gratify her son, in spite of being 'gorgée de mangeaille' [gorged with pigswill] (*MCE* 257). NDiaye's habit of following through an idea to fantastic excess is in evidence here: not only are wild animals eaten but their heads decorate the walls of the dining hall along with colonial-style photographs celebrating the kills; the couple dress in leather and wrap themselves in furs; the mansion has a vast charnel pile in its back garden and is stagnant with the smell of 'le dépeçage, la découpe, le hâchage de trop de viandes mêlées' [the jointing, carving and mincing of too many mingled meats] (*MCE* 283). What is more, this orgy of carnivorous consumption is further troubled by the taboo of cannibalism. Has Wilma eaten Nadia's daughter-in-law Yasmina? Has she concocted a terrine from Souhar, the little granddaughter whom Nadia has never met? If thus far in the novel Nadia has balked at admitting Souhar into her mouth (that is, as discussed in Chapter 2, at speaking her distinctively un-French name) now she imagines eating the infant's cooked and pressed flesh, a fantasy of assimilation, union and osmosis that is entangled with both disgust and desire and that relates to Jean Baudrillard's characterization of racism as a '[p]sychodrame de l'introjection et de l'éjection perpétuelle de l'autre' [psychodrama of the perpetual introjection and ejection of the other].[19] The terrine collapses and compresses the disparate emotions that characterize Nadia's (in)hospitality to Souhar: her desire for annihilation of the girl as ethnically-marked, and her repressed longing to take her in and possibly to love her: cannibalism may indeed be a kind of hyperbolical hospitality, an expression, as Derrida notes, of 'la tentation de l'amour même' [the temptation of love itself].[20]

'Eating well' comes within reach at the novel's end when Nadia is at last reunited with her North-African parents and meets her granddaughter. Here the gastronomic excess that has characterized the novel thus far gives way to the implicitly curative, fragrant *semoule* (couscous grain) and vegetables prepared by her mother, and to hospitable feeding and eating. The novel's first glimpse of what commensality at its best might mean, one that manifestly consolidates and celebrates loving social relations rather than disuniting the participants, involves Souhar, not cannibalized after all but being fed in a high chair, eating from the same spoon as her father in joy and complete confidence as her grandparents look on (*MCE* 271). The composition, seen by Nadia as she peers into the kitchen from the street and framed by a doorway seems, like an intimate genre painting, to offer a hypostesization of simple family values, operating un-problematically across the French/North-African ethnic divide.

A final, compact reminder of the heroine's ethical trajectory as expressed by food comes with mention of the aroma of spices, familiar from her childhood in the poor Bordeaux suburb of Les Aubiers, that has guided her to her parents' house in this other land. We learn that this perfume prompts clear and powerful reactions in her as a marker of identity. Here NDiaye evokes racist discourses that focus on cooking smells as 'pollutants' (the bad smell left by Jacques Chirac's infamous 'le bruit et l'odeur' [the noise and the smell] speech of 1991 inevitably lingers around the text at this point) and in this instance shows how the heroine herself reproduced them.[21] Nadia confesses to her former visceral disgust and to how even '*l'apparence ou les vestiges de cette odeur!*' [the appearance or the vestiges of that smell!] (*MCE* 271) would make her turn on her heels in a rejection as extreme as her current attraction. The hunger that she now alludes to expresses an ethical as much as a physical appetite and her evolution in the latter stages of this novel is prompted and given expression by the values that inhere in foodstuffs and commensality. Of her mother's food, she notes: 'je l'absorbe sans arrière pensées ni crainte d'aucune sorte, avec gratitude' [I absorb it without reservation or fear of any kind, with gratitude] (*MCE* 295), the unusual verb 'absorb' underlining the symbolic stakes of accepting food in a way that *manger* [to eat] would not. This final, far from customary reference to eating underscores NDiaye's interest in the anthropology of commensality and in the tangled values and meanings caught up in the broad question of eating well. It draws to a close the author's virtuoso exercise in constructing an ethical tale, and an individual and social drama, around such meanings.

Splitting, Penetration, Touch

NDiaye's alertness to the materiality and vulnerability of bodies and to questions of hospitality raised by touch, skin and penetration are everywhere apparent, yet what Alain Montandon refers to as 'le toucher de l'hospitalité' [hospitable touch] has only fragile status in her world.[22] More often, touch is careless or brutal, sometimes reaching inside, damaging and disturbing the body's integrity. At its most violent extreme this is manifested in a gruesome palimpsest of murders: in *Ladivine* Clarisse Rivière's throat is slit and Marko throws Wellington from a hotel balcony (*L* 133; 257); in *Trois femmes puissantes* Rudy Descas's father drives his truck deliberately over the head of his right-hand man Salif, cracking it open (*TFP* 209); and in *Rosie Carpe* an elderly white tourist is almost cut in two with a single machete blow (*RC* 251). Opened bodies leave hallucinatory legacies: rivers of blood in the case of Clarisse Rivière; indelible stains in the case of Wellington and Salif. Protagonists fantasize about killing or, paralyzed with terror, about being killed and the reader is stranded anxiously between murder as fantastic trope and as literal reality. The remainder of this chapter focuses not on murder but on violently opened, still living bodies and their wounds. In the second epigraph to this chapter Jean-Luc Nancy suggests that in mass graves the wound is divested of its meaning, which seeps away. He proposes as a figure for contemporary human suffering a wound with no significance beyond itself, a secular wound outside structures of religious sacrifice which remains hauntingly open like an unblinking eye. Here I consider NDiaye's interest in un-healing wounds, with some recourse to intertexts that help us to make sense of them.

In Caravaggio's *The Incredulity of Saint Thomas* Jesus pulls back his robes, allowing Thomas to push a grubby finger into the gash that remains open in his side. The painting's focal point is this very graphically rendered place of entry, where the finger disappears into Jesus's livid skin displacing the edges of the tear. Hospitably Jesus guides it into his body, while two further apostles, heads bent, peer closely at the compelling intrusion. NDiaye too depicts protagonists who linger over, finger and scrutinize wounds, although without such tender intent or clarity of purpose. In *Papa doit manger* Papa's painful facial scars, the legacy of a knife attack perpetrated by Maman, are 'bourrelées, mal jointes, mal soignées' [thickened, badly joined, poorly tended] (*PDM* 82), yet Maman repeatedly touches them in a compulsive, disingenuous cycle where each fresh touch is dressed up as a compassionate attempt to calm the pain it exacerbates. The vulnerable place of the wound, even closed, remains inviting, fascinating, an invocation of 'hostipitality' and a marker of human relationships which, in NDiaye, consistently have more to do with cruelty than with healing.

NDiaye might have taken Carravagio's masterpiece as an ironic starting point for the most lingered-over wound in her corpus, that of Ange Lacordeyre in *Mon cœur à l'étroit*. The 'trou sanglant à peu près au niveau de son foie' [bloody hole near to his liver] (*MCE* 17) remains, like the wound in the painting, conspicuously open and conspicuously probed. Visits to Ange's stifling sickroom structure the first two thirds of the novel as protagonists and readers cluster repeatedly around the 'affreuse cavité' [dreadful cavity] (*MCE* 133) with its inexhaustible purulence, foul stench and encrusted lips. Part of the patient's shirt sets into the wound and this, along with the leathery roll of inverted skin that frames it, seems to confirm the impossibility of closure. The lesion calls out not merely for healing but for interpretation, yet its meanings are diffuse, indeterminate and obscure by comparison with those embodied in the religious painting. Caravaggio focuses on the very moment when Thomas's desire for knowledge is gratified through touch, whereas the body opening created by NDiaye remains a hermeneutic puzzle: just as its healing is deferred so, persistently, is our understanding of what it means.[23]

What is clear from the outset is the widespread sense of investment in Ange's wound. Both his attack — a premeditated ritual in which a chisel-like instrument was repeatedly dug into his side — and the opening have powerful but unspecified collective significance. He is referred to as '*notre* blessé' [*our* wounded] (*MCE* 65, my emphasis) by the couple's invasive neighbour, and all protagonists except Nadia, his wife, not only strive to keep his wound open but collude in its further contamination. Nadia harbours obsessive fantasies about those who have access to the sick room grubbing around in the wound and imagines that instead of cleansing and closing it, Noget lies with her husband 'écartant les bords de la plaie, l'infectant de ses mains sales' [separating the edges of the wound, infecting it with his dirty hands] (*MCE* 51), one of several instances of sexual slippage through which NDiaye evokes two vulnerable openings that call for tenderness, the vagina and the wound, in terms of each other.[24] Ange himself demands repeatedly that the wound not be tended, touched or — an ironic request given NDiaye's painterly insistence on it — even looked at, shifting the terms on which it is to be understood from medical to mythical.

Ange's wound also enthrals the reader and sets in train a busy process of thinking about (in)hospitality. We note, for instance, that his wounding connects him to animal suffering: fibrous strips of his flesh (meat?) are pinned to Nadia's coat, while the term Nadia uses for his attack, 'charcuter' (figuratively 'to butcher', but also evoking *charcuterie*, the French term for cold and cured meats) (*MCE* 49) gestures in the same direction. But reminders of the human–animal connection are not enough to explain the wound's meaning. Protagonists skirt tentatively around various implied diagnoses involving the ethical failings of Nadia, Ange or both, without any one interpretation being made explicit. We are nudged towards paths strewn with biblical allusions whose relevance rapidly peters out. These reach a crescendo in Nadia's final viewing of the wound, which Ange has invited her to inspect. Here as he pulls aside the sheets for her, her lips tremble with a 'pitié crucifiante' [crucifying pity] (*MCE* 133) and she glimpses a small bowl placed at his side to capture the running poison, a clear allusion to the Grail with which Joseph caught the blood of Christ. NDiaye's play on the symbols of Christ's suffering is deeply ironic for it is clear that this self-satisfied bourgeois teacher is neither Christ-like nor, even if his name suggests it, 'angelic'; his wound is not holy and any apparent invitation to pursue ideas of Nadia as the tending Mary Magdalene is invalidated on numerous counts, not least that she leaves Ange to face death alone and is not witness to his resurrection (although she does at first fail to recognize him when he returns 'from the dead' at the end of the novel). None of these allusions does any more than raise the dim glimmer of interpretative structures that linger temptingly around but cannot satisfactorily account for this particular wound. One might say as much for the other mythical wounds with moral or religious significance that are irresistibly evoked by NDiaye: the festering sores of Philoctetes's ulcerated foot which test the charity and nobility of Odysseus, or the open wound of Amfortas that is ultimately healed by a compassionate touch from Parsifal's spear.

It is tempting to imagine Jean-Luc Nancy's 'Une plaie' as a spur to NDiaye's thinking and to trace how Ange concretizes the ideas in Nancy's short essay. His open body raises but moves beyond sacred and sacrificial accounts which allow wounds and the wounded to signify; meaning escapes from rather than coalesces in it; it differs from an illness which, as Nancy observes, 'fait signe vers sa cause et vers la santé' [gestures towards its cause and towards health]; it continues to spread, literalizing Nancy's idea of the body in its entirety as a wound (he speaks here of the depersonalization of bodies in mass graves where form and meaning dissolve); and it ushers in an exponential sense of the entire social and global body as irremediably wounding and (self-)wounded, definitively riven with unhealable splits and gulfs.[25] It is precisely this expanded reach of the wound that in *Papa doit manger* leads the racially concerned Zelner to use it as a wholescale trope for black suffering: 'Il n'y a pas d'homme noir. Il n'y a qu'une plaie' [There is no black man. Only a wound] (*PDM* 65).

A further compelling intertext, especially given NDiaye's fondness for its author, is to be found in Kafka's 'A Country Doctor', a short story whose focal point is a similar open wound, in this instance seething with large white worms, in the side of a young boy.[26] NDiaye emulates Kafka's detailed attention to the wound's textures, edges, colours, clots and suppuration as well as to the knot of individuals (the boy's family in Kafka; family and neighbour in NDiaye) who also become 'encrusted' around the wound and part of the scene's meaning. More fundamentally, as both authors bring us together around the wound they also provide us with a model for responding to their text. To consider the text *as* an open wound is to consider it as a place of deliberate fascination and horror, where infection is continually to be detected and ruminated upon even if its causes are not readily diagnosed. The wound gestures darkly to something beyond the narrative and, alarmingly, to the impossibility of healing. In an analysis of 'A Country Doctor', Menninghaus has suggested that the very model of all Kafka's texts is that of 'an infliction of a wound against which any counteraction is thwarted'.[27] The idea fits NDiaye's inhospitable fictions equally well.

It is worth mentioning that the denouement of *Mon cœur à l'étroit* does indicate healing. When Nadia leaves him, Ange's wound is at an advanced stage of infection, Noget is dosing him with morphine and he seems close to death. On the novel's final page, when Nadia catches sight of Ange in rude health and frolicking on a beach with his new partner, he seems at first to have forgotten his wound, then lifts his shirt to reveal a scarcely visible pink scar in his side, which he casually touches with his own finger. There is more than one sign of improbable closure at this point in the book: the final chapter title, 'Tous guéris' [All cured] (*MCE* 292), suggests the (unreliable) narrator's desire to have her ethically messy story knit itself up and scar over, but such willed neatness is unconvincing. The enigma of the wound and its poison remains unresolved, a polysemic pointer to the several stripes of moral rottenness that fester in the novel, including but by no means confined to a largely unavowed and unarticulated racism. The fact that Ange's cure is dependent upon Nadia's expulsion from Bordeaux may be glossed as a condemnation of her own contaminating prejudices or, most unpalatably, as an illustration of cleansing being made possible by expelling the ethnic Other. Whatever the case, the metaphor of the text *as* wound, as a poisonous opening permanently available to scrutiny but whose ills resist diagnosis is, as I have already suggested, a powerfully convincing way of conceptualizing NDiaye's writing as a whole, as well as our reading of it. Rabaté speaks of the 'opacité tyrannique' [tyrannical opacity] that characterizes the author's work, and notes that she wants us to confront the cruelty of her world 'incomplètement, dans un mélange de stupeur et de saisissement' [incompletely, in a combination of stupor and shock]: the wound contributes precisely to such a goal.[28]

One final reading of the wound which Kafka's country doctor cannot close is that it serves as a 'barely concealed screen memory' allowing the protagonist access to a traumatic and violent event — the rape of his servant girl by a groom — and through this to his own nagging but unarticulated desire to penetrate the girl himself.[29] We have seen too that a sexualized reading of Ange's wound is possible. The following section of my argument applies Derrida's claim that 'la conception-appropriation-assimilation de l'autre' [the conception-appropriation-assimilation of the Other] is worked out at body boundaries to sexual (in)hospitality in NDiaye.[30] I have commented elsewhere in this book that NDiaye refers more often to sexual exploitation — even devouring — and to the intricate mechanisms of abuse than to pleasurable consensual relations and that sex, while frequently alluded to in her work, is seldom described in detail. Her interest lies instead in how the vulnerable, especially women or children, may be drawn into economic systems or perverted structures of affect that require them to open their bodies and to be sexually 'hospitable' for the profit of others.[31] The play *Les Grandes Personnes* [The Grown-ups], for instance, which concerns the sexual abuse of primary school children by their teacher, focuses more on the small community's resistance to acknowledging the crime than on the crime itself, so that while it explicitly and graphically mentions rape — notably the rape of one particular boy, Karim, with 'un godemiché dans l'anus' [a dildo in his anus] (*LGP* 33) — the horror of the act itself and the experience of the child are made secondary to the politics and psychology of its revelation. Karim and others like him are sacrificed, their suffering made invisible by parents who wish to see in the teacher only an unimpeachable repository of French Republican values.[32] There are two instances in NDiaye's writing where the author draws our attention in more detail to the very point and experience of unwanted penetration: the fleeting violation of the black protagonist Lagrand by an elderly white French woman in *Rosie Carpe*, and the routinized rape of Khady Demba in *Trois femmes puissantes*. I shall look briefly at both.

Driving reluctantly through one of Guadeloupe's white tourist areas, Lagrand politely accedes to a request for information from one of the scantily-clad, third-age holidaymakers amusing themselves in the heat. When he leans towards the woman from his car window, he is subjected to a symbolic, racially-motivated rape: '[d]'un seul coup elle enfonça sa langue dans l'oreille de Lagrand' [in a single movement, she thrust her tongue in Lagrand's ear] (*RC* 179). She then leaps back triumphantly to gloat over the achievement with her friends, leaving the victim to rub his ear in humiliated rage. In an incident that clearly transposes ear for vagina, spittle for semen and man for woman, NDiaye emphasizes the physical sensations of abuse: Lagrand 'croyait sentir l'odeur meme de la salive de la femme' [thought he could smell the very odour of the woman's saliva] (*RC* 179); his ear burns; he remains aware of the 'infecte écume' [disgusting foam] (*RC* 181) that soaks his eardrum and affects his hearing, and wonders how the woman managed to penetrate his ear so deeply: '[e]lle lui avait ni plus ni moins craché dedans' [she had spat into it, no more no less] (*RC* 180).[33] The attack constitutes material and symbolic evidence of the economy of sexual exploitation that prevails in tourism in *Rosie Carpe*, while Lagrand's humiliation, anger and visceral revulsion map very precisely onto the trauma of a rape victim. This miniature violation, through its insistence on the other *in* the self and on the shameful legacy of such an experience, also constitutes a potent trope for colonial and postcolonial relations. Just as Marguerite Duras in *L'Amant* aligned her colonized Vietnamese lover with the feminine, so Lagrand is feminized here by NDiaye. The violator and her companions assume that he may be penetrated with impunity and are jubilant at a defilement which re-asserts the prevailing power dynamic. We are reminded of the insistence on spittle elsewhere in NDiaye as a defiling bodily fluid reserved for expressions of racially-motivated revulsion, and of Lagrand's own automatic spitting reflex upon his mentioning of white people at the start of the novel (*RC* 15).

With Khady Demba, arguably the most memorable of NDiaye's *Trois femmes puissantes*, the author reduplicates wounds, emphasizing not one but multiple violent breaches made into her heroine's body as she attempts to migrate to Europe. First, her shin is torn by a nail as she instinctively jumps off the fishing boat which she was supposed to board, leaving a gaping wound that is subject to repeated re-openings, each one more painful than the last, and that ultimately will not close at all. Later, when her travelling companion Lamine can no longer provide for her and her sole remaining resource is her body, Khady becomes bound up as currency in the wretched series of exchanges that characterize the impoverished desert town where the pair await the next stage of their journey. In an all-too-familiar scenario, she is coerced into one of the key positions for women within desperate economies: that of sex worker. The owner of a food shack pimps her in exchange for food and a pittance — just enough, over several months, to buy a place on a lorry to take her and Lamine closer to their goal — but Lamine makes off with the money and finds his way to Europe alone, condemning her to further months of prostitution. For over a year shadowy men desperate for home and comfort are persuaded to visit Khady in a little back room not unlike Ange's sickroom inasmuch as it is set aside for the confinement of a body whose openings are a source of fascination, horror and desire.[34] A cruel parody of an odalisque, she remains prostrate day and night on a strip of foam mattress in a sweat-drenched under-slip, fed by her pimpstress who occasionally bathes her inflamed vagina with 'une solicitude toute maternelle' [a quite maternal solicitude] (*TFP* 305), and dresses her wound. Her sexual encounters are abject, perfunctory, emotionally voided and contaminating. NDiaye focuses on the sensations experienced by both partners at the very point of penetration: '[l'homme] la pénétrait en laissant échapper souvent une plainte étonnée car la récente démangeaison qui enflammait et desséchait le vagin de Khady échauffait aussitôt le sexe du client' [[the man] penetrated her often emitting an astonished complaint for the recent itching that enflamed and dried Kady's vagina at once irritated the client's sexual organ] (*TFP* 303).

Pointedly NDiaye makes of Khady's vagina a wound, connecting it to the suppurating opening on her shin which pains her equally and which from the outset is described with graphic attentiveness to its separated lips, its vulnerability to foreign matter, its swollenness — her wound is 'gonflée et nauséabonde' [puffy and sickening] (*TFP* 305); her sex 'boursouflé, ulcéré' [swollen, ulcerated] (*TFP* 306) — and the nuanced qualities of pain it causes. NDiaye insists on Khady's 'vulve gonflée et douloureuse et [...] vagin brûlant, irrité' [swollen and painful vulva and [...] burning, irritated vagina] (*TFP* 296) just as she stresses the un-abating 'suintement rougeâtre, nauséabond' [nauseating reddish weeping] (*TFP* 300) of the gash on her leg whose lips will not knit together however frequently it is bathed and bound. It is remarkable that this, the one place in NDiaye's writing to focus on sensation in a woman's sex, focuses only on pain and on a desperate economic context where hospitality is all but driven out of human relations. There is little to distinguish in the end between the various debilitating holes in Khady's body.

NDiaye's purpose in sticking close to Khady Demba's open wounds is as transparent as her fascination with the wound of Ange is opaque. In both cases body openings reference systemic ills, but in this comparatively realist text the diagnosis and our intended reaction are clear, unusually so for NDiaye. The author creates the conditions for empathy by stressing the particularity of this protagonist; by picking her out of the indivisible, anonymous mass of migrating bodies and, via her persistent, painful opening to the world, making her sensory experience sharply available to us. At the same time, the mechanisms of this literary singling out draw attention to themselves so that we remain aware of the tension between engaging with Khady and losing sight of her altogether. This narrative is underpinned from the start by a desire to counter discourses of migration as anonymous, amorphous flow, to cut across talk of 'waves', 'floods' and 'surges', or 'flocks' to use the narrative's bird imagery, and bring about genuinely hospitable engagement with a specific individual. The goal of singularizing Khady Demba is furthered by the dizzying distribution throughout the text of the heroine's name, by her own insistent, almost aristocratic repetition of it and her own conviction that she is precisely *not* a unit of currency: that 'on ne pouvait la remplacer, elle Khady Demba [...] elle était indivisible et précieuse' [nobody could replace her, she Khady Demba [...] she was indivisible and precious] (*TFP* 254).[35]

While the depiction of Khady Demba's wounds is realist, they are nonetheless also tropes alluding to the ills of a global politico-economic network that pushes the disenfranchised into clandestine circulation. Khady's journey lurches from one scenario of inhospitality to another. She is seen as expendable, assessed in terms of her economic value as either a cost or a money-making opportunity. She costs her in-laws more than she brings in through selling plastic buckets at the market, and so is sent to make her way to Europe; she is pressed into forced prostitution and eventually, all resources gone, she perishes on the razor wire fence that separates her from her goal. The openings made in her body result precisely from the network of exploitative relations in which she is bound up and stand for something larger than themselves. The difference between Khady's wounds and that of Ange, however, lies in this causal and interpretative clarity, as well as in the fact that the shame that keeps hers festering is, quite unambiguously, ours.

It seems curious that this largely realist narrative — and even NDiaye's decision to craft a story around clandestine migration at all — have disappointed certain critics. Moudileno, for instance, criticizes the author for having recourse to a 'sujet surexploité' [overexploited subject] and for adding to the 'flot de fictions et films sur les sans-papiers' [wave of fictions and films on illegal immigrants] that have, since the end of the 1990s, sought to express the human experiences involved.[36] Yet the terrible crisis in clandestine migration to Europe that emerged in the summer of 2015 and the renewed and pressing questions around European hospitality that it has raised surely *ought* to prompt further attempts to engage readers closely with those undertaking such perilous journeys. The subject is as necessary as it is inevitable. And we should not overlook the fact that NDiaye's sacrificial heroine is put to the service of a new, secular myth of considerable irony which crystallizes unspoken aspects of a contemporary phenomenon. Khady's journey reads like a via dolorosa punctuated by her own 'stations of the cross', and ends as she limps along carrying her own makeshift ladder (a substitute cross) to climb to her death. Further, the patient grace — even joy — with which she assumes her suffering, reactions which to the reader are both painful and implausible, suggests the comfort of a religious schema, but with the clear purpose of at the same time negating it. The concrete brutality of a global system based on inhospitality and requiring urgent intervention cannot be resolved by mere faith, and the migrant is not endowed with Christ-like strength but is precisely the same as us. We know this even as we read. And the implausible emotional escape routes that NDiaye writes into her story for us — Khady's superhuman fortitude and the consolation of her final metamorphosis — emerge as such, bearing little credibility by comparison with the realism that holds us as witnesses at the very edge of the heroine's wounds.

Conclusion

I have examined in this chapter some of the ways in which inhospitality in NDiaye is played out at body boundaries, notably by feeding, wounding and sexual penetration. I have argued that her texts often coalesce around the meaning of sacrificial protagonists whose split and open bodies bear an extraordinary weight of suffering, serving as hermeneutic puzzles and ethical and empathetic magnets.

Where sexual exploitation is concerned, it is interesting that NDiaye sometimes shows it being orchestrated by a woman — potentially a mother figure — who coaxes protagonists into sexual 'hospitality' or abusive proximity. The woman who prostitutes Khady has a maternal touch; in 'Les Garçons' [The Boys], it is Mme Mour who sells her son Anthony over the internet to a woman of her own age, E. Blaye, who will use him for her own erotic gratification; in *Rosie Carpe* it is a middle-aged woman who makes the pornographic films in which she directs Rosie with feigned maternal solicitude, zooming in for a close-up of Rosie's tear-streaked face (*RC* 79); and we have seen that it is an elderly woman who symbolically 'rapes' Lagrand. Relationships with such abhorrent mother figures conjoin cold self-interest with complicated structures of affect and are of a piece with the ambivalence of mothers and mother-child relationships in NDiaye. The next chapter turns precisely to examine the figure of the mother and the complexities of maternal inhospitality in NDiaye's writing.

Notes to Chapter 3

1. Jean-Luc Nancy, 'Une plaie', in *Corpus* (Paris: Éditions Métailié, 2000), pp. 67–71 (p. 70).
2. See F. G. Bailey's edited volume on the competitive and hostile dimensions of everyday exchanges in small communities, *Gifts and Poison: The Politics of Reputation* (New York: Schocken Books, 1971).
3. Matei Candea, 'The Return to Hospitality', in *The Return to Hospitality*, ed. by Matei Candea and Giovanni da Col, special issue of *Journal of the Royal Anthropological Institute*, 18 (2012), 1–19 (p. 9).
4. See Derrida, ' "Il faut bien manger" ou le calcul du sujet'.
5. Ibid., p. 296.
6. Rosello, *Postcolonial Hospitality*, p. 175.
7. Jean Baudrillard, *La Transparence du mal: essai sur les phénomènes extremes* (Paris: Galilée, 1990), p. 144.
8. Marie NDiaye, 'La Gourmandise', in Jean-Pierre Géné and Marie NDiaye, *La Gourmandise* (Paris: Editions du Centre Pompidou, 1996), pp. 46–62.
9. The same voracious, solitary eating is a notable dysfunction of hospitality in Wilma and Nadia of *Mon cœur à l'étroit* and in Antoinette of 'La Gourmandise'.
10. As mentioned in Chapter 2 he will ask Norah, a lawyer, to defend her brother Sony who is accused of a murder committed in fact by their father.
11. For instance Mina, the elder daughter in *Papa doit manger*, notes the impossibility of eluding her father given their shared physiognomy (*PDM* 87).
12. Asibong, *Blankness and Recognition*, p. 123.
13. For readings of the programmatic dimensions of race relations acted out in the play's psychological schemata see Claire Ducorneau, 'Entre noir et blanc: le traitement littéraire de la couleur de peau dans *Rosie Carpe* et *Papa doit manger*', in *Une femme puissante*, ed. by Bengsch and Ruhe, pp. 101–17. See too Asibong, *Blankness and Recognition*, pp. 122–28. Asibong complains that critics' one-dimensional over-racialization of Papa obscures other of his functions, such as his belonging to the panoply of NDiaye's abusive parents, but the play's replication of 'positions' outlined by Césaire (in, for example, *Discours sur le colonialisme* (Paris: Présence Africaine, 1950)) and Fanon (in *Peau noire, masques blancs* (Paris: Seuil, 1952)) clearly invites a focus on race above all else.
14. Via Olga, protagonist of 'Le Jour du président' [The Day of the President] (in Patrick Modiano, Marie NDiaye and Alain Speiss, *Trois nouvelles contemporaines* (Paris: Gallimard, 2006), pp. 51–67) and René from 'Les Garçons' [The Boys] (in *Tous mes amis* [All My Friends] (Paris: Éditions de Minuit, 2004), pp. 81–109).

15. 'La Gourmandise' was published in a small catalogue for an exhibition devoted to the sin of gluttony. The book is the third in a series dedicated to *les péchés capitaux* [the deadly sins] and to art that, as the back cover has it, probes 'les plus obscures zones de la conscience' [the darkest zones of consciousness]. NDiaye's tale draws on the theological idea that greed is a sin against one's neighbour as well as on the spectrum of cultural meanings conveyed by the French term *gourmandise*.

16. See Žižek, 'Neighbours and Other Monsters'.

17. Jean-Jacques Boutaud, 'Le Partage de la table', in *Le Livre de l'hospitalité*, ed. by Montandon, pp. 1711–37 (p. 1713).

18. Antoinette's flesh 'tendait à ressembler aux mets qu'elle désirait si intensément en pensée, figés dans la gelée [...] ou dans de la blanche et orodante graisse de porc' [tended to resemble the foods that she desired so intensely in her thoughts, set in jelly [...] or in white and odorous pork fat] (*G* 49).

19. Baudrillard, *La Transparence du mal*, p. 134.

20. See 'Violences contre les animaux', in Jacques Derrida and Elisabeth Roudinesco, *De quoi demain... Dialogue* (Paris: Fayard Galilée, 2001), pp. 105–27, p. 114.

21. Jacques Chirac, then Mayor of Paris, was referring to immigrants from France's former colonies. See Michael Cronin, 'Cooking the Books: Translation, Food and Migration', *Comparative Critical Studies* 11 (2014), 337–54 for an illuminating study of this speech.

22. See Montandon, 'Le Toucher de l'hospitalité: Gustave Flaubert'.

23. 'Except I shall see in his hands the print of the nails, and put my finger into the prints of the nails, and thrust my hand into his side, I will not believe' (John 20:25).

24. See too Asibong's interpretation of Ange's wound as a 'magical, stigmatized vagina [...] which constantly leaks fluids, confers non-negotiable social inferiority on a previously powerful, conservative man, and which Nadia both longs to look at and cannot bear to see' (*Blankness and Recognition*, p. 96).

25. Nancy, 'Une plaie', p. 71.

26. Franz Kafka, 'A Country Doctor', in *A Country Doctor*, trans. by Kevin Blahut (Prague: Twisted Spoon Press, 1997), pp. 11–22.

27. Winfried Menninghaus, 'The Wound in the Text and the Text as Wound: The Story of "A Country Doctor", in *Disgust: Theory and History of a Strong Sensation*, pp. 318–32 (p. 331).

28. Rabaté, 'Exercice de la cruauté', p. 96.

29. Menninghaus, 'The Wound in the Text and the Text as Wound', p. 321.

30. Derrida, '"Il faut bien manger" ou le calcul du sujet', p. 296.

31. If Nadia mentions in passing her enjoyment of Ange's body (*MCE* 135–36) and Clarisse takes pleasure in caressing Richard Rivière (*L* 91) and Freddy Moliger (*L* 121), instances of exploitative sex are far more frequent, including Fanny's violation by her uncle Georges (*EF* 118) and then by a truck driver who resembles him (*EF* 120); Rosie Carpe's enforced participation in pornographic films (*RC* 77–80); and the sex tourism that is bound up with neo-colonial relations in the same book.

32. I refer the reader once more to Sheringham's 'La Figure de l'enseignant chez Marie NDiaye'. It is worth noting that in 2001 NDiaye's writer husband Jean-Yves Cendrey outed a paedophile teacher in Cormeilles, Normandy, and that the affair found its way into his *Les Jouets vivants* (2005) as well as into NDiaye's work.

33. Anne B. Dalton refers to the eroticization of the ear in an essay on sexual abuse and slavery: '[i]n parables and folklore, the ear has traditionally been one site of the virginal woman's molestation and impregnation' ('The Devil and the Virgin: Writing Sexual Abuse in *Incidents in the Life of a Slave Girl*', in *Violence, Silence and Anger: Women's Writing as Transgression*, ed. by Deirdre Lashgari (Charlottesville & London: University Press of Virginia, 1995), pp. 38–61 (p. 42).

34. Still's observation in *Derrida and Hospitality* that 'Women *are* home — they are home for men in a number of ways' (p. 60) underpins these episodes.

35. NDiaye's strategies of naming are discussed in Chapter 1.

36. Lydie Moudileno, 'Puissance insolite de la femme africaine chez Marie NDiaye', in *Marie NDiaye's Worlds/Mondes de Marie NDiaye*, ed. by Mott and Moudileno, pp. 67–75, (p.75 n. 14).

CHAPTER 4

Mothers, Mothering and Inhospitable Wombs

Il n'était jamais parfaitement sûr [...] qu'elle n'avait pas décidé de l'étouffer
ou de l'étrangler, elle, sa mère, Rosie Carpe. (*RC* 150)

[He was never entirely sure [...] that she had not decided to suffocate him
or strangle him, she, his mother, Rosie Carpe.]

In one of NDiaye's more intimately unsettling threshold scenes a mother sits on one side of a closed door while her adult daughter stands on the other, each pressing their ear to the wooden partition and breathing together in uneasy coexistence (*AV* 78). This uncanny vignette, narrated by the daughter, evokes fusion and alienation, longing and repellence, openness and resistance. Here the domestic threshold is a trope for a specifically maternal membrane and raises the idea of bodily 'hostipitality' as pertaining to the mother. This is one tiny example of NDiaye's fascinated insistence not only on mothers and mothering, but on mother's bodies as ambivalent places of mutual becoming, where the very opportunity for hospitality begins, where the same splits off into strangeness and where self-other distinctions are both challenged and reinforced. NDiaye's unusually intimate body writing, which is characterized as I shall argue by its emphasis on the maternal and on associated relational ethics and affect, constitutes an original literary device for thinking about hospitality and is sharply distinguished from the more sexually-oriented fascination for bodies that one finds in the work of many of her contemporaries.[1] It also raises an often neglected question within thinking on hospitality: that of women's bodies, and especially wombs, as carriers of others and hence primary instances of unconditional hospitality. Thus NDiaye disturbs the habitual emphasis in hospitality theory, which has tended to focus on hospitality between men, and aligns her interrogations with feminist revisions which take account both of the maternal and, critically, of hospitality as it takes place not only outside but within and between bodies.

This chapter, then, further pursues NDiaye's foregrounding of women within scenarios of hospitality by analyzing her almost obsessive fascination with mothers and mothering. In spite of the vignette on which it began, I do not focus in particular on NDiaye's working out of 'mother/daughter plots', however fascinating and intricate the relations depicted undoubtedly are in texts such as *La Sorcière, Rosie*

Carpe, *Autoportrait en vert* and, perhaps notably, *Ladivine* which traces mothers and daughters over four generations, from grandmother to great granddaughter, showing how their relationships are inflected by postcolonial inhospitality.[2] My choice is partly determined by the fact that the terms in which such relationships invite us to analyze them are already very familiar: daughters' fear of engulfment, invasion or contagion; uneasy identification; mingled repulsion and attraction; and mutual disempowerment (especially remarkable in the founding relationship of *Ladivine*), all demarcate the specific difficulties stemming from a struggle for individuation in which, as Laurie Corbin puts it, 'women must turn away from the same'.[3] While there are specific implications for hospitality here, and especially for self-welcome (Irigaray's sense of a possible revolution in mother–daughter interweaving in *Et l'un ne bouge pas sans l'autre* or *Le Corps-à-corps avec la mère* could usefully be enlisted within such a reading), I have decided to sidestep for now the particularities of mother/daughter relations and indeed to downplay the whole question of sexual similarity or difference in favour of a more generic focus on the invitations to hospitality that are inherent in all mother/child exchanges.[4] The two case studies I use in order to show the centrality of the mother to NDiaye's inhospitable fictions both happen to concern the experience of mothers who, unable or unwilling to 'host', abandon their sons.

Maternal Inhospitality and Embodiment

NDiaye's world is thick with mothers and relentless in its depiction of dysfunctional mother/child relations at all stages of the life cycle, seen variously from the point of view of children or of mothers themselves, many of whom remain alert to their own experiences of maternal inhospitality and, typically, reproduce them. Hers is one of the most original and extensive contributions to the new narratives of mothering that began to emerge in France around the turn of the millennium and that collectively have made such great strides in re-articulating what it means to mother. In her study of such texts, Gill Rye notes a number of significant developments such as the emergence of mothers as narrative subjects, their voicing of maternal ambivalence or socially unacceptable feelings about mothering, as well as a growing emphasis on mothering's darker sides.[5] Such features not only apply to, but are routinely magnified in NDiaye. The most original dimension of her approach is her insistence on (in)hospitality and her very deliberate negotiation of the tension between the mother as generic trope for relations of hospitality and mothers as embodied individual women. On the one hand, the idea of the mother raises acutely, even hyperbolically, hospitality's potential rewards, pleasures and dangers, as well as the delicate question of self/other boundaries that is so critical to all relations of hospitality and that, when gone awry (through fusion to the point of suffocation, for example, or through parasitism) can have such devastating effects. If NDiaye is so intent on foregrounding mothers, including several cases of women past child-bearing age who nonetheless (fantastically) conceive and mother again, this is because to carry or raise a child in her fictional world, to 'be with child', is not just a biological and social reality but the exemplification of a range of positions on the spectrum of hospitality relations. And it is not in order to probe the disruption of the family's oedipal configuration that NDiaye insists on paternal absence, but instead to focus uninterrupted on the symbolic stakes of hospitality within mother/child dyads.[6] On the other hand, mothering in her fiction is indeed a biological and social reality, its materiality and the sharpness of its experience for particular mothers drawing us in to contemplate the ambiguities and trials of powerful, singular, lived experience. In her difficult portrayals of mothers NDiaye keeps us, as I argue in this chapter, productively straddling the metaphorical and the material, the abstract and the concrete.[7]

NDiaye's inhospitable fictions focus intensively on mothers who give the lie to 'maternal instinct', mothers like the bullying Isabelle of *La Sorcière* whose son Steve is a veritable whipping boy; like Mme Descas of *Trois femmes puissantes* who prefers other, more 'angelic' boys to her own; or like the mother of the wrenching 'Révélation' [Revelation] (*TMA* 167–74) who takes her mentally disabled son on a bus ride in order to leave him in an institution, before recognizing (too late in the day) that it is she who is the beneficiary of his unconditional love. While NDiaye's corpus does contain instances of tenderness and nurture, it is terrible, abusive and neglectful mothers who are predominant.[8] NDiaye's mothers put themselves first, disown their children, replace them with others, sell them for sexual services, leave them to die when they are sick and invalidate them by a devastating impassivity and unresponsiveness which Asibong, in his psychoanalytically-driven study of lack of affect in NDiaye, terms 'blankness'.[9] Mothers loom even over adult children, inducing overwhelming anxieties of almost cosmic proportions, since they persist in constituting a protagonist's 'landscape' as does a mother to a newborn: the mother is indeed sometimes imagined as a river or a mountain.[10] Accordingly, adult children in NDiaye repeatedly find themselves overwhelmed by aftershocks of pre-Symbolic experience or folded back abruptly, as this chapter's opening tableau suggests, into uterine spaces. Such a move reminds us that the mother is perceived, fantasized, both in theory and in popular consciousness, as what Still calls 'the first sphere of hospitality, before the home, the city, the nation state or the cosmos'.[11]

A number of general objections might legitimately be raised of course. For instance, does it even seem appropriate to speak of 'hospitality' in a relationship as ideally proximate as that between mother and child? The very idea is painful if we think of hospitality in its (weaker) sense as codified behaviour designed to navigate more socially distant human relations. And can we detach NDiaye's depiction of mothering from the wearisome yet tenacious tendency to mother-blame, an issue that is raised especially sharply in her work, given that the horror induced by bad mothering far exceeds anything occasioned by her catalogue of self-centred absentee fathers? Such questions inevitably become part of our reading as we juggle with the interference between mother as metaphor, the social construction of mothers, NDiaye's fantastic imaginings and real practices of mothering, both terrible and enriching, in particular social contexts. As I have begun to suggest though, this interference is precisely the point. As NDiaye's unmotherly mothers perturb our ideals, appearing impervious to the regulatory pressures that seek to coerce them into selflessness, we are not predominantly called upon to determine which of them are 'bad', 'good' or, *pace* Donald Winnicott, 'good enough' (although of course we do), but to consider how they speak to us eloquently of the multiple challenges of hospitality.[12] The mother figure is particularly good to think with. She reminds us, for instance, that at its core hospitality is proximate: to send a gift is not to be hospitable; to invite somebody in, and particularly to touch and feed them is, or can be. In her ideal(ized) incarnation, the mother is the very origin of that unstinting, unconditional giving (of the self), beyond any care for reciprocity, that is hospitality's unrealizable essence and its unquestionable Law. As such she opens not just the home, but her body 'à l'autre absolu, inconnu, anonyme' ('to the absolute, unknown, anonymous other'), in other words to the child as stranger-guest who requires a hospitality that is not easy or straightforward.[13] She is invested with a charge, power and responsibility that are persistently activated by NDiaye and she initiates the pattern for hospitality as something intimately experienced, intensely embodied and, a critical point, potentially life-giving or annihilating.

Maternal inhospitality in NDiaye sets in train a veritable obsession with the minute scrutiny of bodies, so that protagonists read them closely in a combination of yearning, anxiety, incomprehension and sometimes disgust. This urgent attentiveness, sustained throughout numerous texts, often strikes us as an unusual way to take account of the other, especially given its implied proximity and the peculiar features singled out such as dry or flushing skin, sweating or shivering, evidence of excretions, minute tics or changes in facial expression and subtle physical odours. Protagonists' alertness to bodies seems repeatedly to reinstate what Alison Stone has referred to as 'maternal time': a time distinguished by the merging of past and present perceptions, which she sees as particular to the layered experience of mothering, but which NDiaye's writing seems to invite us to understand as more generalized, applying also to the perceptions and memories of children who are not themselves mothers and characterizing more broadly the ways in which protagonists interact with each other.[14] Mother-child alertness entails 'bodily closeness, non-verbal forms of communication, affective rawness, and a constant presence of basic somatic issues around food, sleep, excretion'.[15] While such attentiveness does not necessarily mean that protagonists welcome each other, it nonetheless speaks to a common vulnerability, a sharp awareness of the other's and one's own *need* for hospitality, and sometimes to revulsion at the prospect. As I shall argue shortly, readers too are caught up in this pattern of gazing that is part of 'maternal time' and are required to remain responsive to bodies in this anxiously relational way.

Much contemporary thought concerning the openness and mutuality, as well as the ambivalence, of what Lucy Armitt refers to as 'that first other-place and space, one which we alternately shun and desire', finds echoes in NDiaye.[16] The symbiosis that Julia Kristeva refers to as the 'chora', a private, pre-Symbolic communicative space inhabited by the mother/child dyad, is also evoked and remembered — although significantly as a fearful experience — by several of her protagonists: thus the adult Lagrand is inhabited by vivid residual impressions of infantile oneness

with his crazed mother, and of struggling to share her oxygen and heartbeat in their
tiny dwelling (*RC* 195); while Malinka's reluctant monthly return to her mother's
single room is insistently framed as a series of suffocating uterine re-absorptions
(*L* 18–25).[17] Irigaray's assertion of the mother's potential to 'open within herself a
place of hospitality for the other, without appropriation, fusion or confusion',[18] and
her idea of mother and child engaged from conception in a mutual becoming, both
newly born in a co-created, shared 'third world' are put to the test in NDiaye and
conspicuously shown to fail.[19]

Antoinette Fouque's recent thinking on the womb, and specifically on the special
qualities of hospitality that it affords, constitutes a further relevant step in establishing
women's bodies as critical places and functions — at once politically and ethically
charged — for thinking about hospitality.[20] In a chapter entitled 'La Gestation
comme paradigme de l'éthique' [Gestation as a paradigm of ethics],[21] Fouque
speaks of '*l'hospitalité charnelle*' [fleshly hospitality], argues for proper recognition of
'échanges intra-utérins' [intra-uterine exchanges] and posits the womb, 'l'organe
de culture de l'humanité' [humanity's organ of culture] as the universal site and
condition of the first exchange relationship: that between woman and embryo.[22]
Gestation, she argues, since it is the very paradigm of giving wherein the mother's
body affords its bone and tissue, accepts within itself what is in essence a foreign
being, and creates in collaboration with it a placenta so that it may be nourished,
ought surely to be incorporated within the anthropological scale of gift-giving; and
yet, she complains, Marcel Mauss, chief anthropologist of the gift, does not give it
a single mention.[23] Again, such insistence on the mother's body as the very origin
of unconditional hospitality helps us to interpret NDiaye's persistent return to it.
We might compare her reflections with other telling exercises in thinking about
hospitality via the inner body as host, such as Jean-Luc Nancy's *L'Intrus*, wherein
the author's heart transplant becomes a powerful and far-reaching trope.[24] Here
a foreign organ is grafted into the host body but it remains alien, unintegrated,
a permanent irritant that requires special measures (immunosuppressant drugs)
in order to avert rejection, even though the survival of the host body is utterly
dependent upon it. By contrast, the mother's body yields a far more positive trope
since it genuinely creates a third, mutually produced and mutually acceptable space.
While the transplant is an instance of conditional hospitality, the mother's welcome,
or accommodation, is in theory absolute.

I turn now to inhospitable mother/child relations in two key texts, *Rosie Carpe*
and *Mon cœur à l'étroit*. These novels are chosen for their particularly detailed and
disturbing depiction of mothering, their almost unrelieved emphasis on maternal
inhospitality and their close focus on mother/child bodily relations, as well as
the indication they give of NDiaye's fertile experimentation with, for instance,
narrative focalization or the fantastic as a way of accessing difficult material. *Rosie
Carpe*, a third-person narrative which incorporates a raft of monstrous mother
figures, centres on the eponymous heroine's attempts to mother. It is partly narrated
from her point of view and provides what remains the most fine-grained account
in NDiaye of mother/infant relations. *Mon cœur à l'étroit* is the first-person interior

monologue of a much older mother, who is grudgingly brought to reckon with the inheritance of her poor mothering and her own filial inhospitality. In this second work, as in a number of other writings by NDiaye, the inhospitality of mother figures is inflected, possibly even generated, by internalized racial prejudice, while in both novels the symbolic and material realities of social class, poverty and marginalization also frame maternal unwelcome.[25] I shall focus especially on NDiaye's minute accounts of fusion and separation between mother/host and child/guest, on how the idea — and the ideal — of the mother's body as hospitable repeatedly resurfaces through adult relations, and on the interpretative challenges associated with this. The first text makes us keenly aware of an infant body; the second of a maternal body. Bodies in both become subtle devices for considering hospitality.

Nothing Nurturing: *Rosie Carpe*

Rosie Carpe is full of swollen bellies, ambivalent conceptions and un-motherly mothers. The eponymous heroine, who is with child for most of the novel, has three unwanted pregnancies: the first goes to term, the second ends in abortion and the third, the origins of which remain obscure even to Rosie, terminates in a violent and bloody miscarriage towards the book's end. The primary instance of maternal inhospitality that structures the novel is that which conditions the relationship between Rosie and her only child Étienne, referred to throughout as Titi. Rosie's story of mothering begins with a starkly realist account, including finely observed passages on the post-natal exhaustion and depression of a single mother in a particularly disadvantaged social context. Scraping a living in a grim hotel on the outskirts of Paris and bereft of support networks, Rosie soon takes refuge in drink. She leaves her infant alone in the flat or, when she goes to hospital for her abortion, in the 'care' of an alcoholic neighbour. Twice she gets pregnant when drunk to the point of unconsciousness, deliriously configuring the second instance — the child in her belly when she and Titi leave France for Guadeloupe — as 'une conception immaculée' [an immaculate conception] (*RC* 23). Titi himself was conceived during the making of one of the pornographic videos into which Rosie was lured, the 'sacred' moment ignominiously captured on film. He is as a consequence irredeemably bound up in one of the many commercial transactions around bodies that are so common in NDiaye. His mother, steeped in an oneiric detachment which seems to be the condition of her survival, is dimly conscious of the unborn Titi as already battling against her unpromising body: he is 'ce qui s'était glissé en elle [...] ce qui avait trouvé la force de s'installer dans son ventre froid, dans sa chair pétrifiée et inhospitalière' [what had slipped into her [...] what had been strong enough to install itself in her cold womb, in her petrified and inhospitable flesh] (*RC* 87).

From the start of the novel, NDiaye tracks minutely Rosie's physical and emotional connection to Titi. She produces keenly accurate accounts of the sudden drying-up of her protagonist's breast milk and her attempts to get Titi to take the bottle. The baby's frustrated sucking and furious rejection of the artificial teat which he thrusts away with a dry, white tongue constitute the book's sole image of him as muscular and energetic. It is as if he exhausts himself definitively in this first and last awakening to the inhospitable conditions into which he has been born. Hereafter he will remain, like his mother, unresponsive and inaccessible. Among all NDiaye's unfortunate children, Titi in particular is emblematic of the special status not just of childhood but more specifically of infancy and babyhood in her work: the tremulous fear with which her protagonists are so often infected seems to render them as vulnerable as newborns, while their submerging in overwhelming emotions and sensations that they seem unable to bring to the level of conscious articulation, let alone analyze, equates them with the pre-linguistic child.[26]

What is striking about NDiaye's approach to Titi is that she requires us to continue responding to him as newly — or even not yet — born, using him persistently to allude to the biological dimension of mothering, to the absolute neediness of the child newcomer and to the potential for hospitality in the mother's body. It is this that the novel foregrounds at the expense of any other roles associated with child care. Educating or socializing receive scant attention; instead the fusional ante-natal and early post-natal relationships are imaginatively extended, furnishing the terms in which mother/child interaction is imagined long after pregnancy and nursing are over. The text is bathed in references to fusion with/separation from the mother's body, so that what remains foregrounded is the hospitality of womb and breast. As if to underscore the scandal of its lack, Titi never quite seems to grow but assumes the characteristics of an eternal foetus, both fascinating and repellent in his neediness, ever present in the text (his incessant 'animal' moaning, equated as we saw in Chapter 2 with the cries of cattle, is an urgent, pre-Symbolic appeal for attention) and yet somehow parenthetical.

The novel's frequent descriptions of Titi imply, and demand, repeated glances in his direction. Again and again our attention is drawn to the boy, inviting us to read with maternal attentiveness, to have a care for him. Fragile, mute and lacklustre, his appeal to protection remains strong. NDiaye stresses his softness, insubstantiality and under-development, alluding throughout the narrative to his large, drooping head, slack flesh, translucent skin, blueish colour, prominent veins, light bones and relative inertia. One thinks of the fragility of a foetus, even an embryo, ideas that are indeed evoked in Lagrand's confession in one of NDiaye's more surprising recourses to the animal world that he always thought of Titi as a 'méduse' [jellyfish] (RC 322) — a gelatinous invertebrate creature perhaps obscurely reminiscent of intra-uterine photographs of embryos with their umbilical cord floating beside them. Even as a six-year-old Titi engages in no play or movement, does not laugh and is unresponsive to Rosie's sporadic attempts to nourish him or to re-invent him by dressing him in sporty tee shirts and shorts. Nothing counters his essential vulnerability and lack of contour.

Rosie's body is also designed perpetually to allude to pregnancy and to the uterine transferral of nourishment between mother and child. Pink or bluish veins near the surface of her pale skin match those of Titi, as do references to her circulation and heartbeat, and the sensitivity of her flushing skin (her name of course is not without relevance here). When, upon the couple's arrival in Guadeloupe the boy sleeps fitfully in the back of Lagrand's car, Rosie confuses her own beating heart with that of her son and, soaked in sweat and tears, feels herself to be floating 'dans une poche d'eau aigre, irritante' [in a pouch of bitter, irritating water] (*RC* 27), a peculiarly amniotic image. In the same passage she sees herself and her son as covered in a sticky, viscous fluid: 'tout englués de poisse' (*RC* 26). The range of meanings of 'poisse' — viscous matter and, figuratively, bad luck and poverty — work here to express the mutual contagion of failure and fear that binds and defines mother and child. Further, when Lagrand expresses later in the novel his sense of being contaminated by the ethical mess surrounding Titi, he too evokes an amniotic pouch, referring to an 'impalpable fluide autour de lui' [impalpable fluid surrounding him] (*RC* 184) made up of all the inhospitable thoughts, memories and desires that people harbour concerning the boy.

Life-giving maternal fluids are exchanged in *Rosie Carpe* for experiences of dehydration. Lagrand becomes dehydrated during an errand to fetch Rosie's egotistical mother, the freakishly rejuvenated and now pregnant Diane Carpe. Twice Rosie allows Titi to dehydrate to the point of death: first, in the chaos of early mothering when she ceases to lactate and, second, after a night the boy spends vomiting and sweating in fever. Titi, who is uninterested in solid food and who, as Lagrand remarks, 'ne mange rien, n'aime rien' [eats nothing, likes nothing] (*RC* 272) suddenly attempts to self-nurture (or perhaps to self-harm; we cannot know as we have no access to his inner world) by eating rotten guava which is soaked in rat urine. Rosie leaves him lying in the sun, waiting precisely and very consciously for him to die and to release her from the (mutually) debilitating fusional relationship that she sees as blighting her existence. She begins, somewhat vampirically, to bloom as Titi fails and we read in horror, buffeted between metaphor and realism, as the mother almost suffocates with joy in anticipation of her child's death.

At last Titi's function as touchstone of (in)hospitality works its way to the surface of the text, and of our consciousness, and is articulated in a metatextual aperçu by Rosie herself: 'la vérité, c'est que Titi est un agneau. Il a le sort qu'on réserve aux agneaux' [the truth is that Titi is a lamb; his fate is that reserved for lambs] (*RC* 290). The child's incessantly live fear receives here its *raison d'être* as Rosie repeatedly imagines him as a bound animal that senses the approach of the knife. We have seen that Rosie Carpe as fictional mother and *Rosie Carpe* as text are both deeply inhospitable to Titi; neither provides the conditions for him to emerge as a fully-fledged protagonist with psychological depth and a complex inner world. His role is solely that of the Other whose need for hospitality is manifest and who calls unheeded for it. Even Lagrand, the text's moral compass, is obliged to acknowledge his failings with regard to Titi, most especially his sluggishness in saving the boy's life, for he stops to eat lunch rather than drive the child straight to hospital and, we later learn, does not return to check on his progress. 'Comment', he asks himself, 'était-ce possible, cette répugnance envers un petit garçon?' [How was it possible, this repugnance towards a little boy?] (*RC* 184). An innate distaste for the Other on grounds that are scarcely explicable to the self is a facet of inhospitality that is recurrent in NDiaye.

Importantly, Titi also challenges the hospitality of the reader since we too become weary of his neediness, finding his limpness rebarbative yet being all the while obliged to have a care for him. Because NDiaye gives us access to Titi through Rosie, we find ourselves scrutinizing, touching, carrying and assessing the child in a reading whose rhythm of attentiveness is maternal. He remains in our consciousness and unpleasantly proximate throughout, while his alienating, animal lamentations — 'Titi mugit comme les boeufs' [Titi lows like the cattle] (*RC* 32) — test our empathy far more than human crying. The lowing comes to stand more generally for the stranger's urgent plea, made from pressing need in a language that we cannot understand. It arouses our sense of personal responsibility, while suggesting too that this stranger is somehow 'animal', not like us, which relieves us from the obligation to heed his call. It is in this sense that Titi arouses in Lagrand conflictual feelings of responsibility yet 'une énigmatique et fâcheuse repulsion' [an enigmatic and irritating repulsion] (*RC* 183). In the inhospitable world of NDiaye's fiction the vulnerable and needy, epitomized here by Titi, attract not empathy but cruelty, neglect and distaste.

The novel's fourth and final part offers an alternative perspective on what mother and son make of each other. Now a grandmother, living in inhospitable isolation in Titi's house where she is effectively held hostage, Rosie finds herself at the centre of a symbolic system in which she is deemed 'untouchable': 'Personne ne s'approche de Maman. C'est la règle' [Nobody is to go near Mother. It's the rule] (*RC* 328) explains Titi to Lagrand. Her grandchildren may not touch her and she must eat at a separate table away from the family. Titi is unable to explain the rationale for this segregation, although he and Rosie alike concur that it is nothing to do with love. It is more likely that Titi's own internalized sense of being 'untouchable', transmitted to him in numerous ways in infant sensations and feelings, is turned against Rosie as he replies to her idiom of grudging hospitality with his own ritualized version. Such tactile isolation is a punishment fitting the crime, for the interdiction of touch recognizes that touch is a mother's prerogative. When Irigaray observes that 'the tactile nature of the environment seems to change' with the onset of motherhood, she is putting her finger on a key connection between women's perceptual/ethical experience of the world and the practice of hospitality more generally.[27] Rosie is henceforth removed from the circuit of mutual nurture in its broadest sense and from its various physical and emotional exchanges.

Titi's re-framing of Rosie may also be read as an ironic gloss on how mothers have been conceptualized via the two extremes of idealization and demonization. Throughout *Rosie Carpe* the eponymous heroine self-consciously sees herself as a magnet for the kind of stigmatizing labels that mothers so easily attract: single, irresponsible, alcoholic and prone to bouts of promiscuousness, she is aware of herself as an archetypal 'bad' mother. Yet at the same time, in a bizarre and fantastical move, she aligns herself with the Virgin Mary, insisting on the miraculous conception of the 'saint enfant' [holy child] (*RC* 23) she is carrying on her arrival in Guadeloupe.[28] The adult Titi constructs around her an unstable myth, setting her apart qua mother as somewhere between sanctified and polluting, under so rigid a prohibition that when Lagrand eventually touches her, her son's horror is absolute and her grandchildren whine with fear. Titi's configuration of Rosie as mother, as symbol rather than as complex individual, is a reminder of the loaded construction of the figure of the mother outside the textual world, and in turn of the inhospitality often meted out to mothers as such.

Typically, NDiaye's novels contain secondary instances or echoes of a central scenario of inhospitality and there are several examples of inhospitable mothering in *Rosie Carpe*, beginning with Mme Carpe who abandons Rosie and her brother Lazare, re-invents herself as a fantastically rejuvenated mother and gives birth to a stunning new daughter, Rose-Marie (Rosie's original name) whom she proceeds to pimp. I conclude this section with some comments on how Lagrand's abandonment by his own crazed mother surfaces with overwhelming force as he acknowledges Rosie's decision to let Titi die.[29] Lagrand maps his history onto theirs, finding multiple points of identification, notably his residually live sense of dependence on his mother's body.

Lagrand easily recaptures his infant perception of the tiny house in Boissard (once again, the house becomes metaphor for the maternal body) where the two had lived 'presque comme un seul être' [almost as a single entity] (*RC* 232). So complete is their fusion that the child is entirely subsumed by his mother 'comme s'il avait été l'un de ses membres ou de ses organes, comme si elle avait été seule' [as if he had been one of her limbs or her organs, as if she had been alone'] (*RC* 245). This is a most curious observation, taking no cognizance of the child as a separate being in need of individuation. Lagrand similarly conceptualizes himself as her flesh, accepts that in breathing she takes all the oxygen in the house, waits for her to exhale before taking some himself and believes throughout his childhood that her heart is the organ sending blood round both their bodies. The memory provoked by Rosie's abandonment of Titi stirs the adult Lagrand to visit his mother in the asylum for the first time. In one of NDiaye's stock-in-trade bathetic 'recognition' scenes, he is excited by Mme Lagrand's immediate response to him as 'mon fils' [my son] (*RC* 221), only to find that in her madness she uses this form of address as a generically hospitable greeting for all of the men on her ward and does not in fact know him. So powerfully destabilizing is the rekindled sense of unwelcome that the adult Lagrand urinates in his trousers, contributing to the novel's bathing in bodily fluids as well as to the jaundiced or acid yellow colour that is its 'tenor' and that thus seems connected to inhospitable mothering.[30] In *Sharing the World* Irigaray articulates a question that is posed by parenting a newborn child: 'How can we place ourselves in relation to the appeal that we have perceived'?[31] In *Rosie Carpe* NDiaye offers us a sequence of mothers whose inadequate responses or complete imperviousness to this appeal keep Irigaray's question powerfully and urgently before us.

The Menopausal Threshold in *Mon cœur à l'étroit*

Like *Rosie Carpe*, *Mon cœur à l'étroit* depicts the consequences of a mother's unavailability to her son. This novel too evokes uterine (in)hospitality, anxious infant/
mother bodily relations and the keenness of their legacy into adult life. A first
person interior monologue, it takes the shape of a grudging maternal confession
(or perhaps, until the novel's final pages, an anti-confession) by Nadia a woman
who, like several NDiayean mothers, has re-invented herself at the expense of her
family. As readers privy only to Nadia's consciousness, we fail at first to tune in
to her self-deception and it takes us some time to realize that, as we first saw in
the Introduction, the condition of her re-branding as a member of the Bordeaux
bourgeoisie was the effective 'erasure' of her past, including her parents, husband,
child, social class and, significantly, ethnic origin. Nadia's maternal story is
complicated, indeed structured as I shall discuss at the end of this section, by the
inhospitalities of racism which she has internalized and by the fact that her body
is ethnically marked. It is also characterized by an intensive focus on her body as
menopausal.

The repository of a complicated spectrum of meanings, Nadia's body is clearly
to be read as multiply hysterical. Since she cannot mentally process or bring to
expression either her internalized racism or her maternal inhospitality — except
via NDiaye's subtle inclusion of occasional italicized passages which indicate the
surfacing of unwelcome material and which nudge her protagonist towards self-
awareness — the particularity of her psycho-social situation is played out on a
physical level. The hysterical body and the anti-confession go hand in hand. The
text is accordingly driven by an inquiry into Nadia's body, which is scrutinized
by the heroine herself, by secondary protagonists and by the reader, and which is
required to carry a great burden of collective significance. NDiaye's approach to the
female body in this text shares the minutely graphic quality of much contemporary
experimental body writing by women, but is distinguished from them by its
unusual focus on what is dysfunctional, unhealthy, un-erotic, un-reproductive and
unattractive. *Mon cœur à l'étroit* requires us to tune in to the rhythms and sensations
of a middle-aged body labouring in fat and on the cusp of the climacteric; in other
words a body as distant from euphoric *jouissance* or from the physically celebratory
mode of *écriture féminine* as is imaginable. Nadia has outbreaks of sweating and
difficulty in walking, breathing and fastening her clothes. Our attention is drawn to
her trembling flesh and swelling belly, and to the repressed shame and un-avowed
disorder inherent in her physical self-neglect.

How, more precisely, are we encouraged to understand Nadia's body? Significantly
the novel's title, *Mon cœur à l'étroit*, sets the body's inner workings centre stage,
singling out for attention a so-called organ of hospitality, the metaphorical seat of,
inter alia, love, charity, openness, generosity and courage. Yet the title is itself a
characteristic instance of Nadia's propensity to self-blinding and a double diversion.
First, although it alludes to a dysfunction or blockage, it explicitly frames this as
something beyond Nadia's control (she is not 'hard-hearted'; instead her heart is
'constricted'). Second, it is not so much the heart that is at stake as the organ of

hospitality in this narrative as the womb. NDiaye accordingly draws Nadia (and us) back to the womb, and if one of the novel's arresting features is its plethora of overt references to the heart (references which 'beat' insistently on almost every page, covering a wide spectrum of literal and metaphorical uses which Nadia draws upon to account for herself) we also find within it numerous buried references to gestation and intra-uterine life, a bodily connection to practices of hospitality that the heroine is far less prepared to articulate.[32] Insistently NDiaye evokes the uterus in Fouquian/Irigarayan perspective as a foundational humanizing and hospitable space, cleverly situating her heroine at a biological juncture which mirrors her ethical trajectory. Nadia's body is on the cusp of closure to new life but there is also much speculation that her corpulence may be evidence of a late pregnancy, a renewed opportunity for hospitable maternal opening.

Chapters 2 and 3 of this book explored the construction of Nadia as animal/ stranger and her relationship to food in various parts of the novel. Here I focus on the novel's final section once the heroine has left Bordeaux and arrived in the unnamed, part fantastical land which is the home of her adult son, Ralph. This section of the work is rich in maternal considerations. In it, Nadia re-connects with her son as well as with her own mother and granddaughter, undergoes a pre-natal gynaecological examination, gives birth once more in a weirdly horrific scene at the novel's conclusion and finally generates one of the few chapter titles in the novel that is clear-sighted and that indicates a protagonist prepared to challenge herself: 'Qu'ai-je fait de ce garçon?' [What have I done to this boy?] (*MCE* 273). It is in this last part of the narrative that the ethical charge of the womb is underscored with maximum force, that Nadia is persistently addressed as 'maman', and that we are directed specifically to her inner body. It is striking, incidentally, that Nadia's progression towards hospitality is dependent upon her leaving French soil.[33] Already on the train and sea voyage, we see her extending maternal hospitality to strangers: she 'reads' the bodies — first of the unhappy fellow passenger Natalie (*MCE* 195– 96), then of a distressed chambermaid whom she finds sitting in her cabin and holds to her breast (*MCE* 216) — with the same closeness of concern ideally extended to a child. As if a former perceptive habit were being re-awakened, perhaps prompted by what may indeed be her own pregnancy, she provides them with tender, explicitly maternal, comfort.

Nadia's reunion with Ralph, a typically uneasy NDiayean set piece, involves a succession of regressive moments wherein early patterns of maternal rejection, hostility and failed recognition are re-activated and their consequences deeply felt. In the bustling port not only do mother and son not recognize each other, they do not see each other and literally collide, the jolt throwing Nadia's spectacles to the ground (*MCE* 221). When she bends to retrieve them, her teeth strike the man's collar bone (surely a nod to NDiaye's avowed interest in the figure of the vampiric mother).[34] As Nadia rises, scanning the stranger's body in extreme close up, she does not perceive it as the body of a man but recognizes it as that of her infant son. A powerful physical flashback that recurs more than once in the novel transports her to the poor suburb of Les Aubiers and to a violent incident when Ralph gripped her body with his tiny legs, only to find himself thrown to the floor by his mother, his head smashing on the tiles (*MCE* 226). The unusual, almost erotic physicality of Nadia's perception in this encounter with her adult boy is NDiaye's way of insisting that the emotional economy of hospitality is persistently underwritten and shaped by early bodily memories of how mother and child interweave.

No sooner has Nadia arrived at the (distinctly Gothic) home of her estranged son and his partner Wilma — who is at once huntress, cannibal and medic — than we are invited to consider the inside of her body in an unusual scene of gynaecological scrutiny. Due to the agitation in Nadia's womb, Wilma proposes an internal examination, which NDiaye uses to provoke a telling conjunction of fantastic and clinically precise approaches to the female reproductive body, alluding to superstition, science, the uneasy interface between the two and the inhospitality frequently experienced by women as a result of both (*MCE* 246–51). Significantly, Nadia's examination is anything but private, for the designer consulting room with its sleek furnishing and fuchsia-coloured bed has large, curtain-less windows open to potential onlookers.[35] At this moment of utter exposure, with legs in stirrups and speculum opened wide inside her, Nadia senses that there is an audience for her mothering body, that she is public property, a shared resource, and that the consulting room is full of people (readers?) ready to engage in mother-blame (*MCE* 249). The speculum that opens her cervix is one way of trying to understand Nadia, as if the truth about her were necessarily located in the capacious, muscular space of her womb.[36]

Yet is this perspective not reductive? For a moment, our focus on the inhospitality *of* mothers wavers and we begin to reflect on the inhospitality *to* mothers that is inherent in the way society persistently frames them. Packaged within a Russian-doll set of imperatives to unconditional hospitality, mothers are entrapped by a configuration that is itself inhospitable, a socio-ethical prison constructed of unrealizable demands. And if the scene of clinical examination appears at first to bring about a sharp shift of register away from the murky, psychoanalytically-driven tropes of the Gothic that dominate in this section of the text, its view of the female inner body as darkly potent and terrible is in fact entirely consistent with them.[37] The gynaecologist's observations are, furthermore, not medical but moral in nature: recoiling before she takes a further incredulous look at the 'diabolical' entity within, Wilma is reproachful and angry: 'Avec qui vous avez fait ça, maman? Qu'est-ce que vous avez fait de votre vie?' [Who did you create this with, mother? What have you done with your life?] (*MCE* 249).

The final pages of *Mon cœur à l'étroit* contain a darkly fantastic birthing scene (*MCE* 295–96), the only one to date in NDiaye excepting the bloody miscarriage in *Rosie Carpe*, narrated sketchily by Rosie's brother Lazare (*RC* 310–13). Both scenes bypass the possible establishment of hospitable relations with new life and both imply, metaphorically, inhospitable uterine conditions. Rosie's miscarriage is depicted in realist terms, with unbearable cramping and heavy bleeding. The baby and tissue, referred to in disgust by Lazare as 'ce qu'elle avait expulsé' [what she had excreted] (*RC* 313) are left on the floor of the Toyota pick-up where she loses the child. Nadia's birthing scene is a more surprisingly horrid affair, a rapid expulsion that the narrator struggles to depict in three short, reluctant bursts. It takes place at night as Nadia, now reconciled with her parents, undresses in the bedroom at their house. On one level it resonates with realist accounts of unplanned births or miscarriages that mothers endure alone and disavow, scarcely believing in the event and disposing of its traces.[38] Nadia refers to her mucus-covered offspring as a 'chose' [thing] and asks incredulously, 'd'où aurait-elle pu jaillir, sinon de mon corps?' [where could it have sprung from, if not from my body?] (MCE 295). She at once scrubs the floor with a sponge and seeks to reassure herself that the thing is gone and cannot be connected with or returned to her.

We share Nadia's abhorrence not only at the indeterminate nature of the thing, which she likens to a thick, furry eel, but at the unnatural features of the 'birth' and of the gestation that it implies. The foetus defies the mutuality of intra-uterine exchange mechanisms, which is doubtless one reason for the gynaecologist's horror. It moves in Nadia's belly 'd'une vie propre, chaotique' [with independent, chaotic life] (MCE 256) and tortures her with 'des coups de griffes intérieurs, farouches, forcenés' [fierce, frenzied internal clawing] (MCE 259). It is monstrous in part because it is already self-reliant, rendering completely redundant any notion of the womb as a 'lieu de réciprocité absolue' [place of absolute reciprocity].[39] Its coming into the world has none of what Rye calls 'the enormity of the bodily experience of birth' and is devoid of either violence or pleasure.[40] Monstrously, this un-needy newborn that squatted in Nadia's womb, that could not be aborted but had to go 'to term', is utterly independent from her body as a mother's body; it parts company with her at once, slinking across the floor and out of the door, requiring no labour, nurture, hospitality, welcome or accommodation. Nadia's body shows no signs of early motherhood (her breasts do not fill with milk, for instance), nor is there any umbilical cord to sever or any trace of a placenta.

This expulsion in fact is less reminiscent of a birth than of the excretion of waste matter, aligning the 'newborn' with, for instance, the 'faecal animal' believed by the Ajamaat Diola of southern Senegal to be a kind of double produced from a person's faeces, an entity 'that runs off and seeks shelter in the house of a female relative, as though a "birth" has taken place'.[41] Alternatively we might think of parasites that slip away from their host once they have taken from it everything they need for independent life or exhausted its resources. It is indeed the hospitality-defying model of the parasite/host relationship that seems best to account for what takes place in Nadia's womb, the entity that had 'pris possession' [taken possession] (MCE 295) of it doubtless finding there an appropriate carrier.

Nadia herself frames the birth as an exorcism, a definitive 'cure', and indeed certain elements of the novel's conclusion do strain towards resolution: take the (overly optimistic) final chapter heading 'Tous guéris' [All cured] (MCE 292), the related snippets of her mother's celebratory song, 'La misère est sortie de moi | Et je peux danser maintenant' [Misery has left my body | and I can dance now] (MCE 295) or her sponging clean away of the thing's bloody trail. The narrative nonetheless leaves a dark residue that exceeds such neatness and it is the unanswered questions raised by the 'thing' and its contaminating, inhospitable potentiality that are the text's parting shot. It is thus with recourse to a familiar trope from horror and science fiction that NDiaye affirms the residual power of inhospitality at the end of *Mon cœur à l'étroit*. The dreadful fantasy of something dark, unstoppable and inhuman that lurks beyond the bounds of the familiar is well-worn. When used to evoke inhospitality it becomes newly chilling, especially — as in the sci-fi horror film *Alien* (and it should be noted that NDiaye is far from averse to making allusions to popular fiction and film) — given its gestation inside a mother's body, precisely in defiance of the invitation to primary hospitality that inheres in the womb.

At the start of my analysis of Nadia as maternal figure I argued that NDiaye conjoins and connects in her protagonist both maternal and (disavowed) racial inhospitality. Nadia's unavailability to Ralph, a corollary of her urge to autonomous selfhood outside of the constraints of her social class and ethnic belonging, is ultimately a product of the more widespread structural inhospitality in Nadia's 'ville déloyale' [disloyal town] (*MCE* 122) to people of North-African origin such as her.[42] It is only towards the book's conclusion that this scarcely articulated postcolonial undercurrent, entailing both shame and a repellently vigorous internalized racism on Nadia's part, is made available for articulation, in italics, by the protagonist herself. Nadia, one of NDiaye's extensive cast of morally questionable (French) schoolteachers, considers her inhospitality to certain of the little children who were her charges and acknowledges that she was, in truth, '*ni juste, ni hospitalière, ni correcte*' [neither fair nor hospitable nor proper] with those who reminded her of herself, '*souhaitant au fond de moi leur élimination*' [wanting, in my heart of hearts, to have them eliminated] and imagining them as pigeons one might shoot with impunity '*tant ils sont nombreux et sales et superflus*' [so numerous, dirty and superfluous are they] (*MCE* 286).[43] This shocking confession, evocative of the worst excesses of racial persecution (and surely spurred by NDiaye's growing alarm, discussed elsewhere in this book, at the rise of racist discourse in France while she was writing this novel) is a form of inhospitality to self as well as to Other — to self *as* Other — which, as the italics indicate, Nadia scarcely dares to formulate.[44] The question of ethical responsibility in the story is thus complex and diffuse and spreads far beyond Nadia's maternal body, which one might argue is ultimately as much a sacrificial body as that of Titi. In her study of mothering in contemporary French women's writing, Rye speaks of 'the remarkable, albeit rather harrowing, ways in which the figurative power of the female reproductive body is being both problematized and taken to new horizons in contemporary women's writing in France'.[45] Nadia's body, used by NDiaye to focus on questions of hospitality that are inherent in but extend way beyond the maternal, is precisely such an example.

Conclusion

NDiaye's work offers one of the most intensive focuses on mothering to have emerged in recent women's writing in French. Inhospitable forms of mothering are elaborated in almost every text that she has written to date. They dominate in her major novels and constitute both the ethical wellspring and, to a large extent, the emotional draw of her writing. I have shown in this chapter some of the ways in which hospitality is at stake on the uncomfortable interpretative threshold where her examples of aberrant and abhorrent mothering hold us. I have also argued that the meaning of mothering in her work is productively unstable; that she holds the fantastic and the hyper-real in constant mutual interference (some of the most horrific instances of abusive mothering, the stuff of nightmares, are in fact scarcely removed from stories that we read about in the newspaper); and that inhospitality *to* mothers may also be teased out of the mix. My central points, however, relating to what I argue is Marie NDiaye's core concern for hospitality, are that her recurrent focus on mother/child relations draws us back insistently to what we are invited to imagine as the touchstone of hospitality in its absolute unconditional form, and that it does so thanks to a series of violent departures from the idea.

Notes to Chapter 4

1. It is worth noting that this fascination includes consideration of specifically sexual hospitality in works such as Catherine Millet's *La Vie sexuelle de Catherine M* (Paris: Seuil, 2001) and Anna Rozen's *Plaisir d'offrir, joie de reçevoir* (Paris: Éditions J'ai Lu, 1999).
2. I allude here to Marianne Hirsch's seminal *The Mother/Daughter Plot: Narrative, Psychoanalysis, Feminism* (Bloomington: Indiana University Press, 1989).
3. Laurie Corbin, *The Mother Mirror: Self-Representation and the Mother-Daughter Relation in Colette, Simone de Beauvoir and Marguerite Duras* (Oxford: Peter Lang, 1996), p. 119.
4. Luce Irigaray, *Et l'un ne bouge pas sans l'autre* (Paris: Éditions de Minuit, 1979); *Le Corps-à-corps avec la mère* (Montreal: Éditions de la pleine lune, 1981). In the latter Irigaray imagines 'un rapport de réciprocité de femme à femme [avec nos mères], où ells pourraient aussi éventuellement se sentir nos filles' [a relationship of reciprocity of woman to woman [with our mothers], wherein they could also perhaps feel as if they were our daughters] (p. 86).
5. See Rye, *Narratives of Mothering: Women's Writing in Contemporary France* (Newark: University of Delaware Press, 2010).
6. Women habitually bring up children alone in NDiaye's world. There is no father around to, as Irigaray puts it, 'trancher ce lien trop étroit avec la matrice originelle' [sever this overly tight link with the original womb] (*Le corps-à-corps avec la mère*, p. 20) and even fathers who have not abandoned their offspring tend to be background figures.
7. On such tensions see Still, 'Maternity as hospitality', in *Derrida and Hospitality: Theory and Practice*, pp. 125–32.
8. Demonstrated by Lucie in *La Sorcière* (see Gill Rye, *Narratives of Mothering: Women's Writing in Contemporary France* (Newark: University of Delaware Press, 2010), pp. 77–87); Norah and Fanta in *Trois femmes puissantes*; the elder and younger Ladivine in *Ladivine*; and the autofictional mother narrators of *Autoportrait en vert* and *Y penser sans cesse*. The latter text, which is bilingual, raises the problem of hospitality as articulated beyond the mother tongue. The mother narrator wonders how she and her little boy will stay close when the words to 'open' to each other are lost, questioning his ability to 'rentrer à la maison dans notre langue d'autrefois' [return home in our former language] (*YPSC* 42) and asserting: 'je ne lui dirai pas Mein Leibling' [I will not say 'Mein Leibling' to him] (43).
9. Asibong reads NDiaye's mothers through the prism of psychoanalyst André Green's 'dead mother' complex. On the psychic damage caused by 'dead' mothers see Asibong's *Marie NDiaye: Blankness and Recognition* and 'Autour de la mère morte', in *Une femme puissante*, ed. by Bengsch and Ruhe, pp. 243–62.
10. In *Autoportrait en vert* the Garonne is specifically seen as a (dangerously) pregnant woman threatening to burst her banks (*AV* 8); in 'Une journée de Brulard' the protagonist's dead mother survives as a 'montagne sévère' [severe mountain] (*TMA* 135).
11. Still, *Derrida and Hospitality*, p. 22.

12. D. W. Winnicott, 'Transitional Objects and Transitional Phenomena', *International Journal of Psychoanalysis*, 34 (1953), 89–97.

13. Derrida and Dufourmantelle, *De l'Hospitalité*, p. 29; *Of Hospitality*, p. 25. In an unpublished seminar Derrida uses the term 'absolute' to characterize both child/guest and mother/host: the former is 'l'arrivant absolu' [the absolute guest] and the latter *une figure absolue de l'hospitalité* [an absolute figure of hospitality]. See Michaud, '"Un acte d'hospitalité ne peut être que poétique"', in *Le Dire de l'hospitalité*, ed. by Gauvin, L'Hérault and Montandon, p. 54.

14. See Alison Stone, *Feminism, Psychoanalysis and Maternal Subjectivity* (New York & London: Routledge, 2012), notably the chapter entitled 'Maternal Time' (pp. 128–47).

15. Ibid., pp. 128–29.

16. Lucy Armitt, *Contemporary Women's Fiction and the Fantastic* (Basingstoke: Macmillan Press, 2000), p. 233.

17. Julia Kristeva, *Revolution in Poetic Language* (New York: Columbia University Press, 1984), p. 26.

18. Irigaray, *Sharing the World*, p. xiv.

19. Ibid., p. 23.

20. Antoinette Fouque, *Génésique. Féminologie III* (Paris: Des femmes, 2012). Writing powerfully against the many ways in which the womb has been colonized, pillaged, prostituted or neglected in philosophy and theory, Fouque argues for its centrality in any consideration of giving.

21. Ibid., pp. 15–88. Fouque is especially concerned too with the ethics and politics of surrogacy as practiced outside of commercial relationships, which she sees as a supreme instance of giving as well as a form of liberation from alienating phallocentric structures whose purchase on procreation has been immense.

22. Ibid., pp. 22; 27; 19.

23. Ibid., p. 24.

24. Jean-Luc Nancy, *L'Intrus* (Paris: Éditions Galilée, 2000).

25. The socio-cultural contexts that give meaning to mothering are various in NDiaye, showing women's awareness of how being with child re-valorizes them and often implying their configuration of the child as resource. In *Rosie Carpe* Diane Carpe's late pregnancy is a 'luxury' allowing her to sell her daughter's sexual favours; Rosie Carpe observes that the state takes care of single mothers and sees her unborn child as 'mon petit capital' [my little asset] (*RC* 16); while for Khady Demba in the Senegalese setting of *Trois femmes puissantes* the cultural and economic imperatives to mother are paramount: being sterile leads to social exclusion and the enforced journey to Europe around which her story is based.

26. Certain hyperbolic outsiders such as NDiaye's woman-fish in *La Naufragée* remain open to such a reading throughout, while other protagonists slip into provisional states of absolute helplessness. In the case of *Autoportrait en vert* the book's physical characteristics might even be seen to evoke mother/newborn relations for its photographic material repeatedly depicts inaccessible women who are out of focus, half gone from the frame, or have their backs to the (desiring) camera whose gaze they do not return.

27. Irigaray, *Sharing the World*, p. 32.

28. For Rosie's identification with Marian mythology and her persistence in offsetting her expected 'divine' child against Titi, see Pauline Eaton, 'Rosie Carpe and the Virgin Mary: Modelling Modern Motherhood', in *Religion and Gender*, 6 (2016), 29–46.

29. Sarah Burnautzki's reading of Mme Lagrand's madness connects it to the history of slavery. See 'Le Motif de la folie dans *Rosie Carpe*: réminiscences de la littérature antillaise', in *Quand la folie parle: The Dialectic Effect of Madness in French Literature from the Nineteenth Century*, ed. by Gillian Ni Cheallaigh, Laura Jackson and Siobhàn McIlvanney (Newcastle upon Tyne: Cambridge Scholars Publishing, 2014), pp. 172–89.

30. Urinating as a regressive response to parentally-generated fear recurs in other adult protagonists, for instance Norah in *Trois femmes puissantes* (*TFP* 65–66; 87). As Jérusalem notes more generally of primal fluids in NDiaye, 'Urine, bon et mauvais sang, forment [...] le liquide amniotique de l'œuvre de Marie NDiaye' [Urine, good and bad blood, form [...] the amniotic fluid of Marie NDiaye's work], 'Des larmes de sang au sang épuisé dans l'œuvre de Marie NDiaye (*hoc est enim corpus meum*)', p. 85.

31. Irigaray, *Sharing the World*, p. 12.
32. In conjunction with the womb the beating heart takes on, as we have already seen in this chapter with both Rosie and Lagrand, a further resonance as the familiar sound that the infant hears in uterine space.
33. And perhaps notably the city of Bordeaux, a favourite French setting for NDiaye, whose hidden historic link to the transatlantic slave trade 'hovers over the lives of its inhabitants like a phantom' (Asibong, *Marie NDiaye: Blankness and Recognition*, p. 94).
34. In an early interview NDiaye observed that vampirism was the central motif in her work. See Catherine Argand, 'Entretien: Marie NDiaye', *Lire*, April 2001, p. 6. On the vampiric 'feeding' of what he refers to as 'convex' protagonists on 'concave' ones, see Christoph Meurée, 'Au diable le sujet: le concave et le convexe dans le théâtre de Marie NDiaye', in *Marie NDiaye: l'étrangeté à l'œuvre*, ed. by Asibong and Jordan, pp. 119–36. Meurée's comments are not confined to mothers, but the figure of the life-sapping mother is the most troubling iteration of the 'convex'.
35. Thus NDiaye opens the inner body of both Nadia and Ange to public scrutiny for signs of an infection or abnormality that seems obscurely to allude to an inner core of inhospitality within French society at large. See Chapter 3 for Ange's wound.
36. It is important to stress that NDiaye is not *reducing* woman to her womb; instead her insistence on the womb as trope makes available a way of thinking about an ideal of hospitality in embodied, proximate form.
37. See my 'Fantastic Spaces in Marie NDiaye'.
38. One thinks perhaps of accounts of terminations in Annie Ernaux's *L'Événement* (2000) or Lorette Nobécourt's *La Conversation* (1998).
39. Fouque, *Génésique*, p. 38.
40. Rye, *Narratives of Mothering*, p. 74.
41. This '"faecal animal" [...] is bigger than normal, with a stubby tail, acts strangely, and lives unusually close to people as though somewhat domestic', Shepard, *The Others*, p. 72.
42. On the NDiayean spectrum of racial disavowal, Nadia sits somewhere between Fanny (*En famille*) whose denial of her ethnic origin is absolute, and Malinka/Clarisse (*Ladivine*) who is openly motivated by her desire to be unlike her (black) mother. *Mon cœur à l'étroit* is also a repeat, in miniature, of the pattern within NDiaye's œuvre as a whole, which moves from sublimation to overt expression of racist inhospitality.
43. See Chapter 1 note 20.
44. See Chapter 5.
45. Rye, *Narratives of Mothering*, p. 74.

CHAPTER 5

Author, Market, Reader

Ce bouquet de chardons [...] à qui vas-tu l'offrir? (GP 21)
[To whom will you offer [...] this bouquet of thistles?]

It might be argued that we host authors and they host us. One of NDiaye's hospitality scenes stands out for its attentiveness to the relationships that are negotiated not in, but around, stories. When Ladivine junior and her family take a vacation in an unnamed African destination, they are invited to share a simple family meal in the home of strangers (*L* 240–54). In response to an old woman's question about a lavish wedding and her mistaken assumption that Ladivine had attended it, the latter embroiders an account full of intricate detail from the number of fish courses to the bride's flowers. Here NDiaye recalls the classic function of the traveller's story as part exchange for food or shelter. That Ladivine allows her account to pass as factual seems of little importance to her; as an offering it is as sincere as it is vibrant and it responds to the old woman's request as surely as the lamb and sweet potato respond to her own hunger. As she warms to her role, the whole table becomes privy to her narrative flight, which is caught up in local politics in ways she could not have anticipated. Her host, angry about the dubious origin of the money that funded the wedding, takes offence, the atmosphere turns 'soudain inhospitalière' [suddenly inhospitable] and the family is turned out in the street 'comme des chiens' [like dogs] (*L* 253).

Underscored here are the pleasures and responsibilities of narration, the listener's sense of investment in both tale and author, the difficult snagging of stories between truth and fiction and the fragility of the conditions of reception. In this small incident NDiaye alludes to an oral tradition which makes manifest the social relations inherent in storytelling. Caught up in a differently complex, market-driven system of producing written stories for a mass audience via corporate intermediaries who have their own agenda, the author nonetheless finds herself entangled within competing imperatives in ways that recall Ladivine's experience, especially as regards the politicization of her fiction and a marked desire to position the teller vis-à-vis her tales.

In this chapter I apply ideas of hospitality to the construction of the author and the activity of reading. The first part analyzes the reception of the author in France. To explore the terms on which her writerly persona has been negotiated is to trace what amounts to a richly complex narrative of 'hostipitality', one which takes shape via both textual and paratextual material and which reveals the often unspoken values underpinning the French literary establishment's effusive endorsement of the author. The second part focuses on NDiaye's invitations to hospitable reading.

Constructing the Author

From the outset, NDiaye has been constructed as both 'foreign' and 'French'. While critics frequently analyzed her early writings without reference to racialized otherness — perhaps astonishingly when one considers the reading of race to which *En famille* implicitly but insistently invites us — it is also true that her books were erroneously shelved in the Francophone section of the major bookshop Fnac on the grounds of her name alone and that there were attempts to align the fantastical elements of her texts with African tradition.[1] In short, '[n]otre sorcière bien aimée' [our beloved witch], as she was referred to on the publication of *La Sorcière*, brought with her a whiff of alterity.[2] At the same time NDiaye's stories afforded the kind of universal relevance associated with the best in French literature and her staple settings and protagonists were un-exotic, mundanely French and rooted in the quotidian goings on of small-town or suburban life. Furthermore, the singular Frenchness of NDiaye's classically polished literary style was indisputable. Lydie Moudileno argues persuasively that the author's prodigious accomplishment in this regard constituted a bid for belonging within the French canon on her own chosen terms, terms that pointed away determinedly from the question of race.[3]

This authorial self-positioning was supported by the disappearing act of the embodied writer and NDiaye became notorious for self-effacement. The strategies of silencing, erasure and blurring that characterize the working out of race in her texts, cannily replicating (or parodying) French Republican egalitarian pretentions, were perpetuated by her inscrutability in interviews and her keenness to elude attempts to align her with any identity categories. In 2007 she affirmed 'Je ne me vois ni comme une femme qui écrit ni comme une femme noire qui écrit' [I see myself neither as a woman writer nor as a black woman writer] and concluded in a perplexing bid for her person to be overlooked, 'en fait, je ne me vois pas' [in fact I don't see myself].[4] This willed invisibility and determination to be, as Danielle Deltel puts it, 'Ni Noire ni Blanche' was well-served by the house style of her chosen publishers:[5] no photograph of the author figured on dust jackets; instead the plain white covers of prestigious Les Éditions de Minuit, then from 2007 the clotted-cream of Gallimard's Collection Blanche, gave nothing away.[6] Any attempts to give an autobiographical gloss to the anxiety resulting from racial difference which threads through her work, or even to discuss it openly were, then, headed off at the pass. The author clearly could not be aligned with contemporaries such as Calixthe Beyala or Marima Bâ given that, as Nicki Hitchcott observed in 2000, 'her fiction is not recognizable as that of an African author', having 'neither African context nor African characters'.[7]

To critics seeking to pigeon-hole her as African, NDiaye was swift in her rebuttal: raised and educated solely in France she was, she declared, not to be considered 'a Francophone novelist, that is a French-speaking foreigner' but rather a French writer.[8] Further, as she remarked in one notably acerbic riposte, she was so 'superficiellement africaine' [superficially African] as not to qualify under the meaning of the act.[9] Indeed she insisted that the white French filmmaker Claire Denis, with whom she wrote the screenplay for the 2009 film *White Material* and who spent her childhood in West Africa, was more authentically African than NDiaye herself could ever be.[10] There are some notable, and enjoyable, moments where NDiaye confronts within her fiction the frustrations resulting from critics' misplaced projections. To return briefly to *Un temps de saison*, one could add to the analysis of this book given in Chapter 1 a further level of interpretation: NDiaye's heavy-handed insistence on the characteristics of a provincial France in which she herself is culturally saturated, her mischievous decision to make this familiar environment anthropologically strange and to have it investigated by research methods associated with colonial arrogance, serve to some degree to parody the often wilful othering of a writer conscious only of being unequivocally French. The author's critical engagement with what Graham Huggan refers to as 'Western anthropological metaphors and myths' as well as her cannily exoticized version of Normandy may be read precisely as an early rejoinder to critics who sought to elaborate an exoticized (African) version of the author and her work.[11] Reading *Un temps de saison* in this way also releases a further perspective on Herman the teacher protagonist, for we might interpret his trajectory as that of an overly self-assured (Parisian) critic wrong-footed by a world upon which he projects, inhospitably, too simple an interpretation and is brought to challenge certain of his 'paresseuse[s] hypothèse[s]' [lazy hypotheses] (*UTS* 26).

Further ways in which NDiaye has resisted straightforward packaging include the manipulation of her patronym and her excitingly bewildering exercise in self-portraiture, *Autoportrait en vert*. I have already mentioned NDiaye's interest in the potency of names. In changing her own Senegalese patronymic name from N'diaye — an accepted orthography in French terms — to NDiaye, a less 'digestible' name, she sets herself apart while making an ironic nod to colonial orthography. The apostrophe in N'diaye represents a French solution to the difficult co-sounding of two consonants, producing a (non-authentic) pronunciation beginning with 'en-' and symbolically injecting a breach or division into what once was whole. In eliminating the apostrophe NDiaye re-appropriates the name with a gesture that at once recalls and rejects colonial manipulation.[12] Her determination to dictate the terms on which we may know her is no less palpable in her response to the commission for a contribution to Mercure de France's *Traits et portraits* series, a series inviting authors to produce text-image combinations which reveal their 'face cachée, pudique' [hidden, private face].[13] The resulting phototext, *Autoportrait en vert*, shows NDiaye putting the brief to elusive purposes, playing autofictional cat and mouse with readers hungry for knowledge of her innermost life and evading the 'dual processes of commodification and surveillance' that Graham Huggan associates with the 'cult of authenticity' in ethnic autobiography.[14]

Critics have been fascinated by this unyielding self-portrait. Noelle Giguere sees it as driven by a sharp awareness of 'the risks of self-definition';[15] for Asibong it rehearses some 'skilful subversions and manipulations of racialized representation (and occlusion)';[16] while Daisy Connon reads it, enticingly, as an exercise in 'self-hospitality' attained through problematizing 'textual domestication'.[17] My own argument is that *Autoportrait en vert* very determinedly steers us away from the writer as private individual and towards a portrait of the writer *as* writer.[18] While a number of verifiable biographemes are teasingly offered up, including the location of NDiaye's home, her marriage to author Jean-Yves Cendrey, her experience of mothering young children, and her strained relationship with her distant Senegalese father, these details are repeatedly submerged by something far more intriguing as a mutating cast of 'femmes en vert' [women in green] and 'femmes vertes' [green women] (women 'of colour', ironically enough) unsettles our focus and supplants the narrator as the centre of interest. They, like her, are ungraspable: 'à la fois êtres réels et figures littéraires' [at one and the same time real beings and literary tropes] (*AV* 88). To compound the slipperiness of the work, the photographs dispersed enigmatically through it are in no way documentary evidence of NDiaye's life, but fantastical spurs to our engagement with the much broader appeal of her textual world.[19] At a time, then, when life-writing of all stripes is being written, read and analyzed at full throttle, NDiaye uses *Autoportrait en vert* as a further opportunity to resist the commodification of her life and to have readers conceive of her simply as 'un écrivain face à sa propre identité d'écrivain, et à sa tentative d'universalisation de l'écriture' [a writer contemplating her own identity as a writer and her attempt to universalize writing].[20]

The most remarkable staging post in the ongoing struggle around the articulation of NDiaye's racial identity came in 2009 when she was awarded the Prix Goncourt, France's most prestigious literary prize, for *Trois femmes puissantes*. The establishment's ambivalent embrace now took on a highly — and overtly — politicized dimension with what Dominic Thomas refers to as the 'Marie NDiaye affair', a media storm whipped up after the award was announced.[21] The author and her novel were caught up in a whirlwind of Africanization which NDiaye herself seemed unusually prepared to probe and accept, while the marketing hype itself prompted a flurry of academic analyses.[22] Indeed Asibong suggests that the Goncourt-winning novel might in the long term be 'considered as more noteworthy for what it reveals about French society and its racializing spectacle a decade into the new millennium' than about the text qua text.[23] While such a comment undersells what is a complex and fascinating work, it does indicate the perceived political stakes of the debate. Accordingly, I turn now to examine the climate in which *Trois femmes puissantes* appeared, the reception of the prize-winning work and the often inhospitable controversies that coalesced around both book and author.

The Goncourt Moment

The literary press was in agreement: *Trois femmes puissantes*, a novel comprising three interlinked stories set in contemporary times and concerning individuals whose troubled lives straddle Africa and Europe, allowed NDiaye to be discussed and marketed in overtly postcolonial terms. Not only was the work exquisitely representative of her talents, it melded her staple matter of disturbing family and community relations with an overt focus on Africa, postcolonial violence and global migration. With the wind of the Goncourt machine and the promotional might of the Gallimard publishing house in its sails, this book sealed NDiaye's domestic and international reputation and re-articulated the terms of her reception. One reading of the award is that the French literary establishment waited for NDiaye to accommodate the postcolonial Republic's barely concealed desire for her to be Other before finally canonizing her. The author's uncharacteristic readiness to speak of Africa and her apparent willingness to lend herself to the camera for a clutch of glamorous photographs suggested her consent to the process and to her new status as, in the words of Asibong, 'a brown-skinned poster girl for difference and diversity'.[24] I shall return to these arguments.

It is important first to understand two debates that formed the backdrop to and inflected NDiaye's canonization. One was generated by the 'Pour une littérature-monde en français' [Towards a World-Literature in French] manifesto, launched in 2007, which spoke of a new era of intercultural influence and the erasure of any residue of colonial-era hierarchies in the literary field.[25] The other was the 'Grand débat sur l'identité nationale' [Big debate on national identity] concerning what it meant to be French in a globalizing world at the beginning of the twenty-first century and launched by the Minister of Immigration, Integration, National Identity and Mutually-Supportive Development, Éric Besson, on the very same day in November 2009 that NDiaye was awarded the Goncourt prize. The identity debate, tacitly predicated on a white, Europe-centred sense of Frenchness, inevitably provoked a great deal of unrest and insecurity. The two debates converged with the widely reported, indignant comments about NDiaye made by Éric Raoult, Mayor of Raincy and UMP deputy for the department of Seine-Saint-Denis to the north of Paris. Raoult referred back to an interview with NDiaye published three months earlier in the cult magazine *Les Inrockuptibles*, in which the author characterized the France of President Nicolas Sarkozy as monstrous, castigated his policies for their impact on ethnic minorities and *sans papiers* [illegal immigrants], and denounced the newly created Ministry of Immigration, Integration, National Identity and Mutually-Supported Development as a flimsily disguised opportunity for the promotion of increasingly hard-line racial intolerance.[26] The scandalized (pro-Sarkozy) Raoult accused NDiaye of biting the hand that fed her and even proposed that a 'devoir de réserve' [duty of professional discretion] be a condition of winning the Prix Goncourt. NDiaye was constructed, then, as an ungrateful guest who had insulted the hospitality of her hosts.

In a session devoted to the national identity debate in the National Assembly on 8 December 2009, Besson made a number of claims about identity including, alarmingly, that there was a 'hiérarchie entre les appartenances' [hierarchy of belonging], in essence one of the issues explored in NDiaye's book as protagonists attempt to situate themselves vis-à-vis France, and clearly the issue lying behind Raoult's attack on the author.[27] The spat with NDiaye was provoked by Raoult precisely in order to launch and to raise the temperature of this invidious debate. As Dominic Thomas observes in his detailed account of the affair, the moment the attribution of the Goncourt prize was announced there ensued 'a furore that showed [NDiaye] to be trapped in a web of identity politics which, in the optic of the ["world-literature"] manifesto, had supposedly been consigned to the trash can of history'.[28] Thomas also contends persuasively that this politico-literary spat implicitly casts Marie NDiaye as a 'latter-day évoluée', a claim with potent repercussions in terms of hospitality and its conditions.[29] The term évoluée, formulated by French colonial authorities, belonged to a system of categorizing colonized subjects according to perceived degrees of Frenchness and designated those who, while not considered truly French, were nonetheless distinct from indigènes thanks to their 'exposure to colonial educational and assimilationist mechanisms' and their internalization of French cultural and social norms.[30] As Thomas points out, Raoult was effectively re-activating the validity of this offensive hierarchy and casting NDiaye not only as not-quite-French but as all the more indebted to French generosity given her tenuous belonging. Thomas notes NDiaye's dignified struggle against being labelled peripheral and Raoult's emphatic casting of her as such, as well as his insistence that she should be stripped of her (very French) award 'for not having learned the "assimilation" lesson'.[31] This rather ugly narrative echoes aspects of NDiaye's play Rien d'humain in which the apparently admiring, solicitous and enabling French family that adopts a disadvantaged racially-marked protagonist is in reality made up of self-interested hosts who seek to admire their charge on their own terms, while enjoying the spectacle of their hospitality and the pleasures of serial abuse.[32]

Meanwhile the media made much of the idea of strong black women, marketing NDiaye's book via the three African protagonists — Norah, Fantah and Khady — who give it its title, although without problematizing the nature of their strength as the book clearly requires. The motif is taken up again in 2010 in a special dossier of Le Magazine littéraire, which confirms NDiaye's canonization by picturing her on the front cover beside Mme de Lafayette and Françoise Sagan, all designated as 'femmes puissantes',[33] promotional material which for Asibong purveys 'the ultimate liberal fantasy of a "strong black woman" winning out against the odds'.[34] Asibong goes on to draw a connection between the heroine of the final story in Trois femmes puissantes, Khady Demba, stuck on a stinking mattress as a sex worker in a desert settlement and the Goncourt-winning novel, which he regards as possessed, violated and prostituted by 'a cliché-ridden, neo-colonialist discourse'.[35] If such attacks on the book's politically oversimplified marketing as 'African' have some validity it is my contention that the criticisms of NDiaye's attempts to approach Africa with greater directness in her writing do not.

Inhospitable Criticism

The paratextual feeding frenzy around *Trois femmes puissantes* ran on in academia via a clutch of powerfully articulated critiques fuelled by a deep sense of investment in NDiaye's exploration of race and by indignation at the perceived blind spots not only of the literary establishment but also of the author. NDiaye's explicit, if tentative treatment of Franco-African relations, and her 'collusion' in her Africanization were seen as cynical marketing strategies pandering to what Huggan has called 'the alterity industry'.[36] If Moudileno applauds the author's 'mouvement vers des sujets, projets et personnages africains'[37] as well as a certain maturity in her growing preparedness to explore her own identity as Franco-African and, at the Goncourt moment, to welcome 'the postcolonial origin [...] back into her private and professional identity',[38] other critics are severe about the author's succumbing to 'the temptation of celebrity' on a Francophone ticket.[39] Burnautzki contends that NDiaye uses markers betokening African belonging as a bid to increase the appeal of her book in a market that is avid for (literary) expressions of multiculturalism and notes that in this sense the author 'profits' from her identity as *métisse* which is taken as a guarantor of authenticity of the African dimension of the work.[40] In addition, Burnautzki criticizes NDiaye for focusing on movement between France and Africa instead of tackling what she regards as a more challenging subject: the experiences of black people who have lived in France for generations.[41] Thomas charges NDiaye with ignorance of other writers of migration and, although he stops short of this accusation, wonders whether her work reproduces rather than challenges reductive and negative representations of Africa.[42] Meanwhile Asibong provides an extended and impassioned critique of what he calls NDiaye's 'Africanizing turn' as a market-driven fall from grace.[43]

For all its politically sticky unevenness however, NDiaye's attempt to approach Africa in *Trois femmes puissantes* surely deserves more sympathetic readings. Thomas notes the violence, despair and 'overwhelming range of negative representations and stereotypes' that predominate in her representation of African socio-cultural dynamics, but it is my view that the accusations levelled at her would have been fiercer still had she *not* represented the violence and despair experienced by her protagonists.[44] And we ought not to forget that NDiaye's French-based narratives too are overwhelmingly negative and equally riddled with violence and despair: what of the despair of the white, petit-bourgeois French man Rudy Descas, all but overlooked in this rash of criticism, who is also adrift, uprooted from Senegal and now desperate and out of place in his 'home' country? Overlooked too is the potential irony that shoots through the work's title, an irony that operates differently in English according to whether 'puissance' is translated as 'strength' or 'power' (in French both options are potentially in play).[45] There is an obvious fault line between the agency asserted in the book's title and the lives of these three women, such that the text unpicks the terms of its own packaging if we stay with the term 'power', although strength, residing in an unshakable sense of self even in the face of disempowerment and humiliation, is a different matter. NDiaye decides here to elaborate a new model of heroine: one who is not dogged by being self-consciously 'lesser than' or subject to the crippling confusion and self-doubt — even self-loathing — experienced by Fanny, Rosie, Nadia and later Malinka/Clarisse, but who remains clear-sighted and sure of her own identity and capabilities. She explains that she toyed with terms such as 'force intérieure' [inner strength] and much more curiously 'grâce' [grace] to characterize the special quality of these new, overtly African heroines,[46] the latter term so unexpected and, in the optic of the current study, so interestingly evocative of Derrida's recourse to ideas of grace and the gracious to refer to hospitality or forgiveness.[47] The terms and nature of the strength demonstrated by these women are, however, certainly neither clear nor 'uplifting' and none of them 'win[s] out' (Asibong's words) in any simple way.[48]

The reception of NDiaye is, then, caught up in the intractable identity maze created around her *métissage*. If, as Asibong comments, she has made a specialism of creating 'hybrid protagonists' who routinely '[absorb] the fantasies and projections of the white world in which they must move', she has also herself become such a figure: subject to the 'fantasies and projections' of readers and critics, she seems damned if she does and damned if she does not explore the African part of her heritage.[49] As far as her attempts to do so are concerned, I should like to contribute some further, perhaps more hospitable thoughts. We might now read the author's earlier declaration that in her case an 'origine africaine n'a pas vraiment de sens' [African origin really makes no sense] not as closing down but rather as opening up an avenue of investigation, since much of her writing patently seeks precisely to find a direction (one of the meanings of the French word *sens*) towards an Africa that remains only sketchily present for her and, particularly as she matures, to give it meaning.[50]

There is much in NDiaye that alludes to desires for connection to, yet uncertainty about, Africa. The novels that precede and follow *Trois femmes puissantes* both connect self-discovery and reconciliation with imagined African recovery or discovery, albeit in quiet or nebulous ways. *Mon cœur à l'étroit* concludes with Nadia's small song of welcome that sends shivers of pleasure through her grandchild Souhar and that is not only an inheritance from her North-African mother but specifically refers to the balafon, an African percussion instrument associated with the very performance of Africanness and the transferral of power (*MCE* 267). *Ladivine* includes a journey to Africa whose emotional texture is quite new in NDiaye. When Ladivine junior holidays in an unspecified part of the continent, this third-generation, mixed-race woman experiences self-recognition and a sense of home in a place that she has never previously visited or thought about. The package tour offers something she had not bargained for: a feeling of well-being and at-oneness; a desire to open intimately to her new environment; even a sense of déjà vu (she 'recognizes' the woman selling mango juice in the market, as well as the new taste of the juice itself) (*L* 156–58). In short, her trip is presented as a journey not of discovery but, uncannily, of recovery. It is in this imaginary Africa that the sole completely hospitable gift in NDiaye's entire corpus — a pair of sandals — is offered (*L* 305–06). It is also here that Ladivine undergoes a redemptive metamorphosis, following on from the positive shape-shifting that was a new development in NDiaye's fantastic imaginings in *Trois femmes puissantes*.[51] A third unexpected dimension lies in this book's untethering of Africa from the father: if previous journeys to the continent made by NDiaye's heroines are motivated by failed attempts to connect with the composite African father who repeatedly surges up in her work, the young Ladivine's African experience is entirely unhindered by this complication.

It is impossible to ascertain the degree of authorial projection in this imaginative leap towards Africa, or indeed to gauge whether NDiaye intends this depiction of an authentic 'embrace' between person and place to be read as slightly ironic or entirely straight. In *Trois femmes puissantes* Norah too is taken aback by an unexpected African connection: a blurry photograph supplied by her father appears to situate her in a house in Dakar which she protests she has never visited (*TFP* 78–79). This sensible professional woman nonetheless experiences a creeping sense of familiarity when she does eventually visit the place, so that her father's claim appears, proleptically, to have some substance. The indelible imprint of Africa in Marie NDiaye's family history, body and social persona has made it important for her not to recover some non-existent 'roots', and certainly not to put herself forward as a spokeswoman on account of some ready-made 'certificat d'authenticité "africaine"', but instead to reckon with ideas of Africa, to invite a relationship with and tentatively to find a direction towards it.[52] Rather, then, than read *Trois femmes puissantes* as NDiaye 'selling out', I prefer to explore the work and the impassioned debates that it generated as one episode in an ongoing, faltering process of the author's exploration of the terms of her Franco-Senegalese identity.

Thomas asks: 'at what point [...] does NDiaye stop being a French novelist and *become* an African one?'[53] I would argue that there is no such point; that NDiaye is neither an African writer, nor a writer of Africa, nor a writer who has effected an 'African turn', but instead that she sometimes writes *towards* Africa, quite legitimately exploring even from her early works an evolving sense of personal connection with, and an interest in, the continent whether this suits her critics or not. It is of the strangeness of both France and Africa, of being 'out of joint' in both places yet seeking to accommodate both, that Marie NDiaye's texts speak. The uneasy, violent variants of betweenness portrayed in *Trois femmes puissantes* are not out of line with experiences that are repeatedly explored in her writing and perhaps substantiate the claim made by Migraine-George that the post-Goncourt NDiaye has managed to forge for herself 'both a central and "other" space in the French literary and cultural landscape'.[54] One final point needs to be made: NDiaye's move to Berlin in 2007, her working of contemporary Germany into the fabric of her texts,[55] her configuration as Franco-German spokesperson,[56] her shortlisting for the Man Booker International Prize in 2013 and the increasing translation of her books into ever more languages are all indicative of her enmeshing in what Françoise Lionnet has called a 'becoming-transnational' of literature, suggesting that she will no longer be so dependent upon France but on a diverse set of circuits for her reception.[57] It will be fascinating to follow the terms of her future construction — her 'welcome' — in this regard.

Hospitable Reading

In their introduction to a study concerning accounts of hospitality, Lise Gauvin and Pierre L'Hérault contend that 'l'acte meme d'écrire [...] est d'abord et avant tout une demande d'hospitalité adressée au lecteur' [The very act of writing [...] is first and foremost a request for hospitality addressed to the reader].[58] Does it make sense to apply ideas of hospitality to the relationships in which readers become bound up as they navigate a text? If so, what kind of thinking about reading does such a perspective open up? And what can be gained in our appreciation of NDiaye's bitter and exacting tales by thinking about author-reader or reader-protagonist relationality in terms of thresholds and hosts, invitations and guests? Here I pursue the idea of hospitable reading and argue that NDiaye intends us to read for hospitality, and also to read hospitably. I begin by addressing issues of hospitality and reading in NDiaye more broadly, before providing some more personal thoughts on their application to one particular text, the second story of *Trois femmes puissantes*.

My first point is that NDiaye's writing is unusually testing. Participants in a round table discussion of *Ladivine* noted that reading the author's 'cold prose' is 'sometimes an unpleasant experience' or a 'taxing' one, 'by turns bracing and unpleasant'.[59] Not only does she depict situations of inhospitality, she situates readers in such a way as to challenge and test our own hospitable impulses. Take for example the way in which the icy accuracy of her depiction of the popular milieux of provincial France, a depiction which we might interpret as inhospitable or even cruel, entraps us into collusion with its implicit distaste. Critics who have commented on the distinctive experience of reading NDiaye frequently emphasize a kind of ethical cornering. Nora Cotille-Foley refers to NDiaye's subtle positioning of the reader, such that the issue of reader responsibility becomes live. Speaking of the unarticulated prejudices that are at work in *En famille*, she notes that the reader navigates this epic 'sous le joug du doute, de l'hésitation' [under the yoke of doubt and hesitation] and must, without the assistance of guidance or elucidation from an overarching consciousness, 'assumer la responsabilité de son interprétation et des préjugés qui la conditionnent' [accept responsibility for her/ his interpretation and the prejudices that influence it].[60] Similarly, referring to the depiction of traits pertaining to a nebulously depicted 'Africa' where Fanny visits her father, she observes that it is up to the reader to stand back and take stock of the stereotypes about the continent that the text re-hashes, and that the latter is plunged into 'le malaise d'une confrontation à son propre entendement' [the discomfort of a confrontation with his/her own understanding].[61] The point is not dissimilar to Joseph Hillis Miller's notion in his discussion of the ethics of reading of the 'irresistible demand' made by texts and the responsibility that readers must take for formulating their response.[62] In NDiaye's case the demand is heightened as the text slows us down and sucks us in, its often protracted sentences anatomizing complex textures of affect and tugging at our sleeve to stop us from racing ahead and reading for plot. In his psychoanalytic approach to NDiaye, Asibong too makes strong claims about a certain intensity of personal engagement experienced by her readers, suggesting somewhat programmatically that they '*must* actively insert themselves' in the 'zones of seeming affectlessness, absence and invisibility' (what I would consider zones of disavowal) of the author's work,[63] and that attending to these zones offers a possibility for growth, or even 'enlightenment'.[64]

Dominique Rabaté, the finest commentator on the particular experience of reading NDiaye, focuses on the author's call to empathy and her exercise of cruelty, both unusually heightened features of her work.[65] His analysis draws on a discourse of obligation, indicating what is demanded of us and what we are compelled to do by the force and subtlety of NDiaye's disquieting appeal. Thus 'l'œuvre de Marie NDiaye *exige* de nous [une] plongée dans le chaos des consciences qui cherchent à surnager dans le flot des affects violents qui s'emparent d'elles' [Marie NDiaye's work *demands* that we plunge into the chaos of consciences which are trying to keep afloat in the torrent of violent affects that seize them];[66] we must be ready not necessarily to understand — since we are seldom given the information to make this possible — nor even to like her protagonists, but to lend ourselves to them even in the absence of understanding; to have stirred in us a readiness to listen to 'la plainte d'autrui' [the other's complaint] which is, even if we would sooner not acknowledge it, not so removed from our own.[67] We are encouraged merely to open to the Other, the protagonist who is presented as and remains a stranger, and to 'tendre l'oreille' [lend an ear].[68] Significantly too Rabaté configures empathy via the terminology of hospitality: we do not simply read about NDiaye's protagonists, we are held on a threshold where the idea of welcoming them becomes live thanks to the author's very powerful ability to 'toucher en nous — jusqu'à ses limites — *notre capacité à accueillir l'autre*' [touch within us — to its very limits — *our capacity to welcome the other*].[69] Here Rabaté's analysis edges towards the idea of a special compassion; something that distinguishes this welcome from the relationship we may set up with other, perhaps more comprehensively portrayed and coherently developed literary protagonists — with a Jane Eyre or a Julien Sorel who are not depicted as in need of welcome in the same manner and who gratify us in more habitual ways. It is not so much NDiaye's protagonists as fully rounded characters with whom we engage, but the dark psychic spaces and ethical challenges which they make palpable and for which they are vehicles.

Turning to the idea of narrative cruelty, Rabaté notes that not only are readers spared little (we flinch as we read), but that the author's impassive, deadpan style, the 'neutralité narrative' [narrative neutrality] and 'froideur quasi cynique' [almost cynical coldness] with which she depicts monstrous thoughts and acts (without furthermore subjecting them to critique) seems in itself a kind of cruelty and an odd companion to the call to empathy which her writing, and the extremity of her protagonists' suffering, also issue.[70] If this combination constitutes a kind of realism, a lucid reproduction of 'les mécanismes déréglés de notre monde actuel' [the malfunctioning mechanisms of today's world], it also makes our position as readers distinctively uncomfortable, for NDiaye's cold detachment seems to cut across and interfere with her call for empathic involvement.[71]

This book has raised further ideas about how NDiaye alludes to or directs our reading. In Chapter 3 I explored the trope of a running sore or open wound as metaphor for her fictional world, and imagined as readers those who gathered in the sickroom, driven by compulsion and disgust to contend with the 'negative glamour' of this noxious hole.[72] In Chapter 4 I noted NDiaye's insistence on drawing readers into close physical proximity with protagonists, arguing that she nudges us towards a physical empathy, encouraging a solicitous, even maternal gaze and care. We might extend the point about maternal care by noting that the shadowy residue of children's *contes* [tales] is a recurring feature of NDiaye's writing for adults, providing a reading model that she manipulates with extraordinary subtlety and to great effect. The *conte* welcomes children into some of the ethical complexities of the adult world, yet makes them navigable and (relatively) safe. When written for adults, without ethical resolution or safety net, the *conte* becomes uncannily horrific, one of NDiaye's ways of stressing how a child-like sense of vulnerability remains active in adults, as well as a latent reminder of how children are in reality betrayed and damaged by the adult world. Memories of being read to, of the hospitality of adults — often parents — protecting and educating by reading, and of the secure environment and knowledge furnished by sharing a safely formulaic text, only compound the inhospitality of the adult tales which we approach with the assistance of no warm intermediary, but with only the detachment of an apparently indifferent narrative voice.

The above observations mark out issues of hospitality and reading in NDiaye as very different indeed from, for instance, those outlined by Rosello in the works she analyzes in *Postcolonial Hospitality*. In the Introduction I referred to two complex incidents of failed hospitality across cultures analyzed by Rosello: the authors' refusal to take tea with Madame Zineb in François Maspero and Anaik Frantz's *Les Passagers du Roissy Express* (1990), and in Yamina Benguigui's collection of interviews, *Mémoires d'immigrés* (1997), the rejection of a plate of cakes baked for Eid and offered by two girls to their non-Muslim neighbours.[73] In her discussion of these incidents, Rosello argues that the text and film themselves take on the role of host, resolving the cross-cultural misunderstandings that they explore and offering a new, hospitable space propitious to mutual understanding and welcome. Thus *Les Passagers du Roissy Express* 'welcomes Madame Zineb into [its] multifaceted history of the Paris *banlieue*, where she becomes an important character',[74] while *Mémoires d'immigrés* 'magnifies the private ceremony between the two little girls and makes it public, shareable by a new community of readers who belong to different ethnic and religious groups'.[75] Not merely literature, but 'gesture[s] of reconciliation', these texts translate unfamiliar cultural practices for the reader and 'function like a new gift, a new invitation [...] open[ing] a door between two communities that cannot easily talk to each other'.[76] By contrast, situations of botched hospitality in NDiaye are not bridged, 'broken goodwill' is not resolved and her work is not reparative in the way that Rosello outlines.[77] It rarely depicts cross-cultural misunderstandings of this order and does not seek to mediate or enhance the understanding of a given set of hospitality practices. It is not about hospitality as a particular set of recognizable rituals or laws, but as a universal proposition. As we have seen NDiaye prefers to render the codes of hospitality unfamiliar, even fantastic, and to detach them from, rather than root them in, a given culture. She offers no solution to the ills she depicts and if her inhospitable fictions are gifts, each in its own way is a 'bouquet of thistles': architecturally marvellous and surprisingly beautiful, but prickly, unpleasant, rough and dangerous to handle — at once gift and poison, we might say.

Nor can reading NDiaye be aligned with the kind of proximate appreciation that Still describes with reference to reading (and) hospitality in Derrida and to the particular intensity of affectionate relationship that this, for her, entails. Still asks: 'What is it [...] to be *formed* as a reader by a text — to be host and guest with respect to a text?'[78] The ideas generated by Derrida's hospitable writing that a text might 'welcome you in and give you sustenance, warmth and shelter' and that as reader you in turn might 'welcom[e] it reciprocally, without prejudice, into your heart' are markedly inapplicable to NDiaye's texts which, while they certainly stand in permanent relation to hospitality and are, I have argued, *about* hospitality (and its opposite), are not in themselves hospitable to readers.[79] Perhaps in fact we are NDiaye's hostages rather than her guests, for we are sucked into and worry over the text's unexplained dimensions, especially since we sense their relevance to us, and we cannot detach ourselves from the overwhelming suffering of her world.

Reading Rudy Descas

Here I use as a case study the story of forty-three-year-old Rudy Descas, which covers a day in the protagonist's life. What might it mean to read this narrative hospitably? Descas, a failed fitter of rustic kitchens and former teacher of medieval literature, is a humiliated and envious man with a propensity to anger. His story, the second of the three in *Trois femmes puissantes* (TFP 95–245), is complex in emotional scope and, like so much in NDiaye, it is underwritten with a corrosive postcolonial pre-history which festers in its folds. Propelled forward by Descas's anxiety, the narrative is bleak and wounding and it holds in store for us innumerable ethical tremors or shocks.

Through a third-person narrative which is entirely focalized via Descas, we accompany him on what is by any standards a dreadful day. We share his transitory thoughts, emotions and sensations as he drives around the Aquitaine region mulling over his misfortune, visits a dissatisfied client, breaks into the home of the sculptor Gauquelan (creator of a public statue whose perceived resemblance to him infuriates and humiliates Descas) and — the still point of the story's turning world — stands over the man contemplating murder before stealing away to pick up his small son Djibril from school. As these events unfurl, Descas struggles against three interrelated flashbacks connected to a previous life in Senegal: the murder by his father Abel Descas of his friend and right-hand man Salif in Dara Salam (the most deeply buried memory); his own attack years later on one of his pupils — a boy from Dara Salam who refers to him as 'Fils d'assassin' [Son of a murderer] (TFP 179) — resulting in the loss of his career and his return to France; and his odiously racist, knee-jerk injunction that very morning to his Senegalese wife Fanta, 'Tu peux retourner d'où tu viens' [You can go back to where you came from] (TFP 106).

NDiaye's story is densely constellated with vignettes and scenarios wherein hospitality between protagonists is at stake, situations into which we project ourselves and which continuously prompt an ethical reading. Descas's interactions with his wife, son and mother, with his boss, colleagues, clients and neighbour, as well as with strangers, are all invitations to us, however apparently anodyne and fleeting, to read for hospitality and to take a stance. Systemic inhospitality is on occasion quite obviously in evidence — for instance where we are confronted with the racist assumptions of Descas's mother about the incapacity of the Senegalese for friendship, fidelity or love: 'L'amitié, ça n'existe pas là-bas [...] Même l'amour, ça n'existe pas là-bas' [Friendship doesn't exist over there [...] Even love doesn't exist over there] (TFP 243). Typically however, the protagonist draws us into more subtle thoughts and enactments that teeter on the cusp of hospitality. Descas's apprehension of and engagement with other people are rendered in terms that evoke Levinas's idea of the call to interpersonal ethics as experienced through face, the acute sense of another's singular presence as we take account of them even in the most ordinary everyday interactions. This is forcefully conveyed by NDiaye. The Other surges into Descas's consciousness through intimate sensory detail: the smell of coffee on his boss's breath; the overpowering pinkness of his colleague's clothes; the bubble of saliva forming on the lips of the sleeping Gauquelan; or the soiling hands of the shopkeeper which touch indiscriminately bread, ham and money as she prepares him a sandwich. Almost invariably, the protagonist gives way to irritation, distaste or disgust. In other words, he fails the challenge to hospitality of these everyday micro encounters while we in turn assess his failure. The real challenge that NDiaye has set for us as 'hospitable readers', however, is whether we can be hospitable to Rudy Descas himself.

NDiaye ensures that we stick close to Descas. Our experience of him is immersive, if not suffocating. Within seconds we are gripped by him and sucked into the dense complexity of his singular consciousness, a consciousness that is struggling to self-welcome and torn between self-loathing and self-exoneration. His shameful rumination, while it is neither self-consciously focused nor perspicacious enough to constitute a confession, is nonetheless a trial of sorts — 'son propre tribune intérieur' [his own inner discussion forum] (TFP 96) — and we are called upon as if to a hearing.[80] In other words, Descas makes ethical demands on us from the outset. Reeling from his comment to Fanta, stricken with terror that she may in fact leave him, the protagonist asks himself how he has become this unthinkable person and how he might get others, including Fanta, to love him again. The question of whether he can indeed be loved or liked is asked on the first page and is clearly intended to engage the reader immediately in a challenge: can I, in spite of everything (I don't know all the details yet but have a bad feeling), open to Rudy Descas? I certainly cannot validate the positive self-image he struggles to hold on to as he takes the temperature of his self-worth, asking, for instance, 'n'était-il pas, en un sens, à présent plus digne d'être aimé que ce matin-là seulement?' [was he not, in a sense, now worthier of being loved than he had been only that morning?] (TFP 220), or returns over and over to his name like a mantra in order to test in imagination the degree of hospitality that others are able to extend to him. In Chapter 1, I noted that repeated naming keeps us locked into a relationship and even a sense of responsibility with regard to certain protagonists. Descas's story is a key instance of this. The subtle modulations of his self-naming (by turns 'Rudy', 'Rudy Descas', or 'Descas'), aided by the supple vantage point provided by NDiaye's free indirect discourse, conveys a kaleidoscopic range of more or less welcoming 'takes' on the self, as the protagonist struggles to hold himself to account and tests his name against the person he has become and the person he intended to be. Descas's repeated name calls him to trial and also calls me — if I can muster it — to empathy.

Much is, of course, stacked against my empathy: even as she asks me to project myself into the intimacy of this suffering subject, NDiaye withdraws the conditions for empathy, or at least makes it tricky to achieve. She creates in Descas an unpalatable protagonist, seeing to it that he is both prone to and beset by a humiliation that enrages him. She devises trials that emasculate and belittle him, compounding his awareness of material and emotional failure, stoking his sense of victimhood and thus making it all the more likely that he will give in to his violent impulses. She has him cuckolded by Manille, his boss. She makes him cruelly bewildered by the contrast between the possessions of others and his own lack of material success, a sense of failure that is underscored by his being a loser in a globalizing, liberal economy: Americans or Australians now own the small local château he once coveted; the gypsies in a nearby camp have mobile telephones while he has none; and his clapped-out Nevada, stigma of his social failure, contrasts starkly with the sleek vehicles of his colleagues. Further, NDiaye ensures that Descas's body is mired in discomfort. He not only suffers from the intolerable heat of the day, but is visited with the maddening itch of haemorrhoids, giving rise to further humiliation. This affliction, along with the fantastical buzzard which attacks Descas in the second part of the narrative — a further device sent by NDiaye to plague her protagonist in this punishing story — tests my compassion, leaving me suspended between a temptation to laughter and something more hospitable which may be pity.

I cannot like Descas, this disturbing 'arrivant' (to use Derrida's term) offered to me by NDiaye; I find it hard to be hospitable to him.[81] His propensity to violence against the weak, which keeps company with a propensity to self-pity and sentimentality, horrifies me. He fits the mould, in fact, of a self-pitying bully. I am involved intensely with him, but do not wish to identify with him. I am conflicted and disturbed, attracted and repulsed. I read Descas with distaste and a certain detachment that confirms to me that I do not bully the weak and am better than he (I cannot answer for how he might be read by readers who are themselves violent, sentimental bullies). But I am at the same time aware that the text asks me to do him justice and to avoid my own knee-jerk reactions. And although I cannot like Descas, I am in some ways like him. I can identify with some of his traits. His struggle between lucid self-criticism and wholesale self-exoneration is perhaps not as strange to me as I would like to think. His deep insecurities, his rehearsing of different versions of the self in search of one with which he can identify, his massaging of reality to make it more comfortable, his neediness and fear, the agonies of incommunicability that he shares with others of NDiaye's protagonists (rivalled only perhaps in the fiction of Nathalie Sarraute) are all to some degree uncomfortably familiar and keep me close to him.

There are micro epiphanies in Descas's story, transitory acts of thinking beyond the self which redeem him a little in my eyes. One of the greatest challenges held out to him, and perhaps the greatest opportunity in ethical terms, is located in his relationship with his little boy Djibril. We have seen that the ethical charge of NDiaye's writing is frequently generated by adult/child relationships and here some of the most important questions Descas asks himself are related to fatherly love and to the problem of how to father. Early on in the story Decas instrumentalizes the boy, using him as a pawn to prevent Fanta from leaving. When he takes the unusual step of picking Djibril up from school, it becomes clear that father and son are afraid of each other, but the small beginning of a more ethically-driven opening to the world takes place in a moment when Descas inwardly welcomes Djibril as an independent being with an inner life as complex as his own. Advances in the shifting father/son relationship are conveyed powerfully through touch, gesture and bodily reaction. If Djibril is physically wary of his father, it may be in part that the little boy intuits the shame that his father experienced as he acknowledged inwardly that the intense physical pleasure he felt as he half-strangled the boy from Dara Salam was in fact shot through with thoughts of his then two-year-old son's tender body. Towards the end of the story a sudden impulse of the couple to touch each other unleashes a quite different sense of wonder: 'Djibril laissa aller sa tête contre le ventre de son père et Rudy fouilla de ses doigts les cheveux bouclés et soyeux, tâtant le crâne bien lisse, parfait, miraculeux' [Djibril let his head drop against his father's tummy and Rudy ran his fingers through the curly, silky hair, feeling the smooth, perfect, miraculous skull] (*TFP* 235). The brief description falls like a revelation, producing in my reading a breath-taking moment of grace — something that in another fictional universe might be commonplace — wherein father and son welcome each other in reciprocal trust.

Can I say that keeping company with Rudy Descas, sharing his day of acid purgatory and allowing my intimacy to be breached by him, has a real impact on me in ethical terms? Is this simply too much to ask from a story? On the question of literature's active presence in our lives, I note that NDiaye weaves into Descas's self-scrutiny a series of allusions to the thirteenth-century trouvère Rutebeuf, the former teacher's specialist author whose *Complainte de Rutebeuf* details a series of (self-induced) misfortunes that have reduced him to abject destitution. The intertext determines much of what NDiaye sets out for Descas and also the way in which he sees himself. It would not be too great a stretch of the imagination to see this entire narrative as a satirical, postcolonial re-working of the tale, but my purpose here in noting the intertext is different. Descas turns to Rutebeuf intensively as implied interlocutor and touchstone for his own life, using the story — a reminder of his lost glory as a teacher — to stoke self-pity and identifying with the protagonist's rhetorical questions about his destitution and friendlessness.

NDiaye's use of the story cruelly cuts across Descas's self-indulgence and competes with his own recourse to it (for instance, she latches on to the ribald physicality of the tale, injecting something similar into Descas's story by focusing on the over-sized scrotum of Gauquelan's statue, or the inflated idea of Manille as a centaur covering Fanta), but the overriding point is that we do use literature actively to feel our way forward through the ethical challenges of our own lives, and we may host Descas for this purpose. And the fact is that I do think of Rudy Descas — and other of NDiaye's protagonists — very often indeed; they are vivid companions not merely in the walk of academic life, notably thanks to their vulnerabilities which I share and recognize. While all literature throws us back upon ourselves, NDiaye is particular in the persistence and depth of ethical searching that our keeping company with her protagonists engenders. In a study of how ethical issues are encountered and made live in and through the work of South-African writer J. M. Coetzee, Derek Attridge notes a powerful reciprocity: 'we perform them and they perform us, as we read'.[82] The same kind of process takes place, in renewed and somewhat different form each time I open to, and am tested by, the inhospitable fiction that is the story of Rudy Descas.

Conclusion

I have argued in this final chapter that it is profitable to consider two sets of relationships through the prism of hospitality: that between the author and the various institutions and individuals involved in her reception; and that between reader and text. I have shown how ideas of hospitality are pertinent to the construction of Marie NDiaye as an author and to her reception in France. I have also argued that NDiaye's writing engages the reader in distinctive ways, promoting intense involvement and an ethics of reading which is precisely related to the question of hospitality that this book has pursued. I have argued that NDiaye makes available the conditions for hospitable reading in a number of ways: by filling her texts with ethically aversive matter; by negative examples against which we test ourselves; by the absence of a meta-voice telling us what to believe or think (we are made alert and responsible); and by a surfeit of suffering and the incessant, if sometimes problematic, appeal to empathy that is thereby made, which takes us to a difficult meeting place 'aux limites de notre Moi' [at the limits of our Self].[83] And what emerges from our encounter is certainly the possibility of change. On the last of her visits to her grossly inhospitable father, the narrator of *Autoportrait en vert* muses 'à quoi bon venir et que rien ni personne n'en soit modifié?' [what's the point of coming if nothing and nobody is changed by it?] (*AV* 85). The same question might be asked of our reading, as we navigate the shocks of NDiaye's inhospitable fiction

Notes to Chapter 5

1. Lucie Clair, 'Écrire, quoi d'autre?', *Le Matricule des Anges*, 107 (2009), 20–24 (p. 22).
2. Jean-Baptiste Harang, 'Notre sorcière bien aimée', *Libération*, 12 February 2004, <http://remue.net/cont/NDiaye/html> [accessed 5 March 2016].
3. Moudileno, 'L'Excellent Français de Marie NDiaye', in *Marie NDiaye: l'étrangeté à l'œuvre*, ed. by Asibong and Jordan, pp. 25–38. On NDiaye's determination to be received as French see too Odile Cazenave, 'Marie NDiaye ou une aspiration à "l'universel"', in *Afrique sur Seine: une nouvelle génération de romanciers africains à Paris* (Paris: L'Harmattan, 2004), pp. 73–78. Significantly, Cazenave's study of NDiaye appears in the section of her book entitled 'Roman du détachement et refus de la communauté africaine' (pp. 41–77).
4. Asibong and Jordan, 'Rencontre avec Marie NDiaye', in *Marie NDiaye: l'étrangeté à l'œuvre*, pp. 187–99 (p. 199).
5. Danielle Deltel, 'Marie NDiaye: l'ambition de l'universel', *Notre librairie: Revue du livre: Afrique, Caraïbes, Océan Indien*, 118 (1994), 111–15 (p. 112). Deltel notes on the same page the reaction of black magazines which 's'étonnent que [NDiaye] taise sa négritude' [are astonished that [NDiaye] should conceal her negritude].
6. On the Minuit cover see Lydie Moudileno, 'Délits, détours et affabulation: l'écriture de l'anathème dans *En famille* de Marie NDiaye', *The French Review*, 71:3 (1998), 442–53 (p. 451). It is with the cheaper, more widely circulated pocket-sized editions of NDiaye's works that covers begin to tether texts to marketable 'meanings'.
7. Nicki Hitchcott, *Women Writers in Francophone Africa* (Oxford: Berg, 2000), p. 24.
8. Beverley Ormerod and Jean-Marie Volet, *Romancières africaines d'expression française: le sud du Sahara* (Paris: L'Harmattan, 1994), p. 111.
9. NDiaye, 'Lettre de Marie NDiaye à Jean-Marie Volet 2 January 1992', quoted by Lydie Moudileno in 'Marie NDiaye: entre visibilité et réserve', in *Une femme puissante*, ed. by Bengsch and Ruhe, pp. 159–76 (p. 164).
10. Kapriélian, 'Marie NDiaye aux prises avec le monde', p. 32.
11. Huggan, *The Postcolonial Exotic*, p. 40.
12. Thanks to Toby Garfitt for his helpful observations on this issue.
13. Tirthankar Chanda, 'L'Essentiel d'un livre: portrait de l'écrivain en vert', *MFI HEBDO* (April 2005), p. 1, <http://www.rfi.fr/Fichiers/Mfi/CultureSociete/1455.asp> [accessed 10 November 2007].
14. Huggan, 'Ethnic Autobiography and the Cult of Authenticity', in *The Postcolonial Exotic*, pp. 155–76 (p. 155).
15. Noelle Giguere, 'Strange and Terrible: Understanding the Risks of Self-Definition in Marie NDiaye's *Autoportrait en vert*', in *Women Taking Risks in Contemporary Autobiographical Narratives*, ed. by Anna Rocca and Kenneth Reeds (Newcastle upon Tyne: Cambridge Scholars Publishing, 2013), pp. 59–70.
16. Andrew Asibong, 'The Spectacle of Marie NDiaye's *Trois femmes puissantes*', *Australian Journal of French Studies*, 50 (2013), 385–98 (p. 390).
17. Connon, 'Marie NDiaye's Haunted House', p. 259.
18. Shirley Jordan, 'Marie NDiaye: énigmes photographiques, albums éclatés', in *Marie NDiaye: l'étrangeté à l'œuvre*, ed. by Asibong and Jordan, pp. 65–82.
19. On photographs in NDiaye see my 'Marie NDiaye: énigmes photographiques, albums éclatés'; and Nora Cotille Foley, 'Optique fantastique, traitement de la photographie et transgression des limites du visible chez Marie NDiaye', *Contemporary French and Francophone Studies*, 13 (2009), 547–54.
20. Deltel, 'Marie NDiaye: l'ambition de l'universel', p. 115.
21. Dominic Thomas, 'The "Marie NDiaye Affair", or the Coming of a Postcolonial *Évoluée*', in *Transnational French Studies: Postcolonialism and Littérature-Monde*, ed. by Alec Hargreaves, Charles Foresdick and David Murphy (Liverpool: Liverpool University Press, 2010), pp. 146–63.
22. In addition to Thomas, 'The "Marie NDiaye Affair"', and Asibong, 'The Spectacle of Marie NDiaye's *Trois femmes puissantes*', see Moudileno, 'Marie NDiaye, entre visibilité et réserve'; and Sarah Burnautzki, 'Jeux de visibilité et d'invisibilité: la production romanesque de Marie

NDiaye à la lumière de la crise du républicanisme français', in *Une femme puissante*, ed. by Bengsch and Ruhe, pp. 141–58.

23. Asibong, 'The Spectacle of Marie NDiaye's *Trois femmes puissantes*', p. 388.

24. Ibid.

25. *Le Monde des livres*, 16 March 2007, <http://www.etonnants-voyageurs.com/spip.php?article1574> [accessed 8 August 2016]. For critical appraisal of reactions, related debates and the ongoing configuration of world literature in French see Jacqueline Dutton, '*État present*: World Literature in French, *littérature-monde*, and the Translingual Turn', *French Studies*, 70 (2016), 404–18.

26. Kaprièlian, 'Marie NDiaye aux prises avec le monde'.

27. See Thomas, 'The "Marie NDiaye Affair"', p. 156.

28. Ibid., p. 146. See too Thérèse Migraine-George, 'A Case-Study in *Littérature-Monde*: The Marie NDiaye Controversy', in *From Francophonie to World Literature in French: Ethics, Poetics, and Politics* (Lincoln & London: University of Nebraska Press, 2013), pp. xii–xvi

29. Thomas, 'The "Marie NDiaye Affair"', p. 146.

30. Ibid.

31. Ibid., p. 156.

32. See Chapter 1 for an analysis of the play.

33. *Le Magazine littéraire*, September 2010. The cover-page headline read 'Les Romancières françaises, Madame de Lafayette, George Sand, Françoise Sagan, Marie NDiaye... Des femmes puissantes'.

34. Asibong, 'The Spectacle of Marie NDiaye's *Trois femmes puissantes*', p. 389.

35. Ibid.

36. Huggan, *The Postcolonial Exotic*, p. x.

37. Moudileno, 'L'Excellent Français de Marie NDiaye', p. 38.

38. Lydie Moudileno, 'Fame, Celebrity and the Conditions of Visibility of the Postcolonial Writer', *Yale French Studies*, 120 (2011), 62–74 (p. 72).

39. Ibid.

40. Burnautzki, 'Jeux de visibilité et d'invisibilité', p. 153.

41. Ibid., p. 154.

42. Thomas, 'The "Marie NDiaye Affair"', p. 153.

43. Asibong, 'The Spectacle of Marie NDiaye's *Trois femmes puissantes*', p. 395.

44. Thomas, 'The "Marie NDiaye Affair"', p. 154.

45. On the discomfort provoked by this title, see Moudileno, 'Puissance insolite de la femme africaine chez Marie NDiaye'.

46. See NDiaye's interview with Sylvain Bourmeau, 'Le Goncourt pour *Trois femmes puissantes* de Marie NDiaye', *Mediapart*, 2009, <http://www.mediapart.fr/journal/culture-idees/150709/avec-troi-femmes-puissantes-marie-ndiaye-domine-la-litterature-contemp> [accessed 7 June 2013].

47. Derrida speaks of hospitality 'gracieusement offerte au-delà de la dette et de l'économie' ('graciously offered beyond debt and economy') in Derrida and Dufourmantelle, *De l'hospitalité*, p. 77; *Of Hospitality*, p. 83.

48. Asibong, 'The Spectacle of Marie NDiaye's *Trois femmes puissantes*', pp. 383; 389.

49. Ibid., p. 397.

50. Kaprièlian, 'Marie NDiaye aux prises avec le monde', p. 32.

51. See Chapter 2 of this book.

52. Burnautzki, 'Jeux de visibilité et d'invisibilité', p. 153.

53. Thomas, 'The "Marie NDiaye Affair"', p.150.

54. Thérèse Migraine-George, 'Writing as Otherness: Marie NDiaye's Inalterable Humanity', in *From Francophonie to World Literature in French*, pp. 63–91 (p. 89).

55. In both *Ladivine* and the bi-lingual phototext *Y penser sans cesse*.

56. NDiaye was interviewed in this capacity in the radio programme *Comme on nous parle*, broadcast on France Inter on 22 January 2013, which celebrated Franco-German cooperation on the occasion of the fiftieth anniversary of the Traité de l'Elysée [the Elysée Treaty].

57. Françoise Lionnet, 'Introduction', in *Francophone Studies: New Landscapes*, ed. by Françoise Lionnet and Dominique Thomas, special issue of *Modern Language Notes*, 18 (2003), 783–86 (p. 784).

58. Lise Gauvin and Pierre L'Hérault, 'Introduction', in *Le Dire de l'hospitalité*, ed. by Gauvin, L'Hérault and Montandon, pp. 7–15 (p. 9).

59. Amy Gentry, Jeffrey Zuckerman and Aaron Bady, 'A Roundtable on Marie NDiaye's *Ladivine*', *The New Inquiry*, 30 May 2016, <http://thenewinquiry.com/features/spaces-where-identity-stutters-and-goes-silent-a-roundtable-on-maria-ndiayes-ladivine/> [accessed 10 August 2016].

60. Nora Cotille-Foley, 'Les Mots pour ne pas le dire: ou encore l'indicibilité d'une visibilité frottée de fantastique dans les œuvres de Marie NDiaye', in *Marie NDiaye: l'étrangeté à l'œuvre*, ed. by Asibong and Jordan, pp. 13–23 (p. 14).

61. Ibid., p. 18.

62. Joseph Hillis Miller, *The Ethics of Reading: Kant, De Man, Eliot, Trollope, James and Benjamin* (New York: Columbia University Press, 1987), p. 43.

63. Asibong, *Blankness and Recognition*, p. 169.

64. Ibid., p. 174.

65. See Dominque Rabaté, '"Qui peut l'entendre? / Qui peut savoir?"', in *Marie NDiaye* (Paris: Éditions Textuel, 2008), pp. 55–65, a study of the call to empathy in *Rosie Carpe*; and 'Exercice de la cruauté', in *Marie NDiaye's Worlds/Mondes de Marie NDiaye*, ed. by Mott and Moudileno, pp. 90–96.

66. Rabaté, '"Qui peut l'entendre?"', p. 64 (my emphasis).

67. Ibid.

68. Ibid., p. 65.

69. Ibid., p. 56 (my emphasis).

70. Rabaté, 'Exercice de la cruauté', p. 95.

71. Ibid., p. 96.

72. McGinn uses this term to refer to our response to disgusting stimuli, see *The Meaning of Disgust*, p. 48.

73. See Introduction, note 12.

74. Rosello, *Postcolonial Hospitality*, p. 81.

75. Ibid., pp. 81–82.

76. Ibid., p. 82.

77. Ibid., p. 67.

78. Still, *Derrida and Hospitality*, p. 51.

79. Ibid.

80. Descas's laborious journey towards a more honest self-appraisal resembles Nadia's coming to self-awareness in *Mon cœur à l'étroit*.

81. Derrida refers to the 'arrivant' throughout *De l'hospitalité*.

82. Derek Attridge, *J. M. Coetzee and the Ethics of Reading: Literature in the Event* (Chicago & London: University of Chicago Press, 2004), p. xii.

83. Rabaté, '"Qui peut l'entendre?"', p. 55.

AFTERWORD

In this book I have argued that NDiaye's fiction accumulates examples of behaviour that transgress hospitality's most basic requirements and that the performance of inhospitality in its broadest sense is the staple matter of her writing. I have shown some of the ways in which inhospitality takes shape in her texts, between the pure hospitality of theory and intricately embodied practice, and across the fault lines of race, class, gender and species. I have argued that her creation of a semi-fantastic realm which persistently draws our attention to often uncanny norms, practices and rites amounts to a fantastic anthropology of inhospitality. In discussing what it means to read NDiaye, I have suggested not only that we are repelled by the negative ethics of the author's world, but that her systematic depiction of inhospitality draws us to consider the density of appeals to, or opportunities for, hospitality in which her protagonists — and we — are enmeshed on a daily basis. In other words, to read her makes us alive to the Other's need. It is as if the author's determinedly negative display, her imagining of hospitality's impossibility, were in fact a gift of sorts.

The density of material in NDiaye relating to ideas and practices of hospitality is by no means exhaustively covered in this book: there are many other instances worth considering in the works I analyze, as in the works I do not touch upon. To take one unusual example, the short bilingual phototext *Y penser sans cesse* [To Think of it Ceaselessly], which is set in contemporary Berlin and which ambitiously overlays the author's habitual concerns of home, welcome, empathy and compassion with the problem of Holocaust memory, could be read most productively through the prism of hospitality. To trace the several levels on which this experimental work is conspicuously driven by an active sense of care for where the self ends and the other begins, to analyze the ways in which it hinges on the capacity for hospitality of a child, and to explore its opening both to photographs and to a second language (German) are pleasures, however, that I leave to other readers.[1]

I draw this book to a conclusion by homing in, as NDiaye so frequently encourages us to do, on the ethical charge of a single, small sign of vulnerability. It is a sign which appears as a quiet yet persistent leitmotif in *Trois femmes puissantes* and which stops protagonists in their tracks, producing suspended moments wherein the responsibility that individuals have for each other is deeply felt. The sign — an open hand resting on a lap, its soft palm uppermost — assumes special importance within a text that is especially attentive to hands, and within NDiaye's repertoire of hospitality gestures more broadly, not least because it is not in fact a deliberate gesture or conscious plea, as of a beggar or a busker, but one that simply happens while the subject is sleeping and is thus an invitation offered up by an entirely defenceless creature.

In the story of Khady Demba the up-turned hands of her inhospitable sisters-in-law 'dénonçaient soudain leur mort' [suddenly denoted their death] (*TFP* 257), since they evoke her dead husband's body, described earlier in the story as child-like, 'la main ouverte, paume en l'air, innocente, vulnérable' [hand open, palm in the air, innocent, vulnerable] (*TFP* 250). We note that Khady is receptive to a sense of their vulnerability, while they are not to hers. The story of Rudy Descas harbours a dreadful 'encounter' between Descas and the sleeping Gauquelan where, as we saw in Chapter 5, Descas the intruder stands over the sleeper and contemplates murder (*TFP* 203–09). The outcome is determined by Descas's attentiveness to Gauquelan's hands, 'paumes en l'air, dans une attitude de confiance, d'abandon' [palms upturned, in an attitude of confidence, self-abandonment] (*TFP* 203). At first the abyss between his own alertness and intentions and the sleeping man's 'confidence' (the word implies relationality and is an interesting choice) seems to him grotesque. He profits from his situation of power to imagine the sensations derived from thrusting a knife through the man's skin, muscle and fat to his heart. But a flashback to his father Abel slumbering in his chair evokes a layered memory of the latter's own potential vulnerability and of the anger which led to his murder of the defenceless Salif and ultimately to his suicide in prison. Can one hate a man enough to kill him in his sleep, 'malgré les paumes ouvertes sur les cuisses' [in spite of his palms resting open on his legs] (*TFP* 205)? It is, in the last analysis, Gauquelan's upturned palm that changes the course of Descas's destiny and saves him from becoming like his father. And the coda to his story, a more everyday twist, sees his maligned neighbour Mme Pulmaire wake from a nap and raise her hand to wave, for the very first time, at the strange Senegalese woman next door (Fanta, Descas's wife) who returns the gesture.[2]

NDiaye uses the sleeper's open hand, then, as a form of appeal, an affirmation of our dependence on each other, and an image of the unrealized potentiality that holds us in tension between the abstract idea of pure hospitality — to which it alludes — and contingent hospitality as physically enacted including, for example, waving, holding, touching, caressing and any number of gestures of welcome, forgiveness, protection or invitation. A wave between neighbours may not seem like much to cling on to even if, as in the coda to Rudy Descas's story, it is presented with the force of a minor miracle, and one might argue that NDiaye's fiction is a less than comforting companion in current times. In this book, however, I have argued that her determination to engage us so persistently in the ethics of hospitality makes her one of the most appropriate, and even essential, of contemporary writers.

Notes to the Afterword

1. There is one published study to date on this work: Frédérique Donovan, 'Nouvelles formes et espaces palimpsestes dans *Y penser sans cesse* de Marie NDiaye', *Contemporary French and Francophone Studies*, 17 (2013), 388–95.
2. The palm in NDiaye opens horizons similarly to the palm of the sleeping Japanese lover in Alain Resnais's *Hiroshima mon amour*.

BIBLIOGRAPHY

Works by Marie NDiaye

En famille (Paris: Éditions de Minuit, 1990)

Un temps de saison (Paris: Éditions de Minuit, 1994)

'La Gourmandise', in Jean-Pierre Géné and Marie NDiaye, *La Gourmandise* (Paris: Éditions du Centre Pompidou, 1996), pp. 46–62

La Sorcière (Paris: Éditions de Minuit, 1996)

La Naufragée (Paris: Éditions Flohic, 1999)

Rosie Carpe (Paris: Éditions de Minuit, 2001)

Papa doit manger (Paris: Éditions de Minuit, 2003)

Tous mes amis (Paris: Éditions de Minuit, 2004)

Rien d'humain (Paris: Les Solitaires intempestifs, 2004)

Les Serpents (Paris: Éditions de Minuit, 2004)

Autoportrait en vert, with photographs by Julie Ganzin and anon. (Paris: Mercure de France, 2005)

'Le Jour du président', in Patrick Modiano, Marie Ndiaye and Alain Speiss, *Trois nouvelles contemporaines* (Paris: Gallimard, 2006), pp. 51–67

Mon cœur à l'étroit (Paris: Gallimard, 2007)

'Providence', in Marie NDiaye and Jean-Yves Cendrey, *Puzzle* (Paris: Gallimard, 2007)

Trois femmes puissantes (Paris: Gallimard, 2009)

Les Grandes Personnes (Paris: Gallimard, 2011)

Y penser sans cesse, with photographs by Denis Cointe (Paris: L'Arbre vengeur, 2011)

Ladivine (Paris: Gallimard, 2013)

Interviews with Marie NDiaye

Argand, Catherine, 'Entretien: Marie NDiaye', *Lire*, April 2001, p. 6

Asibong, Andrew, and Shirley Jordan, 'Rencontre avec Marie NDiaye', in *Marie NDiaye: l'Étrangeté à l'œuvre* (Villeneuve d'Ascq: Presses Universitaires du Septentrion, 2009), pp. 187–99

Bourmeau, Sylvain, 'Le Goncourt pour *Trois femmes puissantes* de Marie NDiaye'. *Mediapart*, 2009, <http://www.mediapart.fr/journal/culture-idees/150709/avec-troi-femmes-puissantes-marie-ndiaye-domine-la-litterature-contemp> [accessed 7 June 2013]

Casanova, Pascal, *L'Atelier littéraire* (France Culture, 04/10/2009)

Chanda, Tirthankar, 'L'Essentiel d'un livre: portrait de l'écrivain en vert', *MFI HEBDO* (April 2005), p. 1, <http://rfi.fr/Fichiers/Mfi/CultureSociete/1455.asp> [accessed 10 November 2007]

Clair, Lucie, 'Dossier Marie NDiaye', *Le Matricule des anges: le mensuel de la littérature contemporaine*, 107 (2009), 20–29

Harang, Jean-Baptiste, 'Notre sorcière bien aimée', *Libération*, 12 February 2004, <http://remue.net/cont/NDiaye/html> [accessed 5 March 2016]

KAPRIÈLIAN, NELLY, 'Marie NDiaye aux prises avec le monde', *Les Inrockuptibles*, 716 (2009), 28–33

NICOLAS, ALAIN, 'Le Cœur dans le labyrinthe', *L'Humanité* 1 February 2007, <http://www.humanité.fr/2007–02–01_Cultures_Le-cœur-dans-le-labyrinthe> [accessed 9 February 2007]

Other Works

AGAMBEN, GIORGIO, *L'Ouvert: de l'homme et de l'animal*, trans. by Joël Gayraud (Paris: Bibliothèque Rivages, 2002)

AGAR, MICHAEL H., *The Professional Stranger: An Informal Introduction to Ethnography* (New York: Emerald Group Publishing, 1996)

ARMITT, LUCIE, *Contemporary Women's Fiction and the Fantastic* (Basingstoke: Macmillan Press, 2000)

ASIBONG, ANDREW, *Marie NDiaye: Blankness and Recognition* (Liverpool: Liverpool University Press, 2013)

——'Autour de la mère morte', in *Une femme puissante: l'œuvre de Marie NDiaye*, ed. by Daniel Bengsch and Cornelia Ruhe (Amsterdam & New York: Rodopi, 2013), pp. 243–62

——'The Spectacle of Marie NDiaye's *Trois femmes puissantes*', *Australian Journal of French Studies*, 50 (2013), 385–98

——'Tou(te)s mes ami(e)s: le problème de l'amitié chez Marie NDiaye', in *Marie NDiaye: l'Étrangeté à l'œuvre*, ed. by Adam Asibong and Shirley Jordan (Villeneuve d'Ascq: Presses Universitaires du Septentrion, 2009), pp. 137–52

——'*Moja sestra*: Marie NDiaye and the Transmission of Horrific Kinship', in *Transmissions: Essays in French Thought, Literature and Cinema*, ed. by Isabelle McNeill and Bradley Stephens (Oxford: Peter Lang, 2007), pp. 95–112

ASIBONG, ANDREW, and SHIRLEY JORDAN (eds), *Marie NDiaye: l'étrangeté à l'œuvre* (Villeneuve d'Ascq: Presses Universitaires du Septentrion, 2009)

ATTRIDGE, DEREK, 'Hospitality', in *The Work of Literature* (Oxford: Oxford University Press, 2015), pp. 280–305

——*J. M. Coetzee and the Ethics of Reading: Literature in the Event* (Chicago & London: University of Chicago Press, 2004)

BAHRI, DEEPIKE, *Native Intelligence: Aesthetics, Politics and Postcolonial Literature* (Minneapolis & London: University of Minnesota Press, 2003)

BAILEY, F. G. (ed.), *Gifts and Poison: The Politics of Reputation* (New York: Schocken Books, 1971)

BAUDRILLARD, JEAN, *La Transparence du mal: essai sur les phénomènes extrêmes* (Paris: Galilée, 1990)

BEHAR, CLARISSA, 'Écrire en pays à majorité blanche: *En famille* de Marie NDiaye', in *Une femme puissante: l'œuvre de Marie NDiaye*, ed. by Daniel Bengsch and Cornelia Ruhe (Amsterdam & New York: Rodopi, 2013), pp. 125–39

BENGUIGUI, YAMINA, *Mémoires d'immigrés* (Paris: Canal + Éditions, 1997)

BEN JELLOUN, TAHAR, *Hospitalité française: racisme et immigration maghrébine* (Paris: Seuil, 1997)

BENGSCH, DANIEL, and CORNELIA RUHE (eds), *Une femme puissante: l'œuvre de Marie NDiaye* (Amsterdam & New York: Rodopi, 2013)

BERTRANDIAS, BERNADETTE, 'Le Fantôme: hostilité d'une inquiétante étrangeté', in *Le Livre de l'hospitalité: accueil de l'étranger dans l'histoire et les cultures*, ed. by Alain Montandon (Paris: Bayard, 2004), pp. 1122–41

BIRNBAUM, JEAN (ed.), *Qui sont les animaux?* (Paris: Gallimard, 2010)

BONOMO, SARA, 'La Mise en œuvre de la peur dans le roman d'aujourd'hui: *Rosie Carpe* de Marie NDiaye', *Travaux de littérature* 17, *Les Grandes Peurs 2: L'Autre* (2004), 21–29

BOUTAUD, JEAN-JACQUES, 'Le Partage de la table', in *Le Livre de l'hospitalité: accueil de l'étranger dans l'histoire et les cultures*, ed. by Alain Montandon (Paris: Bayard Éditions, 2004), pp. 1711–37

——'Approches sémiotiques des rituels de commensalité', in *L'Hospitalité: signes et rites*, ed. by Alain Montandon (Clermont-Ferrand: Presses Universitaires Blaise Pascal, 2001), pp. 175–94

BOYER, FRÉDÉRIQUE, 'Un animal dans la tête', in *Qui sont les animaux?*, ed. by Jean Birnbaum (Paris: Gallimard, 2010), pp. 11–25

BRUNS, GERALD L., 'Derrida's Cat (Who Am I?)', *Research in Phenomenology*, 38 (2008), 404–23

——'Becoming-Animal (Some Simple Ways)', *New Literary History*, 38.4 (2007), 703–20

BURNAUTZKI, SARAH, 'Jeux de visibilité et d'invisibilité: la production romanesque de Marie NDiaye à la lumière de la crise du républicanisme français', in *Une femme puissante: l'œuvre de Marie NDiaye*, ed. by Daniel Bengsch and Cornelia Ruhe (Amsterdam & New York: Rodopi, 2013), pp. 141–58

——'Le Motif de la folie dans *Rosie Carpe*: réminiscences de la littérature antillaise', in *Quand la folie parle: The Dialectic Effect of Madness in French Literature from the Nineteenth Century*, ed. by Gillian Ni Cheallaigh, Laura Jackson and Siobhàn McIlvanney (Newcastle upon Tyne: Cambridge Scholars Publishing, 2014), pp. 172–89

CALARCO, MATTHEW, and PETER ATTERTON (eds), *Animal Philosophy: Essential Readings in Continental Thought* (London and New York: Continuum, 2004)

CANDEA, MATEA, 'Derrida en Corse? Hospitality as Scale-Free Abstraction', in *The Return to Hospitality*, ed. by Matei Candea and Giovanni da Col, special issue of *Journal of the Royal Anthropological Institute*, 18 (2012), 534–48

——'The Return to Hospitality', in *The Return to Hospitality*, ed. by Matei Candea and Giovanni da Col, special issue of *Journal of the Royal Anthropological Institute*, 18 (2012), 1–19

CARUTH, CATHY, *Trauma: Explorations in Memory* (Baltimore, MD, & London: Johns Hopkins University Press, 1995)

CAZENAVE, ODILE, 'Marie NDiaye ou une aspiration à "l'universel"', in *Afrique sur Seine: une nouvelle génération de romanciers africains à Paris* (Paris: L'Harmattan, 2004), pp. 73–78

CÉSAIRE, AIMÉ, *Discours sur le colonialisme* (Paris: Présence Africaine, 1950)

CONNON, DAISY, 'Marie NDiaye's Haunted House: Uncanny *Autofiction* in *Autoportrait en vert*', in *Redefining the Real: The Fantastic in Contemporary French and Francophone Women's Writing*, ed. by Margaret-Anne Hutton (Oxford: Peter Lang 2009), pp. 245–60

——*Subjects Not-at-home: Forms of the Uncanny in the Contemporary French Novel: Emmanuel Carrère, Marie NDiaye, Eugène Savitzkaya* (Amsterdam & New York: Rodopi, 2010)

CORBIN, LAURIE, *The Mother Mirror: Self-Representation and the Mother-Daughter Relation in Colette, Simone de Beauvoir and Marguerite Duras* (Oxford: Peter Lang, 1996)

COTILLE-FOLEY, NORA, 'Permanence et métamorphose: l'évolution du lieu de mémoire Paris-Province de J.-K. Huysmans à Marie NDiaye', *Essays in French Literature*, 43 (July 2006), 47–63

——'Optique fantastique, traitement de la photographie et transgression des limites du visible chez Marie NDiaye', *Contemporary French and Francophone Studies*, 13 (2009), 547–54

——'Les Mots pour ne pas le dire: ou encore l'indicibilité d'une visibilité frottée de fantastique dans les œuvres de Marie NDiaye', in *Marie NDiaye: l'étrangeté à l'œuvre*, ed.

by Andrew Asibong and Shirley Jordan (Villeneuve d'Ascq: Presses Universitaires du Septentrion, 2009), pp. 13–23

CRONIN, MICHAEL, 'Cooking the Books: Translation, Food and Migration', *Comparative Critical Studies*, 11 (2014), 337–54

DALTON, ANNE B., 'The Devil and the Virgin: Writing Sexual Abuse in *Incidents in the Life of a Slave Girl*', in *Violence, Silence and Anger: Women's Writing as Transgression*, ed. by Deirdre Lashgari (Charlottesville & London: University Press of Virginia, 1995), pp. 38–61

DANTA, CHRIS, '"Like a Dog, Like a Lamb": Becoming Sacrificial Animal in Kafka and Coetzee', *New Literary History: A Journal of Theory and Interpretation*, 38 (2006), 721–37

DARRIEUSSECQ, MARIE, *Truismes* (Paris: P.O.L., 1996)

DAMLÉ, AMALEENA, *The Becoming of the Body: Contemporary Women's Writing in French* (Edinburgh: Edinburgh University Press, 2014)

DAVIS, COLIN, 'Diasporic Subjectivities', *French Cultural Studies*, 17.3 (2006), 335–48

DELEUZE, GILLES, 'A comme animal', in *Abécédaire* (DVD: Editions Montparnasse, 2004)

DELEUZE, GILLES, and FÉLIX GUATTARI, *A Thousand Plateaus: Capitalism and Schizophrenia*, trans. by Brian Massumi (Minneapolis: University of Minnesota Press, 1987)

——*Kafka: Toward a Minor Literature*, trans. by Dana Polan (Minneapolis: The University of Minnesota Press, 1986)

DELTEL, DANIELLE, 'Marie NDiaye: l'ambition de l'universel', *Notre librairie: Revue du livre: Afrique, Caraïbes, Océan Indien*, 118 (1994), 111–15

DERRIDA, JACQUES, 'Nombre de Oui', in *Psyché: inventions de l'autre* (Paris: Galilée, 1987), pp. 639–50

——'A Number of Yes', in *Psyche: Inventions of the Other*, ed. Peggy Kamuf and Elizabeth Rottenberg, 2 vols (Stanford, CA: Stanford University Press, 2007), I, 231–40

——'Hospitality, Justice and Responsibility: A Dialogue with Jacques Derrida', in *Questioning Ethics: Contemporary Debates in Philosophy*, ed. by Mark Dooley and Richard Kearney (London: Routledge, 1999), pp. 65–83

——*L'Animal que donc je suis* (Paris: Galilée, 2006)

——'The Animal That Therefore I Am (More to Follow)', trans. by David Willis, *Critical Inquiry*, 28 (2002), 369–418

——'Hostipitality', in *Jacques Derrida: Acts of Religion*, ed. by Gil Anidjar (New York: Routledge, 2002), pp. 356–420

——'"Il faut bien manger" ou le calcul du sujet', interview with Jean-Luc Nancy, in Jacques Derrida, *Points de suspension: entretiens* (Paris: Éditions Galilée, 1992), pp. 269–301

——'"Eating Well", or the Calculation of the Subject', in *Points... Interviews, 1974–1994*, ed. by Elisabeth Weber, trans. by Peggy Kamuf (Stanford, CA: Stanford University Press, 1995), pp. 255–87

DERRIDA, JACQUES, and ANNE DUFOURMANTELLE, *De l'hospitalité* (Paris: Calman-Lévy, 1997)

——*Of Hospitality*, trans. by Rachel Bowlby (Stanford, CA: Stanford University Press, 2000)

DERRIDA, JACQUES, with ELISABETH ROUDINESCO, 'Violences contre les animaux', in Jacques Derrida and Elisabeth Roudinesco, *De quoi demain... Dialogue* (Paris: Fayard Galilée, 2001), pp. 105–27

DETEL, DANIELLE, 'Marie NDiaye: l'ambition de l'universel', *Notre librairie*, Nouvelles Écritures Féminines, 2 (1994), 111–15

DEVI, ANANDA, *Moi, l'interdite* (Paris: Dapper, 2000)

DONOVAN, FRÉDÉRIQUE, 'Nouvelles formes et espaces palimpsestes dans *Y penser sans cesse* de Marie NDiaye', *Contemporary French and Francophone Studies*, 17 (2013), 388–95

DUCORNEAU, CLAIRE, 'Entre noir et blanc: le traitement littéraire de la couleur de peau dans *Rosie Carpe* et *Papa doit manger*', in *Une femme puissante: l'œuvre de Marie NDiaye*, ed. by Daniel Bengsch and Cornelia Ruhe (Amsterdam & New York: Rodopi, 2013), pp. 101–17

DUTTON, JACQUELINE, '*État present*: World Literature in French, *littérature-monde*, and the Translingual Turn', *French Studies*, 70 (2016), 404–18

EATON, PAULINE, 'Rosie Carpe and the Virgin Mary: Modelling Modern Motherhood', *Religion and Gender*, 6 (2016), 29–46

FANON, FRANTZ, *Peau noire, masques blancs* (Paris: Seuil, 1952)

FASSIN, DIDIER (ed.), *Les Nouvelles Frontières de la société française* (Paris: Éditions de la découverte, 2010)

FASSIN, DIDIER, and PATRICE BOURDELAIS (eds), *Les Constructions de l'intolérable: études d'anthropologie et d'histoire sur les frontières de l'espace moral* (Paris: Éditions la Découverte, 2005)

FASSIN, DIDIER, ALAIN MORICE and CATHERINE QUIMINAL (eds), *Les Lois de l'inhospitalité: les politiques de l'immigration à l'épreuve des sans papiers* (Paris: Éditions La Découverte, 1997)

FONTENAY, ELISABETH DE, *Le Silence des bêtes: la philosophie à l'épreuve de l'animalité* (Paris: Fayard, 1998)

FORSDICK, CHARLES, and DAVID MURPHY (eds), *Postcolonial Thought in the French-Speaking World* (Liverpool: Liverpool University Press, 2009)

FOUQUE, ANTOINETTE, *Génésique. Féminologie III* (Paris: Des femmes, 2012)

GAENSBAUER, DEBORAH, 'Further outside the Bounds: Mobilization of the Fantastic as Trauma Narrative in Marie NDiaye's *En famille*', in *Redefining the Real: The Fantastic in Contemporary French and Francophone Women's Writing*, ed. by Margaret-Anne Hutton (Oxford: Peter Lang 2009), pp. 207–24

GALLI PELLEGRINI, ROSA, 'Marie NDiaye: de l'abandon à la (ré)-appropriation', in *Trois études sur le roman de l'extrême contemporain: Marie NDiaye, Sylvie Germain, Michel Chaillou*, ed. by Rosa Galli Pellegrini (Italy: Schéna Editore/Presses de l'Université Paris-Sorbonne, 2004), pp. 11–49

GAUVIN, LISE, PIERRE L'Hérault and Alain Montandon (eds), *Le Dire de l'hospitalité* (Clermont-Ferrand: Presses Universitaires Blaise Pascal, 2004)

GEERTZ, CLIFFORD, *The Interpretation of Cultures* (New York: Basic Books, 1973)

GENTRY, AMY, JEFFREY ZUCKERMAN and AARON BADY, 'A Roundtable on Marie NDiaye's *Ladivine*', *The New Inquiry*, 30 May 2016, <http://thenewinquiry.com/features/spaces-where-identity-stutters-and-goes-silent-a-roundtable-on-maria-ndiayes-ladivine/> [accessed 10 August 2016]

GIGUERE, NOELLE, 'Strange and Terrible: Understanding the Risks of Self-Definition in Marie NDiaye's *Autoportrait en vert*', in *Women Taking Risks in Contemporary Autobiographical Narratives*, ed. by Anna Rocca and Kenneth Reeds (Newcastle upon Tyne: Cambridge Scholars Publishing, 2013), pp. 59–70

GOTTMAN, ANNE, *Le Sens de l'hospitalité: essai sur les fondements sociaux de l'accueil de l'autre* (Paris: Presses Universitaires de la France, 2001)

HAHN, ALOïS, 'L'Hospitalité et l'étranger', in *Mythes et représentations de l'hospitalité*, ed. by Alain Montandon (Clermont-Ferrand: Presses Universitaires Blaise Pascal, 1999), pp. 9–22

HARGREAVES, ALEC G., *Voices from the North African Community in France: Immigration and Identity in Beur Fiction* (New York & Oxford: Berg, 1991)

HENKE, SUZETTE A., *Shattered Subjects: Trauma and Testimony in Women's Life Writing* (Charlottesville & London: University of Virginia Press, 2002)

HIDDLESTON, JANE (ed.), *The Postcolonial Human*, special issue of *International Journal of Francophone Studies*, 15 (2012), 363–74

HILLIS MILLER, JOSEPH, *The Ethics of Reading: Kant, De Man, Eliot, Trollope, James and Benjamin* (New York: Columbia University Press, 1987)

HIRSCH, MARIANNE, *The Mother/Daughter Plot: Narrative, Psychoanalysis, Feminism* (Bloomington: Indiana University Press, 1989)

HITCHCOTT, NICKI, *Women Writers in Francophone Africa* (Oxford: Berg, 2000)

HUGGAN, GRAHAM, *The Postcolonial Exotic: Marketing the Margins* (London & New York: Routledge, 2001)

HUTTON, MARGARET-ANNE (ed.), *Redefining the Real: The Fantastic in Contemporary French and Francophone Women's Writing* (Oxford: Peter Lang 2009)

IRIGARAY, LUCE, *Sharing the World* (London: Continuum, 2008)

——'Animal Compassion', in *Animal Philosophy*, ed. by Matthew Calarco and Peter Atterton (London: Continuum, 2004), pp. 195–201

——*Le Corps-à-corps avec la mère* (Montreal: Éditions de la pleine lune, 1981)

——*Et l'un ne bouge pas sans l'autre* (Paris: Éditions de Minuit, 1979)

JACKSON, ROSEMARY, *Fantasy: The Literature of Subversion* (London & New York: Methuen, 1981)

JÉRUSALEM, CHRISTINE, 'Des larmes de sang au sang épuisé dans l'œuvre de Marie NDiaye (*hoc est enim corpus meum*)', in *Marie NDiaye: l'étrangeté à l'œuvre*, ed. by Andrew Asibong and Shirley Jordan (Villeneuve d'Ascq: Presses Universitaires du Septentrion, 2009), pp. 83–91

JORDAN, SHIRLEY, 'Marie NDiaye: la puissance de Khady Demba', in *Une femme puissante: l'œuvre de Marie NDiaye*, ed. by Daniel Bengsch and Cornelia Ruhe (Amsterdam & New York: Rodopi, 2013), pp. 263–83

——'Chronicles of Intimacy: Photography in Autobiographical Projects', in *Textual and Visual Selves*, ed. by Natalie Edwards, Amy L. Hubbell and Ann Miller (Lincoln: University of Nebraska Press, 2011), pp. 51–77

——'Telling Tales: Marie NDiaye's Mythopoeic Imagination', in *Contemporary French Women's Writing: Women's Visions, Women's Voices, Women's Lives* (Oxford: Peter Lang, 2004), pp. 164–67

——'Fantastic Spaces in Marie NDiaye', *Dalhousie French Studies*, 93 (2010), 97–108

——'Marie NDiaye: énigmes photographiques, albums éclatés', in *Marie NDiaye: l'étrangeté à l'œuvre*, ed. by Andrew Asibon and Shirley Jordan (Villeneuve d'Ascq: Presses Universitaires du Septentrion, 2009), pp. 65–82

——'La Quête familiale dans les écrits de Marie NDiaye: nomadisme, (in)hospitalité, différence', in *Nomadismes de romancières contemporaines de langue française*, ed. by Anne Simon (Paris: Presses Sorbonne Nouvelle, 2007), pp. 143–53

KAFKA, FRANZ, 'Investigations of a Dog', in *The Great Wall of China and Other Short Works*, trans. by Malcolm Pasley (London: Penguin, 1991) pp. 141–77

——'A Country Doctor', in *A Country Doctor*, trans. by Kevin Blahut (Prague: Twisted Spoon Press, 1997), pp. 11–22

KOLNAI, AUREL, 'The Standard Modes of Aversion: Fear, Disgust, and Hatred', in *On Disgust*, ed. by Barry Smith and Carolyn Korsmeyer (Chicago & La Salle, IL: Open Court, 2004), pp. 93–108

KRISTEVA, JULIA, *Revolution in Poetic Language* (New York: Columbia University Press, 1984)

LEVINAS, EMMANUEL, *Autrement qu'être ou au-delà de l'essence* (Paris: Kluwer Academic, 1996)

——*Otherwise than Being, or Beyond Essence*, trans. by Alphonso Lingis (Pittsburgh, PA: Duquesne University Press, 1998)

——*Difficult Freedom: Essays on Judaism*, trans. by Seán Hand (Baltimore, MD: Johns Hopkins University Press, 1990)

LIONNET, FRANÇOISE, 'Introduction', in *Francophone Studies: New Landscapes*, ed. by Françoise Lionnet and Dominique Thomas, special issue of *Modern Language Notes*, 18 (2003), 783–86

LOUDEN, BRUCE, 'Theoxeny', in *Homer's Odyssey and the Near East* (Cambridge: Cambridge University Press, 2010), pp. 30–56

MANOLESCU, CAMELIA, 'L'Espace clos ou le thème du village dans le roman *Un Temps de saison* de Marie NDiaye', *Language and Literature: European Landmarks of Identity*, 2 (2010), 196–201

MANZI, JOACHIM, and FRÉDÉRIQUE TOUDOIRE-SURPALPIERRE, 'L'Inconnu qui frappe à ma porte', in *Le Livre de l'hospitalité: accueil de l'étranger dans l'histoire et les cultures*, ed. by Alain Montandon (Paris: Bayard, 2004), pp. 1108–21

MAUSS, MARCEL, *Essai sur le don* (Paris: PUF, 1925)

MASPERO, FRANÇOIS, and ANAIK FRANTZ, *Les Passagers du Roissy Express* (Paris: Seuil, 1990)

McGINN, COLIN, *The Meaning of Disgust* (Oxford: Oxford University Press, 2011)

MELLIER, DENIS, *La Littérature fantastique* (Paris: Editions du Seuil, 2000)

MENNINGHAUS, WINFRIED, *Disgust: Theory and History of a Strong Sensation*, trans. by Howard Eiland and Joel Golb (Albany: State University of New York Press, 2003)

—— 'The Wound in the Text and the Text as Wound: The Story of "A Country Doctor"', in *Disgust: Theory and History of a Strong Sensation*, trans. by Howard Eiland and Joel Golb (Albany: State University of New York Press, 2003), pp. 318–32

MEURÉE, CHRISTOPH, 'Au diable le sujet: le concave et le convexe dans le theâtre de Marie NDiaye', in *Marie NDiaye: l'étrangeté à l'œuvre*, ed. by Andrew Asibong and Shirley Jordan (Villeneuve d'Ascq: Presses Universitaires du Septentrion, 2009), pp. 119–36

MICHAUD, GINETTE, '"Un acte d'hospitalité ne peut être que poétique": seuils et délimitations de l'hospitalité derridienne', in *Le Dire de l'hospitalité*, ed. by Lise Gauvin, Pierre l'Hérault and Alain Montandon (Clermont-Ferrand: Presses Universitaires Blaise Pascal, 2004), pp. 33–60

MIGRAINE-GEORGE, THÉRÈSE, 'A Case-Study in *Littérature-Monde*: The Marie NDiaye Controversy', in *From Francophonie to World Literature in French: Ethics, Poetics, and Politics* (Lincoln & London: University of Nebraska Press, 2013), pp. xii–xvi

—— 'Writing as Otherness: Marie NDiaye's Inalterable Humanity', in *From Francophonie to World Literature in French: Ethics, Poetics, and Politics* (Lincoln & London: University of Nebraska Press, 2013), pp. 63–91

MILLER, SUSAN B., *Disgust: The Gatekeeper Emotion* (London: Routledge, 2004)

MILLET, CATHERINE, *La Vie sexuelle de Catherine M* (Paris: Seuil, 2001)

MONTANDON, ALAIN, 'Le Toucher de l'hospitalité: Gustave Flaubert', in Alain Montadon, *Désirs d'hospitalité: de Homère à Kafka* (Paris: Presses Universitaires de France, 2002), pp. 127–51

—— (ed.), *Littérature et anthropologie* (Paris: Société Française de Littérature Générale et Comparée, 2006)

—— (ed.), *Le Livre de l'hospitalité: accueil de l'étranger dans l'histoire et les cultures* (Paris: Bayard, 2004)

—— (ed.), *Espaces domestiques et privés de l'hospitalité* (Clermont-Ferrand: Presses Universitaires Blaise Pascal, 2000)

—— (ed.), *Hospitalité: signes et rites* (Clermont-Ferrand: Presses Universitaires Blaise Pascal, 2001)

—— (ed.), *Mythes et représentations de l'hospitalité* (Clermont-Ferrand: Presses Universitaires Blaise Pascal, 1999)

MOUDILENO, LYDIE, 'Délits, détours et affabulation: l'écriture de l'anathème dans *En famille* de Marie NDiaye', *The French Review*, 71 (1998), 442–53

——'L'Excellent Français de Marie NDiaye', in *Marie NDiaye: l'étrangeté à l'œuvre*, ed. by Andrew Asibong and Shirley Jordan (Villeneuve d'Ascq: Presses Universitaires du Septentrion, 2009), pp. 25–38

——'Marie NDiaye, entre visibilité et réserve', in *Une femme puissante: l'œuvre de Marie NDiaye*, ed. by Daniel Bengsch and Cornelia Ruhe (Amsterdam & New York: Rodopi, 2013), pp. 159–76

——'Puissance insolite de la femme africaine chez Marie NDiaye', in *Marie NDiaye's Worlds/Mondes de Marie NDiaye*, ed. by Warren Mott and Lydie Moudileno, special issue of *L'Esprit Créateur*, 53 (2013), 67–75

——'Fame, Celebrity and the Conditions of Visibility of the Postcolonial Writer', *Yale French Studies* 120 (2011), 62–74

NANCY, JEAN-LUC, *L'Intrus* (Paris: Éditions Galilée, 2000)

——'Une plaie', in *Corpus* (Paris: Éditions Métailié, 2000), pp. 67–71

NGAI, SIANNE, *Ugly Feelings* (Cambridge, MA: Harvard University Press, 2005)

NUSSBAUM, MARTHA C., *Hiding from Humanity: Disgust, Shame and the Law* (Princeton, NJ, & Oxford: Princeton University Press, 2004)

ORMEROD, BEVERLEY, and JEAN-MARIE VOLET, *Romancières africaines d'expression française: le sud du Sahara* (Paris: L'Harmattan, 1994)

PITT-RIVERS, JULIAN, 'The Stranger, the Guest and the Hostile Host: Introduction to the Study of the Laws of Hospitality', in *Contributions to Mediterranean Sociology*, ed. by J.-G. Peristiany (Paris & The Hague: Mouton & Co, 1968), pp. 13–30

——'The Place of Grace in Anthropology', in *Honour and Grace in Anthropology*, ed. by J. G. Peristiany and J. Pitt-Rivers (Cambridge: Cambridge University Press, 1992), pp. 215–46

RABATÉ, DOMINIQUE, *Marie NDiaye* (Paris: Éditions Textuel, 2008)

——'Exercice de la cruauté', in *Marie NDiaye's Worlds/Mondes de Marie NDiaye*, ed. by Warren Mott and Lydie Moudileno, special issue of *L'Esprit Créateur*, 53 (2013), 90–96

REECE, STEVE, *The Stranger's Welcome: Oral Theory and the Aesthetics of the Homeric Hospitality Scene* (Ann Arbor: University of Michigan Press, 1993)

RICHARD, JEAN-PIERRE, 'Le Trouble et le partage', in *Terrains de lecture* (Paris: Gallimard, 1996), pp. 161–86

RICHARDS, DAVID, 'Postcolonial Anthropology in the French-Speaking World', in *Postcolonial Thought in the French-Speaking World*, ed. by Charles Forsdick and David Murphy (Liverpool: Liverpool University Press, 2009) pp. 173–84

ROSELLO, MIREILLE, *Postcolonial Hospitality: The Immigrant as Guest* (Stanford, CA: Stanford University Press, 2001)

——'Immigration: discours et contradictions', in *Le Livre de l'hospitalité: accueil de l'étranger dans l'histoire et les cultures*, ed. by Alain Montandon (Paris: Bayard, 2004), pp. 1516–28

ROZEN, ANNA, *Plaisir d'offrir, joie de recevoir* (Paris: Éditions J'ai Lu, 1999)

RUHE, CORNELIA, 'La Poétique du flou de Marie NDiaye', in *Une femme puissante: l'œuvre de Marie NDiaye*, ed. by Daniel Bengsch and Cornelia Ruhe (Amsterdam & New York: Rodopi, 2013), pp. 17–33

RYE, GILL, *Narratives of Mothering: Women's Writing in Contemporary France* (Newark: University of Delaware Press, 2010)

SANSAVOIR, EVA, *Maryse Condé and the Spaces of Literature* (Oxford: Legenda, 2012)

SCHÉRER, RENÉ, *Zeus hospitalier* (Paris: Armand Colin, 1993)

SÉRY, MACHA, 'Tous des monstres!', *Le Monde des livres*, 18 January 2013, pp. 2–3

SHEPARD, PAUL, *The Others: How Animals Made Us Human* (Washington, DC: Shearwater Books, 1996)

SHERINGHAM, MICHAEL, 'The Law of Sacrifice: Race and the Family in Marie NDiaye's

En famille and *Papa doit manger*', in *Affaires de famille: The Family in Contemporary French Culture and Theory*, ed. by Marie-Claire Barnet and Edward Welch (Amsterdam & New York: Rodopi, 2007), pp. 23–38

—— 'Space, Identity and Difference in Contemporary Fiction: Duras, Genet, NDiaye', in *French Global: A New Approach to Literary History*, ed. by Christie McDonald and Susan Rubin Suleiman (New York: Columbia University Press, 2010), pp. 437–52

—— 'La Figure de l'enseignant chez Marie NDiaye', in *Marie NDiaye's Worlds/Mondes de Marie NDiaye*, ed. by Warren Mott and Lydie Moudileno, special issue of *L'Esprit Créateur*, 53 (2013), 97–110

—— 'Ambivalences de l'animalité chez Marie NDiaye', in *Une femme puissante: l'œuvre de Marie NDiaye*, ed. by Daniel Bengsch and Cornelia Ruhe (Amsterdam & New York: Rodopi, 2013), pp. 51–70

SLATER, MICHELLE B., 'Rethinking Human-Animal Ontological Differences: Derrida's "Animot" and Cixous' "Fips"', in *Human-Animal*, ed. by Roger Célestin, Eliane Dalmolin and Anne Simon, special issue of *Contemporary French and Francophone Studies*, 16 (2012), 685–93

STILL, JUDITH, 'Love and Money in Marie NDiaye's *Ladivine*', in *Derrida and Other Animals: The Boundaries of the Human* (Edinburgh: Edinburgh University Press, 2015), pp. 337–45

—— '"Welcoming animals" bei Derrida und Irigaray — unter besonderer Berücksichtigung des Hundes in Marie NDiaye's Roman *Ladivine*', in *Perspektiven europäischer Gastlichkeit: Geschichte — Kulturelle Praktiken — Kritik*, ed. by Burkhard Liebsch, Michael Staudigl and Philipp Stoellger (Weilerswist-Metternich: Velbrück Wissenschaft, 2016), pp. 374–94

—— 'Being a Guest: From Uneasy Tourism to Welcoming Dogs in Marie NDiaye's *Ladivine*', in *Hospitalities: Bodies and Texts, Transitions and Transgressions*, ed. by Merle A. Williams and Russell West-Pavlov (Berlin: de Gruyter, forthcoming in 2017)

—— *Derrida and Hospitality: Theory and Practice* (Edinburgh: Edinburgh University Press, 2010)

—— '*Sharing the World*: Luce Irigaray and the Hospitality of Difference', *L'Esprit Créateur*, 52 (2012), 40–51

STONE, ALISON, *Feminism, Psychoanalysis and Maternal Subjectivity* (New York & London: Routledge, 2012)

SYLLA, ABDOULAYE, 'La Négoce de la distance', in *Une femme puissante: l'œuvre de Marie NDiaye*, ed. by Daniel Bengsch and Cornelia Ruhe (Amsterdam & New York: Rodopi, 2013), pp. 201–15

THOMAS, DOMINIC, 'The "Marie NDiaye Affair", or the Coming of a Postcolonial *Évoluée*', in *Transnational French Studies: Postcolonialism and Littérature-Monde*, ed. by Alec Hargreaves, Charles Forsdick and David Murphy (Liverpool: Liverpool University Press, 2010), pp. 146–63

TODOROV, TZVETAN, *The Fantastic: A Structural Approach to a Literary Genre*, trans. by Richard Howard (Ithaca, NY: Cornell University Press, 1975)

WEIL, PATRICK, *La République et sa diversité: immigration, intégration, discriminations* (Paris: Éditions du Seuil, et La République des Idées, 2005)

WINNICOTT, D. W., 'Transitional Objects and Transitional Phenomena', *International Journal of Psychoanalysis*, 34 (1953), 89–97

ŽIŽEK, SLAVOJ, 'Neighbours and Other Monsters: A Plea for Ethical Violence', in Kenneth Reinhard, Eric L. Santner and Slavoj Žižek, *The Neighbour: Three Inquiries in Political Theology* (Chicago: University of Chicago Press, 2005), pp. 134–90

INDEX

Printed by BoD™in Norderstedt, Germany